REMAKING HISTORY

Dia Art Foundation

Discussions in Contemporary Culture

Number 4

REMAKING HISTORY

Edited by Barbara Kruger and Phil Mariani

BAY PRESS   SEATTLE   1989

Printed in the United States of America
95 94 93 92 91 5 4 3 2 1

Bay Press
115 West Denny Way
Seattle, Washington 98119

Design by Bethany Johns
Typesetting by The Sarabande Press, New York
Printing by Edwards Brothers, Lillington, North Carolina
Set in Perpetua

Library of Congress Cataloging-in-Publication Data
(Revised for no. 4)

Discussions in Contemporary Culture.

Nos. 1-2 edited by Hal Foster. No. 3 edited by Gary Garrels. No. 4
edited by Barbara Kruger and Phil Mariani.
Contents: no. 1 [without special title].—no. 2. Vision and visuality.—
no. 3. The work of Andy Warhol.—no. 4. Remaking history.
1. History and culture.   2. Historiography.
I. Kruger, Barbara.   II. Mariani, Phil. III. Dia Art Foundation.
N72.S6D57 1987   700'.1'03   87-71579
ISBN 0-941920-12-0 (no. 4: pbk.)

Carol Squiers's article, "At Their Mercy," is a compilation and edited
version of articles published in Artforum, Summer 1988, September
1988, November 1988, and March 1989. © Artforum and the author
1988, 1989; reprinted here by permission of the author and Artforum.
Homi K. Bhabha's article, "Remembering Fanon," originally appeared
as the preface to the British edition of Frantz Fanon's Black Skin, White
Masks (London: Pluto Press Limited, 1986), and is reprinted by
permission of the author.

CONTENTS

A NOTE ON THE SERIES

In 1987, the Dia Art Foundation initiated a commitment to critical discussion and debate through a program of lectures and symposia, with related publications in some cases, called "Discussions in Contemporary Culture." Events in the series are organized usually by artists, scholars, and critics from outside the Dia Foundation. More ambitious lectures or symposia are transcribed and edited, sometimes with related contributed essays, furthering the "Discussions in Contemporary Culture" publication series. We look forward to the continuation of this series as a chronicle for topics of concern to cultural communities in downtown Manhattan and, through our publications, to broader national communities.

This is the fourth volume we have published. It documents lectures that took place over several months in 1987-88, and includes several commissioned essays, all of which treat from various perspectives alternatives to the received, standard, or official histories of different cultures, eras, ideas. We are very grateful to the lecturers who participated in the series and the writers who contributed to this publication for their research and thought on the question of "remaking" history. The entire project was conceived and organized by Barbara Kruger and Phil Mariani. Phil Mariani also acted as coordinator of this publication, and we are particularly grateful to her for her careful and thoughtful work. The Dia staff worked under pressure both in the planning of the lecture series and in the production of the publication. We also thank Bethany Johns, our designer, and Thatcher Bailey, our publisher at Bay Press.

As always, the continued support of our programming by the Board of Directors of the Dia Foundation has made this project possible.

Charles Wright
Executive Director
Dia Art Foundation

5

INTRODUCTION

The Questions: What administers the souls of the dead? What is the euphoria of the panorama? What is the neatly voluptuous plenitude which, arranging sequences and ordering events, locks in the world? What revels in the site of the so-called objective with the abandon usually reserved for the body, but has no body? The Answer: History. There is only one answer because there has purportedly been only one history: a bulky encapsulation of singularity, a univocal voice-over, an instructor of origin, power, and mastery. History has been the text of the dead dictated to the living, through a voice which cannot speak for itself. The ventriloquist that balances corpses on its knee, that gives speech to silence, and transforms bones and blood into reminiscences, is none other than the historian. The keeper of the text. The teller of the story. The worker of mute mouths.

But what happens if the answer to the preceding questions is not a singular response which is "history," but a chorus of commentaries, a crowd of reckonings. What might be attempted is this: a display of expository moments and happenings which tell not only of events and proper names, but of their places within a broader construct of forces and relations. What happens when the formalities and franchises of "history" are displaced into a dispersal of stories? Who has stories to tell? What are their methodologies? How do they speak to their readers? What are the tones of their voices?

If traditional history writing has been in a sense a process of collecting, it has also been a process of marginalizing, omitting. Still, it speaks *at* us, if not *to* us, with the authority of all discourses that seek to demonstrate cause-and-effect. The past several years have seen the development of alternate histories, recoveries of neglected and "forgotten" cultures and the recuperation of names and faces. Simultaneous with the elaboration of critical theories problematizing the construction of the subject and the relationship between knowledge and power, this process of recovery has been essential to challenging masculinist and Eurocentric visions that rely on linear narrative and promote totalizing concepts. The foundation of traditional historiography, the *document,* has now become one discursive text among many, and which ones the historian chooses for his or her analysis becomes a crucial issue in itself, bringing into focus such questions as race, gender, class, and institutional affiliation. The awareness of the voices of "others," the plurality of stories to tell, has produced, as Foucault describes it, a "new form of history [that] is trying to develop its own theory" and one in which one works "to specify the . . . concepts that enable us to conceive of *discontinuity.*" And, one might add, difference.

The new historicism is not necessarily a History of the Victors. It disrupts the notion of the "major" event. It is anti-hierarchical and questions the narratives of chronology. It is cross-disciplinary: its most productive tools of analysis are originating in feminist literary-critical studies and in their rereadings of psychoanalytic texts; in poststructural, sociolinguistic examinations of ideology construction and its operation through the political, cultural, and social; out of cultural studies from the perspective of race and experiences of exclusion; and out of a recognition of the power of the image, its centrality in ideological formations and its usefulness in analyzing change and reformation.

Official History, increasingly made for TV, becomes indisputable fact through its repetitions and powerful alignments. One site of struggle against this imperialism that colonizes bodies and minds centers on the text. Texts empower; they grant authority, and their deconstruction from race-gender perspectives has become a kind of anti-imperialist strategy that has reverberations for political action.

This work is ongoing and urgent. The confusion of discourses generated by the publication of Salman Rushdie's *Satanic Verses* is paradigmatic: a "fiction" that includes a critique of Islam is published in the West where racist attitudes toward Iranians have been promoted and utilized with great profit over the past decade. This text provokes violent threats to the author from a religious counterrevolution that cannot bear to be criticized. This text generates a spectrum of corroborations and dissenting opinions from Muslims worldwide. This text is presumably responsible for generating bloodshed that threatens the stability of the regime of a female president of a Muslim country (who, coincidentally, was the subject of one of the author's previous books), that simultaneously, then, raises issues about Islamic attitudes toward women and the complicated conflation of Western feminism and education with imperialism. This text becomes the focus of nightly news accounts as a struggle between liberalism and fundamentalism and their respective stands on "personal freedom," "individualism," etc., which leaves little room for discussion of other possible social orders. Conventional methods of historical analysis—which create polarities or tend to choose the most "dramatic" moment or end in the typical trajectory of linearity—cannot excavate and disentangle all the voices in this complicated text.

Which has been and continues to be the motivation behind much of the new historical writing: to allow the chorus of voices to speak, to focus on the process and not just the moment, on the scene and not just the individual, on the body and not just the figure. The new history is not only about the pain of the past, or the struggles of the present, but implicitly and explicitly proposes inclusive definitions for democratic futures.

REMAKING HISTORY

Edward W. Said

YEATS AND DECOLONIZATION

I

Yeats has now been almost completely assimilated to the canon
as well as the discourses of modern English literature, in addition to those of European high modernism. Both of these institutions of course reckon with him as a great modern Irish poet,
deeply affiliated and interacting with his native traditions, the
historical and political context of his times, and the extraor-
dinarily complex situation of being a poet in Ireland writing in
English. Nevertheless, and despite Yeats's obvious and, I would
say, settled presence in Ireland, in British culture and literature,
and in European modernism, he does present another fascinating
aspect: that of the indisputably great *national* poet who articu-
lates the experiences, the aspirations, and the vision of a people
suffering under the dominion of an offshore power. From this
perspective, Yeats is a poet who belongs in a tradition not usually considered his, that of the colonial world ruled by European
imperialism now—that is, during the late nineteenth and early
twentieth centuries—bringing to a climactic insurrectionary
stage the massive upheaval of anti-imperialist resistance in the
colonies, and of metropolitan anti-imperialist opposition that has
been called the age of decolonization. If this is not a customary
way of interpreting Yeats for those who know a great deal more
about him as an Irish European modernist poet of immense stature than I do, then I can only say that he appears to me, and I
am sure to many others in the Third World, to belong naturally
to the other cultural domain, which I shall now try to characterize. If this also sheds more light on the present status of Yeats's

role in post-independence Ireland, then so much the better.

The age of imperialism is conventionally said to have begun in the late 1870s, with the scramble for Africa. Yet it seems to me to be perfectly clear that there are all sorts of cultural as well as political indications that it began a good deal earlier. Even if we speak only about the eighteenth and nineteenth centuries, Britain and France, which dominate the history of European imperialism until World War II (Britain especially), are to be found already present in those very territories that will later become formally central during the heyday of imperialist ideology. India, North Africa, the Caribbean, Central and South America, many parts of Africa, China and Japan, the Pacific archipelago, Malaysia, Australia, North America, and of course Ireland: all these are sites of contention well before 1870, either between various local resistance groups or between the European powers themselves; in some cases, India and Africa for instance, the two struggles are going on simultaneously long before 1857, and long before the various European congresses on Africa at the end of the century. The point here is of course that no matter how one wishes terminologically to demarcate high imperialism—that period when everyone in Europe and America believed him or herself in fact to be serving a high civilizational and commercial cause by having an empire—from earlier periods of overseas conquest, rapacity, and scientific exploration, imperialism itself was a continuous process for at least a century and a half *before* the scramble for Africa. I don't think it much matters to an Indian or an Algerian that in the first half of the nineteenth century he or she did not belong to the age of imperialism whereas after 1850 both of them did. For both of them, their land was and had been dominated by an alien power for whom distant hegemony over nonwhite peoples seemed inscribed by right in the very fabric of European and Western Christian society, whether that society was liberal, monarchical, or revolutionary.

I would also want to say that modern European imperialism itself is a constitutively and radically different type of overseas domination from all earlier forms. Sheer scale and scope are only part of the difference. Certainly neither Byzantium, nor Rome, nor Athens, nor Baghdad, nor Spain and Portugal during the fifteenth and sixteenth centuries controlled anything like the territories controlled by Britain and France during the nineteenth century. The more important differences are first the extraordinary and sustained longevity of the disparity in power between Europe and its possessions, and second, the massively organized rule, which affected the detail and not just the large outlines of life, of that power. By the beginning of the nineteenth century, Europe—and in this Britain leads the way—had begun the industrial transformation of its economies; the feudal and traditional landholding structures were changing; the new mercantilist pattern of overseas trade, naval power, and colonialist settlement was firmly established; the bourgeois revolution had finally entered its triumphant stage. All these things gave the ascendancy of metropolitan Europe over its far-flung and distant possessions a profile of imposing, and even daunting power. By the beginning of World War I, Europe and America held 85 percent of the earth's surface in some sort of colonial subjugation. This, I hasten to add, did not happen in a fit of absentminded whimsy or as the result of a distracted shopping spree.

It came about for a whole series of reasons, which the library of systematic work that now exists on imperialism, beginning with Hobson, Luxemburg, Schumpeter, and Lenin, has ascribed to largely economic and somewhat ambiguously characterized political processes. My own theory, which I put forth in the book from which these comments are an extract, is that culture played a very important, indeed indispensable role. At the heart of European culture during the many decades of imperial expansion lay what could be called an undeterred and unrelenting Eurocentrism. This accumulated experiences, territories, peoples, histories, it studied them, it classified them, it verified them; but above all, it subordinated them to the culture and indeed the very idea of white Christian Europe. This cultural process has to be seen if not as the origin and cause, then at least as the vital, informing, and invigorating counterpoint to the economic and political machinery that we all concur stands at the center of imperialism. And it must also be noted that this Eurocentric culture relentlessly codified and observed everything about the non-European or presumably peripheral world, in so thorough and detailed a manner as to leave no item untouched, no culture unstudied, no people and land unclaimed. All of the subjugated peoples had it in common that they were considered to be naturally subservient to a superior, advanced, developed, and morally mature Europe, whose role in the non-European world was to rule, instruct, legislate, develop, and at the proper times, to discipline, war against, and occasionally exterminate non-Europeans.

From these views that were held in Europe and America there was no significant divergence from the Renaissance on, and if it is embarrassing for us to remark that those elements of a society we have long considered to be progressive were, so far as empire is concerned, uniformly retrograde, we still mustn't be afraid to say it. When I say "retrograde" I speak here of advanced writers and artists, of the working class, and of women, groups whose imperialist fervor increased in intensity and perfervid enthusiasm for the acquisition of and sheer bloodthirsty dominance over innumerable niggers, bog-dwellers, babus, and wogs, as the competition between various European and American powers also increased in brutality and senseless, even profitless, control.

What enables us to say all of those things retrospectively is the perspective provided for us in the twentieth century by theoreticians, militants, and insurgent analysts of imperialism like Frantz Fanon, Amilcar Cabral, C. L. R. James, Aimé Césaire,

Walter Rodney, plus many others like them on the one hand, and on the other, by the great nationalist artists of decolonization and revolutionary imperialism, like Tagore, Senghor, Neruda, Vallejo, Césaire, Faiz, Darwish . . . and Yeats. Yeats, I think, belongs in this group, for all sorts of reasons, although strangely enough he commonly isn't thought of as a natural, or card-carrying member. But let me return to Yeats and the case for him a little later, so that I can now complete the general sketch I have been attempting hitherto. As imperialism increased in scope and in depth, so too, in the colonies themselves, the resistance mounted. Indeed I would go so far as saying that just as in Europe the accumulation on a world scale that gathered the colonial domains systematically into the world market economy was supported and enabled by a culture giving empire an ideological license, so too in the overseas imperium there was a massive political, economic, and military resistance that was itself carried forward and informed by an actively provocative and challenging culture of resistance. It has been the substantial achievement of all of the intellectuals, and of course of the movements they worked with, by their historical, interpretive, and analytic efforts to have identified the culture of resistance as a cultural enterprise possessing a long tradition of integrity and power in its own right, one *not* simply grasped as a belated reactive response to Western imperialism.

A great deal, but by no means all of the resistance to imperialism was conducted in the name of nationalism. Nationalism is a word that has been used in all sorts of sloppy and undifferentiated ways, but it still serves quite adequately to identify the mobilizing force that coalesced into resistance against an alien and occupying empire on the part of peoples possessing a common history, religion, and language. Yet for all its success in ridding many countries and territories of colonial overlords, nationalism has remained, in my opinion, a deeply problematic ideological, as well as sociopolitical, enterprise. At some stage in the anti-

resistance phase of nationalism there is a sort of dependence between the two sides of the contest, since after all many of the
nationalist struggles were led by bourgeoisies that were partly
formed and to some degree produced by the colonial power;
these are the national bourgeoisies of which Fanon spoke so
ominously. These bourgeoisies in effect have often replaced the
colonial force with a new class-based and ultimately exploitative
force; instead of liberation after decolonization one simply gets
the old colonial structures replicated in new national terms.

That is one problem with nationalism: its results are written across the formerly colonized world, usually in the fabrics of
newly independent states whose pathologies of power, as Eqbal
Ahmad has called them, bedevil political life even as we speak.
The other problem is that the cultural horizons of nationalism
are fatally limited by the common history of colonizer and colonized assumed by the nationalist movement itself. Imperialism
after all is a cooperative venture. Both the master and slave par-
ticipate in it, and both grow up in it, albeit unequally. One of
the salient traits of modern imperialism is that in most places it
set out quite consciously to modernize, develop, instruct, and
civilize the natives. An entire massive chapter in cultural history
across five continents grows up out of it. The annals of schools,
missions, universities, scholarly societies, hospitals in Asia, Africa, Latin America, Europe, and North America fill its pages,
and have had the effect over time of establishing the so-called
modernizing trends in the colonial regions, as well as muting or
humanizing the harsher aspects of imperialist domination—all of
them bridging the gap between imperial center and peripheral
territories. In paying respect to it, acknowledging the shared and
combined experiences that produced many of us, we must at the
same time note how at its center it nevertheless preserved the
nineteenth-century imperial divide between native and West-
erner. The great colonial schools, for example, taught generations of the native bourgeoisie important truths about history,

science, culture. And out of that learning process millions grasped the fundamentals of modern life, yet remained subordinate dependents of an authority based elsewhere than in their lives. Since one of the purposes of colonial education was to promote the history of France or Britain, that same education also demoted the native history. There were always the Englands, Frances, Germanys, Hollands as distant repositories of the Word, for all the contradictions developed during the years of productive collaboration. Stephen Dedalus is a famous example of someone who discovers these facts with unusual force.

The culmination of this dynamic of dependence is, I said a moment ago, the resurgent nationalism of the various independence movements. Right across the Third World (including Ireland) in the period from World War I and concluding in the 1940s and 1950s, new national states appear, all of them declaring their independence from the various European powers whose rule of direct domination had for various reasons come to an end. Nationalism in India, Ireland, and Egypt, for example, was rooted in the long-standing struggle for native rights and independence by nationalist parties like the Congress, Sinn Fein, and the Wafd. Similar processes occurred in other parts of Africa and Asia. Nehru, Nasser, Sukarno, Nkrumah: the pantheon of Bandung flourished, in all its suffering and greatness, because of the nationalist dynamic. Crucial works like K. M. Panikkar's *Asia and Western Dominance* (1953), George Antonius's *The Arab Awakening* (1938), and the various works of the Irish Revival were produced out of it. Nevertheless, there were two distinct political moments during the nationalist revival, each with its own imaginative culture, the second unthinkable both in politics and history without the first. One was the period of nationalist anti-imperialism; the other, an era of liberationist anti-imperialist resistance that often followed it. The first was a pronounced awareness of European and Western culture *as* imperialism, as a reflexive moment of consciousness that enabled the

African, Caribbean, Irish, Latin American, or Asian citizen inching toward independence through decolonization to require a theoretical assertion of the end of Europe's cultural claim to guide and/or instruct the non-European or nonmainland individual. Often this was first done as Thomas Hodgkin has argued, "by prophets and priests," among them poets and visionaries, versions perhaps of Eric Hobsbawm's precapitalist protest and dissent. The second more openly liberationist moment occurred during a dramatic prolongation after World War II of the Western imperial mission in various colonial regions, principal among them Algeria, Vietnam, Palestine, Ireland, Guinea, Cuba. Whether in its general statements such as the Indian constitution, or Pan-Arabism and Pan-Africanism, or in its particularist forms such as Cusack's Gaelic or Senghor's *négritude,* the nationalism that formed the initial basis of the second moment stood revealed both as insufficient and yet as an absolutely crucial first step. Out of this paradox comes the idea of liberation, a strong new post-nationalist theme which is already implicit in the works of Connolly, Garvey, Martí, Mariategui, DuBois, for instance, but sometimes requiring the propulsive infusion of theory and sometimes armed, insurrectionary militancy to bring it forward clearly and unmistakably.

Let us look closely at the literature of the first of these moments, that of anti-imperialist resistance. Its literature develops quite consciously out of a desire to distance the native African, Indian, or Irish individual from the British, French, or (later) American master. Before this can be done, however, there is a pressing need for the recovery of the land that because of the presence of the colonizing outsider, is recoverable at first only through the imagination. Now if there is anything that radically distinguishes the imagination of anti-imperialism, it is the primacy of the geographical in it. Imperialism after all is an act of geographical violence through which virtually every space in the world is explored, charted, and finally brought under control.

For the native, the history of his/her colonial servitude is inaugurated by the loss to an outsider of the local place, whose concrete geographical identity must thereafter be searched for and somehow restored. From what? Not just from foreigners, but also from a whole other agenda whose purpose and processes are controlled elsewhere.

Let me give three examples of how complex and how totalizing is the geographical *morte main* of imperialism, and, more important, how radical, how heroic is the effort needed somehow to win back control of one's own territory. The first example is offered in a recent study by Alfred W. Crosby, *Ecological Imperialism: The Biological Expansion of Europe, 900-1900* (1986). Crosby says that wherever they went, Europeans immediately began to change the local habitat; their conscious aim was to transform territories in places as far away from Europe as South America and Australia into images of what they left behind. This process was never-ending, as a huge number of plants, animals, crops, and farming as well as building methods invaded the colony and gradually turned it into a new place, complete with new diseases, environmental imbalances, and traumatic dislocations for the overpowered natives who had little choice in the matter. A changed ecology also introduced a changed political system that, in the eyes of the nationalist poet or visionary, seemed retrospectively to have alienated the people from their authentic traditions, ways of life, political organizations. A great deal of mythmaking went into these retrospective decolonizations, by which the land was seen again, revised so to speak, in a state that antedated its alienation by imperialism. But we must not doubt the extent of the actual changes wrought by imperialism, however much we fault the nationalist poet and writer for his or her excessive romanticism.

A second example is to be found in an extraordinary book by the Indian political theorist and historian, Ranajit Guha, *A Rule of Property for Bengal* (1963). Guha's study is an account of how the Act of Permanent Settlement for Bengal was enacted in 1826 at the instigation of Philip Francis, a functionary of the East India Company. In a painstaking archeological investigation of the legal decree that made all the rents in Bengal permanent and uniform, Guha describes the intellectual background in Europe of so important a piece of legislation for India. Francis was a physiocrat; he was also an Enlightenment rationalist whose ideas were entirely Western, although they acquired the enforceable status in India of an unbreakable law. Thus to Indians the literal worth of their land in currency and produce was determined by Englishmen whose thought—abstract, rationalistic, inflexible—preempted and then displaced the traditional customs of a complex native society.

My last example also derives from recent research. In his book *Uneven Development* (1984), the geographer Neil Smith provides a brilliant formulation of how the production of a particular kind of nature and space under historical capitalism is essential to the unequal development of a landscape that integrates poverty with wealth, industrial urbanization with agricultural diminishment. The culmination of this process is imperialism, which achieves the domination, classification, and universal commodification of all space, under the aegis of the metropolitan center. Its cultural analogue is commercial geography, whose perspectives (for example in the work of Halford J. Mackinder and George Chisolm) justified imperialism as the result of "natural" fertility or infertility, of available sea lanes, of permanently differentiated zones, territories, climates, and peoples (p. 102). Thus is accomplished "the universality of capitalism," which is "the differentiation of national space according to the territorial division of labor" (p. 146).

Following Hegel, Marx, and Lukács, Smith calls the production of this scientifically "natural" world, a *second* nature. To the imagination of anti-imperialism, *our* space at home in the peripheries has been usurped and put to use by outsiders for *their* purpose. It is therefore necessary to seek out, to map, to invent, or to discover a *third* nature, which is not pristine and pre-historical ("Romantic Ireland's dead and gone" says Yeats) but one which derives historically and abductively from the deprivations of the present. This impulse then is what we might call *cartographic,* and among its most striking examples are Yeats's early poems collected in "The Rose," Neruda's various poems charting the Chilean landscape, Césaire on the Antilles, Faiz on Pakistan, and Darwish on Palestine:

> Restore to me the color of face
> And the warmth of body,
> The light of heart and eye,
> The salt of bread and earth . . . the Motherland.
> — "A Lover from Palestine" (p. 23)

With the new territoriality there comes a whole set of further assertions, recoveries, and identifications, all of them quite literally grounded on this poetically projected base. The search for authenticity, for a more congenial national origin than that provided by colonial history, for a new pantheon of heroes, myths, and religions, these too are enabled by the land. And along with these nationalistic adumbrations of the decolonized identity, there always goes an almost magically inspired, quasi-alchemical redevelopment of the native language. Yeats is especially interesting here. He shares with Caribbean and some African writers the predicament of a common language with the colonial over-lord, and of course he belongs in many important ways to the Protestant Ascendancy whose Irish loyalties, to put it mildly, were confused. There is, I think, a fairly logical progression then from Yeats's early Gaelicism, with its Celtic preoccupations and themes, to his later systematic mythologies as set down in pro-grammatic poems like "Ego Dominus Tuus" and in the treatise *A Vision.* For Yeats the overlappings he knew existed between his Irish nationalism and the English cultural heritage that both dominated and empowered him as a writer was bound to cause an overheated tension, and it is the pressure of this urgently political and secular tension that one may speculate caused him to try to resolve it on a "higher," that is, nonpolitical level. Thus the deeply eccentric and aestheticized histories he produced in *A Vision* and the later quasi-religious poems are elevations of the tension to an extra-worldly level.

In what must stand as the most interesting and brilliant account of Yeats's idea of revolution, Seamus Deane in *Celtic Revivals* (1985) has suggested that Yeats's early and invented Ireland was "amenable to his imagination . . . [whereas] he ended by finding an Ireland recalcitrant to it." Whenever Yeats tried to reconcile his occultist views with an actual Ireland—as in "The Statues"—the results, Deane says correctly, are strained. Because Yeats's Ireland was a revolutionary country, Yeats was able to use Ireland's backwardness as the source of its radically disturbing, disruptive return to spiritual ideals that had been lost to an overdeveloped modern Europe. Moreover, in such dramatic realities as the Easter 1916 uprising, Yeats also saw the breaking of a cycle of endless, perhaps finally meaningless recurrence, as symbolized by the apparently limitless travails of Cuchulain. Deane's theory therefore is that the birth of an Irish national identity coincides for Yeats with the breaking of the cycle, although it also underscores and reinforces the colonialist British attitude of a specific Irish national character. Thus Yeats's return to mysticism and his recourse to fascism, Deane says perceptively, are underlinings of the colonial predicament to be found, for example, in V. S. Naipaul's representations of India, that of a culture indebted to the mother country for its own self and for a sense of "Englishness" and yet turning towards the colony: "such a search for a national signature becomes colonial, on account of the different histories of the two islands. The greatest flowering of such a search has been Yeats's poetry." And Deane goes on to conclude that far from representing an outdated nationalism, Yeats's willful mysticism and incoherence do embody a revolutionary potential in the poet's insistence "that Ireland should retain its culture by keeping awake its consciousness of metaphysical questions." In a world from which the harsh strains of capitalism has removed thought and reflection, a poet who can stimulate a sense of the eternal and of death into consciousness is the true rebel, a figure whose colonial diminishments spur him to a negative apprehension of his society and of "civilized" modernity.

This final Adornian formulation of Yeats's quandary as it appears to the contemporary critic is of course powerful and it is attractive. Yet might we not suspect it a little of wanting to excuse Yeats's unacceptable and indigestible reactionary politics—his outright fascism, his fantasies of old homes and families, his incoherently occult divagations—by seeking to translate them into an instance of Adorno's "negative dialectic," thereby rendering Yeats more heroic than a crudely political reading would have suggested? As a small corrective to Deane's conclusion, could we not more accurately see in Yeats a particularly exacerbated example of the *nativist* (e.g., *négritude*) phenomenon, which has flourished elsewhere as a result of the colonial encounter?

Now it is true that the connections are closer between England and Ireland than between England and India, or France and Senegal. But the imperial relationship is there in all cases. The colonized may have a *sense* of England and France, speak and write in the dominant language even as he or she tries simultaneously to recover a native original, may even act in ways that directly conflict with the overall interests of his/her people, and still the divide remains. This, it seems to me, has always been the case in every colonial relationship, because it is the first principle of imperialism that there is a clear-cut and absolute hierarchical distinction between ruler and ruled. Nativism, alas, reinforces the distinction by revaluating the weaker or subservient partner. And it has often led to compelling but often demagogic assertions about a native past, history, or actuality that seems to stand free not only of the colonizer but of worldly time itself. One sees the drive backwards in such enterprises as Senghor's *négritude,* or in Soyinka's explorations of the African past, or in the Rastafarian movement, or in the Garveyite solution, or all through the Islamic world, the rediscoveries of various unsullied, precolonial Muslim essences.

Even if we leave aside the tremendous *ressentiment* often to be found in nativism (for example, in Jalal Al Ahmad's *Occidentosis,* 1984), there are two reasons for rejecting, or at least reconceiving, the nativist enterprise. Deane says that it is incoherent and yet, by its negation of politics and history, also heroically revolutionary. That, it seems to me, is to fall into the nativist position too willingly, as if nativism were the only alternative for a resisting and decolonizing nationalism. The main reason therefore to refuse it is rather that we have enough evidence of its ravages elsewhere to regard it today with very much charity: to accept nativism is to accept the consequences of imperialism too willingly, to accept the very racial, religious, and political divisions imposed on places like Ireland, India, Lebanon, and Palestine by imperialism itself. To leave the historical world for the metaphysics of essences like *négritude,* Irishness, Islam, and Catholicism is, in a word, to abandon history. Most often this abandonment in the post-imperial setting has often led to some sort of millenarianism, if the movement has any sort of mass base, or it has degenerated into small-scale private craziness, or into an unthinking acceptance of stereotypes, myths, animosities, and traditions encouraged by imperialism. No one needs to be reminded that such programs are hardly what great resistance movements had imagined as their goals.

The other reason now for tempering the nativist and, in Yeats's case as formulated by Deane, the specifically Irish colonial attitude with a decent admixture of secular skepticism, is of course that nativism is not the only alternative. Here I return to what I said at the outset, that the first moment of resistance to imperialism brought forth all the various nationalist and independence movements that culminated in the large-scale dismantling of the great classical empires, and the birth of many new states throughout the world. The second moment (liberation), however, still continues with us, and its complexities and turbulence in many instances still defy resolution. In this phase, imperialism courses on, as it were, belatedly and in different forms perhaps, but the relationship of domination continues. Even though there was an Irish Free State by the end of his life, Yeats in fact partially belonged to this second moment; the evidence for it is his sustained anti-British sentiment. And we know from the experiences of numerous colonial regions—Algeria, Vietnam, Cuba, Palestine, South Africa, and others—that the struggle for release continued. It is in this phase that I would like to suggest that *liberation,* and not nationalist independence, is the new alternative, liberation that by its very nature involves, in Fanon's words, a transformation of social consciousness beyond national consciousness.

From the perspective of liberation then, Yeats's slide into incoherence and mysticism, his rejection of politics, and his arrogant but often charming espousal of fascism (or if not fascism then authoritarianism, perhaps even of the South American kind) appear as something not to be excused, something that should not too quickly and alchemically be dialecticized into the negative utopian mode. Later I want to argue that one can quite easily situate and criticize those unacceptable attitudes of Yeats without throwing out the baby with the bath water, without changing one's view of Yeats as a poet of decolonization. But for the moment, I should like to make the case that the way beyond nativism is figured in the great turn at the climax of Césaire's *Cahier d'un retour au pays natal,* when the poet realizes that, after the rediscovery and reexperiencing of his past, after reentering the passions, horrors, and circumstances of his history as a black,

17

after feeling and then emptying himself of his anger, after accepting—

> J'accepte ... j'accepte ... entièrement, sans reserve
> ma race qu'aucune ablution d'hypsope et de lys melés
>   ne pourrait purifier
> ma race rongée de macules
> ma race raisin mûr pour pieds ivres (p. 72)

> I accept ... I accept ... totally, without reservation
> my race that no ablution of hyssop mixed with lilies
>   could purify
> my race pitted with blemishes
> my race a ripe grape for drunken feet

—after all this he is suddenly assailed by strength and life "comme un taureau," and begins to understand that

> il n'est point vrai que l'oeuvre de l'homme est finie
> que nous n'avons rien à faire au monde
> que nous parasitons le monde
> qu'il suffit que nous nous mettions au pas du monde
> mais l'oeuvre de l'homme vient seulement de
>   commencer
> et il reste à l'homme à conquérir toute interdiction im-
> mobilisée aux coins de sa ferveur et aucune race ne pos-
> sède le monopole de la beauté, de l'intelligence, de la
> force

> et il est place pour tous au rendez-vous de la conquête
> et nous nous savons maintenant que le soleil tourne au-
> tour de notre terre éclairant la parcelle qu'à fixée notre
> volonté seule et que toute étoile chute de ciel en terre à
> commandement sans limite. (p. 76)

> for it is not true that the work of man is done
> that we have no business being on earth

that we parasite the world
that it is enough for us to heel to the world
whereas the work has only begun
and man still must overcome all the interdictions
wedged in the recesses of his fervor and no race has a
monopoly on beauty, on intelligence, on strength

and there is room for everyone at the convocation of
conquest and we know now that the sun turns around
our earth lighting the parcel designated by our will alone
and that every star falls from sky to earth at our om-
nipotent command.

The striking part of this are phrases like "à conquérir toute in-
terdiction immobilisée aux coins de sa ferveur" and "le soleil . . .
éclairant la parcelle qu'à fixée notre volonté seule." You don't
give in to the rigidity and interdictions of those self-imposed
limitations that come with race, moment, or milieu; instead, you
move through them to an animated and expanded sense of "au
rendez-vous de la conquête," which necessarily involves more
than your Ireland, your Martinique, your Pakistan, etc.

I don't mean to use Césaire *against* Yeats (or Seamus
Deane's Yeats), but rather more fully to associate a major strand
in Yeats's poetry both with the poetry of decolonization and resistance, and with the historical alternatives to the nativist im-
passe. For in so many other ways, Yeats is very much the same as
other poets resisting imperialism in his insistence on a new narrative for his people, his anger at the scheme for partition (and
enthusiasm for its felt opposite, the requirement of wholeness),
the celebration and commemoration of violence in bringing
about a new order, and the sinuous interweaving of loyalty and
betrayal in the nationalist setting. Yeats's direct association with
Parnell and O'Leary, with the Abbey Theatre, with the Easter
Uprising, bring to his poetry what R. P. Blackmur, borrowing
from Jung, calls "the terrible ambiguity of an immediate experi-

ence." As one reads Yeats's work into the early twenties, there is an uncanny resemblance to the engagement and ambiguities of Darwish's Palestinian poetry half a century later, in *its* renderings of violence, of the overwhelming suddenness and surprises of historical events, of the role of politics and poetry, as opposed to violence and guns (see "Roses and Dictionaries"), of the search for respites after the last border has been crossed, the last sky flown in. "The holy centaurs of the hills are vanished," says Yeats sixty years earlier, "I have nothing but the embittered sun."

One feels in reading poems like "Nineteen Hundred and Nineteen" or "Easter 1916," and "September 1913," not just the disappointments of life commanded by "the greasy till" or the violence of roads and horses, of "weasels fighting in a hole," but also of a terrible new beauty that changes utterly the old political and moral landscape. Like all the poets of decolonization, Yeats struggles to announce the contours of an "imagined" or ideal community, crystallized not only by its sense of itself but also of its enemy. Imagined community, Benedict Anderson's fine phrase for emergent nationalism, is apt here as I have used it, so long as we are not obliged to accept his mistakenly linear periodization of unofficial and official nationalism. In the cultural discourses of decolonization, a great many languages, histories, forms circulate. As Barbara Harlow has shown in *Resistance Literature* (1987), there are spiritual autobiographies, poems of protest, prison memoirs, didactic dramas of deliverance, but in them all is a sense of the instability of time, which has to be made and remade by the people and its leaders. The shifts in Yeats's accounts of his great cycles invoke this instability, as does the easy commerce in his poetry between popular and formal speech, folk tale, and learned writing. The disquiet of what T. S. Eliot called the "cunning history, [and] contrived corridors" of history—the wrong turns, the overlap, the senseless repetition, the occasionally glorious moment—furnish Yeats, as they do all the poets of decolonization, with stern martial accents, heroism, and the grinding persistence of "the uncontrollable mystery on the bestial floor."

II

In the first volume of his memoirs, Neruda speaks of a writer's congress in Madrid held in 1937 in defense of the Republic. "Priceless replies" to the invitations "poured in from all over. One was from Yeats, Ireland's national poet; another, from Selma Lagerlöf, the notable Swedish writer. They were both too old to travel to a beleaguered city like Madrid, which was steadily being pounded by bombs, but they rallied to the defense of the Spanish Republic" (*Memoirs,* p. 130). This passage comes as a surprise to someone who, like myself, had once been influenced by Conor Cruise O'Brien's famous account of Yeats's politics, an essay whose claims are, it seems to me, hopelessly inadequate when contrasted with the information and analysis put forward by Elizabeth Cullingford's *Yeats, Ireland and Fascism* (1981) (which also refers to the Neruda recollection). Just as Neruda himself saw no difficulty in thinking of himself as a poet who dealt both with internal colonialism in Chile and with external imperialism throughout Latin America, we should think of Yeats, I believe, as an Irish poet with more than strictly local Irish meaning and applications. Neruda takes him as a national poet who represents the Irish nation in its war against tyranny and, according to Neruda, Yeats responded positively to that unmistakably anti-fascist call, despite his frequently cited dispositions towards European fascism.

There is a justly famous poem, "El pueblo," by Neruda in the 1962 collection *Plenos Poderes* (a collection translated by Alastair Reid, whose version I have used, as *Fully Empowered,* 1975). The resemblance between Neruda's poem and Yeats's "The Fisherman" is striking, because in both poems the central figure is an anonymous man of the people, who in his strength and lone-

liness is also a mute expression *of* the people; and it is this quality that inspires the poet in his work. Yeats: "It is long since I
began/ To call up to the eyes/ This wise and simple man./ All
day I'd look in the face/ What I had hoped 'twould be/ To write
for my own race/ And the reality." Neruda:

> I knew that man, and when I could
> when I still had eyes in my head,
> when I still had a voice in my throat,
> I sought him among the tombs and I said to him,
> pressing his arm that still was not dust:
> "Everything will pass, you will still be living.
> You set fire to life.
> You made what is yours."
> So let no one be perturbed when
> I seem to be alone and am not alone;
> I am not without company and I speak for all.
> Somcone is hearing me without knowing it,
> But those I sing of, those who know,
> go on being born and will overflow the world. (p. 131)

The poetic calling develops out of a pact made between people
and poet; hence the power of such invocations to an actual
poem as those provided by the popular but silent figures both
men seem to require. But the chain does not stop there, since
Neruda goes on (in "Deber del Poeta") to claim that "through
me, freedom and the sea/ will call in answer to the shrouded
heart," and Yeats in "The Tower" speaks of sending imagination
forth "and call images and memories/ From ruins or from ancient trees." Yet because such protocols of exhortation and ex-
pansiveness are announced from under the shadow of
domination, we would not be wrong to connect them with the
new, and perhaps even underground narrative of liberation de-
picted so memorably in Fanon's *Wretched of the Earth* (1963). For
whereas the divisions and separations of the colonial order

freeze the population's captivity into a sullen torpor, "new outlets . . . engender new aims for the violence of colonized peoples" (p. 59). Fanon specifies such things as declarations of the rights of man, clamors for free speech, trade union demands; later, as the violent confrontation escalates, there is an entirely new history that unfolds subterraneously, as a revolutionary class of militants, drawn from the ranks of the urban poor, the outcasts, criminals, and *déclassés,* takes to the countryside, there slowly to form cells of armed activists, who return to the city for the final stages of the insurgency.

The extraordinary power of Fanon's writing is that it is presented as a surreptitious counternarrative to the aboveground force of the colonial regime, which in the teleology of Fanon's narrative is certain to be defeated. The difference between Fanon and Yeats is, I think, that Fanon's theoretical and perhaps even metaphysical narrative of anti-imperialist decolonization is cadenced and stressed from beginning to end with the accents and inflections of liberation. Fanon's is a discourse of that anticipated triumph, liberation, which marks the second moment of decolonization. Yeats, on the other hand, is a poet whose early work sounds the nationalist note and stands finally at the very threshold it cannot actually ever cross. Yet it is not wrong to interpret Yeats as in his poetry setting a trajectory in common with other poets of decolonization, like Neruda and Darwish, which he could not complete, even though perhaps they could go further than he did. This at least gives him credit, for adumbrating the liberationist and utopian revolutionalism in his poetry that had been belied, and to some extent canceled out, by his late reactionary politics.

It is interesting that Yeats has often been cited in recent years as someone whose poetry warned of nationalist excesses. He is quoted without attribution, for example, in Gary Sick's book, *All Fall Down* (1985), on the Carter administration's handling of the Iranian hostage crisis, 1979-81; and I can distinctly

recall that the *New York Times* correspondent in Beirut in
1975-76, James Markham, quotes the same passages from "The
Second Coming" in a piece he did about the onset of the
Lebanese civil war in 1977. "Things fall apart; the centre cannot
hold" is one phrase. The other is "The best lack all conviction,
while the worst/Are full of passionate intensity." Sick and Markham both write as Americans frightened of the revolutionary
tide sweeping through a Third World once contained by Western power. Their use of Yeats is minatory: remain orderly, or
you're doomed to a frenzy you cannot control. As to how, in an
inflamed colonial situation, the colonized are supposed to remain
orderly and civilized—given that the colonial order has long
since profited the oppressor and has long since been discredited
in the eyes of the colonized—neither Sick nor Markham tells us.
They simply assume that Yeats, in any event, is on our side,
against the revolution. It's as if both men could never have
thought to take the current disorder back to the colonial intervention itself, which is what Chinua Achebe does in 1958, in his
great novel, *Things Fall Apart.*

The point, I believe, is that Yeats is at his most powerful
precisely as he imagines and renders that very moment itself. His
greatest decolonizing works quite literally conceive of the birth
of violence, or the violent birth of change, as in "Leda and the
Swan," instants at which there is a blinding flash of simultaneity
presented to his colonial eyes—the girl's rape, and alongside
that, the question "did she put on his knowledge with his
power/Before the indifferent beak could let her drop?" Yeats situates himself at that juncture where the violence of change is
unarguable, but where the results of the violence beseech necessary, if not always sufficient, reason. More precisely, Yeats's
greatest theme in the poetry that culminates in *The Tower* is, so
far as decolonization is concerned, how to reconcile the inevitable violence of the colonial conflict with the everyday politics of
an ongoing national struggle, and also with the power of each of

the various parties in the colonial conflict, with the discourse of reason, of persuasion, of organization, with the requirements of poetry. Yeats's prophetic perception that at some point violence cannot be enough and that the strategies of politics and reason must come into play is, to my knowledge, the first important announcement in the context of decolonization of the need to balance violent force with an exigent political and organizational process. Fanon's assertion, almost half a century later than Yeats, that liberation cannot be accomplished simply by seizing power (though he says, "Even the wisest man grows tense with some sort of violence"), underlines the importance of Yeats's insight. That neither Yeats nor Fanon offers a prescription for undertaking the transition from direct force to a period *after* decolonization when a new political order achieves moral hegemony, is part of the difficulty we live with today in Ireland, Asia, Africa, the Caribbean, Latin America, and the Middle East.

How one can assure the marriage of knowledge to power, or of understanding with violence, are themes in Antonio Gramsci's work, undertaken and elaborated in a wholly different context. In the Irish colonial setting, Yeats can only pose and repose the question provocatively, using his poetry, Blackmur says, as a technique of trouble. Yeats goes somewhat further than asking questions, however, in great poems of summation and vision like "Among School Children," "The Tower," "A Prayer For My Daughter," "Under Ben Bulben," and "The Circus Animals' Desertion." These are poems most eminently of genealogy and recapitulation of course. In the colonial context their significance is that they reverse the slenderizing, the reductiveness, and the slanderous encapsulation of Irish actualities that, according to a very learned book by Joseph Leerssen (*Mere Irish and Fior-Ghael,* 1986), had been the fate of the Irish at the hands of English writers for eight centuries. Displacing ahistorical rubrics such as "potato-eaters," or "bog-dwellers," or "shanty people," Yeats's poetry joins his people to its history, the more imperatively in that as father, or as "sixty year old smiling public man," or as son and husband, the poet assumes that the narrative and density of personal experience are equivalent to the experience of his people. The range of references in the closing strophes of "Among School Children" suggests that Yeats was reminding his audience that history and the nation were not separable, any more than a dancer was separate from the dance.

The power of Yeats's accomplishment in restoring a suppressed history, and rejoining the nation to it, is rendered dramatic when we recall Fanon:

Colonialism is not satisfied merely with holding a people in its grip and emptying the native's brain of all form and content. By a kind of perverted logic, it turns to the past of the oppressed people, and distorts, disfigures, and destroys it. (p. 210)

What the efforts of Mangan, Ferguson, and Dinneen did in the field of cultural nationalism, Yeats does after them in another, more challenging way. He rises from the level of personal experience to that of national archetype, without losing the immediacy of the former or the stature of the latter. Moreover Yeats's unerring choice of genealogical fables and figures speaks to another aspect of colonialism, as described by Fanon: its capacity for separating the individual from his or her own instinctual life, thereby breaking the generative lineaments of the national identity:

On the unconscious plane, colonialism therefore did not seek to be considered by the native as a gentle loving mother who protects her child from a hostile environment, but rather as a mother who unceasingly restrains her fundamentally perverse offspring from managing to commit suicide and from giving free rein to its evil instincts. The colonial mother protects her child from itself, from its ego, and from its physiology, its biology, and its own unhappiness which is its very essence.

In such a situation the claims of the native intellectual [and

*poet] are not a luxury but a necessity in any coherent program. The
native intellectual who takes up arms to defend his nation's legitimacy,
. . . who is willing to strip himself naked to study the history of his
body, is obliged to dissect the heart of his people.* (p. 211)

No wonder that Yeats instructed Irish poets to

> Scorn the sort now growing up
> All out of shape from toe to top,
> Their unremembering hearts and heads
> Base-born products of base beds.

That in the process, again according to Blackmur, Yeats ended
up creating not individuals but types that "cannot quite overcome the abstractions from which they sprang" (p. 118) is true
to the extent that the decolonizing program and its background
in the history of Ireland's subjugation are ignored, as Blackmur
was wont to do in interpreting poetry so masterfully and yet so
ahistorically. When the colonial realities are taken into account,
we get "insight and experience," and not merely "the allegorical
simulacrum churned with action" (p. 119). I will confess, however, that Yeats's full system of cycles, pernes, and gyres in any
case seems important only as it symbolizes his understandable attempts to lay hold of an extremely distant and extremely orderly
reality felt as a refuge from the colonial turbulence before his
eyes. And when in the Byzantium poems he asks to be gathered
into the artifice of eternity, the need for respite from age and
from what he would later call "the struggle of the fly in mar-
malade" is even more starkly at work. Otherwise it is difficult to
read most of Yeats and not feel that the devastating anger and
genius of Swift were harnessed by him to lifting the burdens of
Ireland's colonial afflictions. True, Yeats stopped short of imag-
ining the full political liberation he might have aspired toward,
but we are left with a considerable achievement in decolonization nonetheless.

Selected Bibliography of Works Cited

Achebe, Chinua. *Things Fall Apart.* London: Heinemann, 1958.

Ahmad, Jalal Ali. *Occidentosis: A Plague from the West.* Trans. Robert Campbell. Berkeley: Mizan Press, 1984.

Anderson, Benedict. *Imagined Communities: Reflections on the Origin and Spread of Nationalism.* London: Verso, 1983.

Antonius, George. *The Arab Awakening: The Story of the Arab National Movement.* London: H. Hamilton, 1938.

Blackmur, R. P. *Selected Essays of R. P. Blackmur.* Ed. Denis Donoghue. New York: Ecco Press, 1985.

Cabral, Amilcar. *Return to the Source: Selected Speeches.* New York: Monthly Review Press, 1973.

Césaire, Aimé. *The Collected Poetry, 1939-1976.* Trans. Clayton Eshleman and Annette Smith. Berkeley: University of California Press, 1983.

Crosby, Alfred W. *Ecological Imperialism: The Biological Expansion of Europe, 900-1900.* Cambridge: Cambridge University Press, 1986.

Cullingford, Elizabeth. *Yeats, Ireland and Fascism.* New York: New York University Press, 1981.

Darwish, Mahmud. *Victims of a Map.* Trans. Abdullah al-Udhari. London: Al Saqi Books, 1984.

Deane, Seamus. *Celtic Revivals: Essays in Modern Irish Literature, 1880-1980.* London: Faber and Faber, 1985.

DuBois, W. E. B. *Color and Democracy: Colonies and Peace.* New York: Harcourt, Brace and Company. 1945.

Faiz, Faiz Ahmad. *Poems by Faiz.* Trans. V. G. Kiernan. London: Allen & Unwin, 1971.

Faiz, Faiz Ahmad. *The True Subject: Selected Poems of Faiz Ahmed Faiz.* Trans. Naomi Lazard. Princeton: Princeton University Press, 1988.

Fanon, Frantz. *The Wretched of the Earth.* New York: Grove Press, 1963.

Garvey, Marcus. *Philosophy and Opinions of Marcus Garvey.* 2 vols. New York: Arno Press, 1968-1969.

Gramsci, Antonio. *Selections from Political Writings, 1910-1920.* Trans. John Matthews. New York: International Publishers, 1977.

Guha, Ranajit. *A Rule of Property for Bengal: An Essay on the Idea of Permanent Settlement.* Paris: Mouton, 1963.

Harlow, Barbara. *Resistance Literature.* New York and London: Methuen, 1987.

James, C. L. R. *The Future in the Present: Selected Writings.* Westport, Conn.: Lawrence Hill, 1977.

Mariategui, José. *Seven Interpretive Essays on Peruvian Reality.* Trans. Marjory Urquidi. Austin: University of Texas Press, 1971.

Martí, José. *Major Poems.* Trans. Elinor Randall. New York: Holmes Meier Publishers, 1982.

Martí, José. *Martí on the U.S.A.* Selected and trans. Luis A. Baralt. Carbondale: Southern Illinois University Press, 1966.

Neruda, Pablo. *Fully Empowered.* Trans. Alastair Reed. New York: Farrar, Straus and Giroux, 1975.

O'Brien, Conor Cruise. *Writers and Politics.* New York: Pantheon Books, 1965.

Panikkar, K. M. *Asia and Western Dominance: A Survey of the Vasco da Gama Epoch of Asian History, 1498-1945.* New ed. London: Allen & Unwin, 1965.

Rodney, Walter. *How Europe Underdeveloped Africa.* Washington, D.C.: Howard University Press, 1972.

Senghor, L. S. *Liberté,* Vol. 1: *Négritude et humanisme.* Paris: Editions du Seuil, 1964.

Smith, Neil. *Uneven Development: Nature, Capital, and the Production of Space.* Oxford: Basil Blackwell, 1984.

Paula A. Treichler

AIDS AND HIV INFECTION IN THE THIRD

WORLD: A FIRST WORLD CHRONICLE

This essay grows out of my struggle to read and interpret widely contradictory reports about AIDS and HIV infection in the Third World. At first I attributed this struggle to my lack of firsthand knowledge of the regions I was reading about. But the more I read, the less this seemed to be the issue. While it is clear that understanding AIDS as a medical phenomenon involves understanding it as a culturally specific phenomenon, it is also clear that excessively positivist notions of cultural specificity limit our ability to recognize AIDS as a complex, contradictory, and multilayered discursive construction. Even Western commentators who readily acknowledge the multiply-complex construction of AIDS in the First World habitually imagine that a single materially grounded truth about AIDS can be established for the Third World. This essay accordingly explores the question of how we are to make sense of AIDS and HIV infection in the Third World, focusing on selected First and Third World publications that attempt to chronicle and conceptualize the AIDS epidemic. I first discuss the general question of AIDS discourse, then use an essay about AIDS in Haiti to explore the discursive construction of Third World AIDS. I review several recent analyses of AIDS internationally, contrasting the statistical chronicle of the epidemic with alternative constructions; these examples show how differing conceptualizations can promote differing material consequences. Further, however, the production of knowledge is a key feature of this international chronicle, and a given Third World country's inability to produce a technically sophisticated account may simultaneously establish its need for external aid and reproduce a legacy of intellectual imperialism. In the final section, I discuss the question of narrative coherence and contradiction in the context of two published reports on the politics of AIDS in Kenya. I suggest in conclusion that understanding the discursive dimensions of the AIDS crisis is a necessary if not sufficient prelude to addressing its conceptual and material complexity.

The Problem of Discourse: The Voice We Hear May Be Our Own

to infect: *to taint with contaminated matter; communicate a pathogen or a disease; invade, usually by penetration; impregnate with deleterious qualities; communicate or affect as if by some subtle contact; deprave. Also to stain or dye.*[1]

All accounts of the AIDS epidemic in the Third World, whether they are medical reports, patient testimony, media observations, investigative journalism, World Health Organization news bulletins, or government reports, are at some level linguistic constructions. These diverse representations of AIDS in the Third World draw their authority from many sources, including the credentials and persuasive powers of individual authors, consistency with accepted beliefs and knowledge about AIDS and about the Third World, compatibility with social and political perspectives, and resonance with established discursive traditions. The influence of discourse is powerful and pervasive, yet is least likely of all these sources of authority to be explicitly recognized by readers, or by writers for that matter. The Third World typically enters First World discourse more or less unconsciously as a stereotypically reliable explanatory figure for the exotic and alien. Reviewing *And the Band Played On,* for example, Randy Shilts's book about the AIDS epidemic in the United States, Frank Browning in *Tikkun* especially praises its dissection of the major interest groups and subcultures involved in the crisis: "To rely on *The Post* or *The Times,* to plow through the scientific journals, or to listen to government officials tell their version of the AIDS story is to read about a people as strange as Bantu twig gatherers."[2]

Browning chastises Western AIDS analysts for constructing the subjects of their discourse (primarily the gay community) as members of an alien culture. As trained anthropologists can explain the strange world of the "Bantu," so Shilts is cast as the expert qualified to decode exotic subcultural practices. Thus stripped of its discursive camouflage, AIDS is laid bare for Browning as a fully comprehensible medical phenomenon. This dismissal of language as camouflage reflects the widespread view among AIDS experts that science can somehow be combined with "accurate information" and "clear communication" to strip AIDS of its politics, its metaphors, its terrifying murkiness, in short its entire connotative life, and at last reveal it as it is, an infectious disease and nothing more. The following statement, from a book on AIDS, ethics, and public policy, is representative of this view:

It is time . . . to speak plainly. There is too much at stake to permit rhetorical flourish to drive our pens . . . AIDS has been permitted and encouraged to carry a moral meaning, but that morality is in our minds, not in the disease. . . . [I]t is time for us to confront the inner meanings our language betrays and then to rid not only our speaking and writing but also our thinking of these metaphors.[3]

For Browning, it is precisely such misguided rhetoric that makes AIDS and HIV transmission confusing. Though he concedes that "innumerable mysteries about AIDS" remain, the arcane circumlocutions of scientists and journalists obfuscate even well-known facts. One of Browning's female colleagues, he tells us, is needlessly perplexed about heterosexual transmission when in fact there is a "rather simple explanation" of why heterosexual women and men are differentially at risk of becoming infected:

Gay men get it because during anal intercourse infected semen can mix with blood once the penis has caused abrasions on the rectal wall. And women are at greater risk because their reproductive systems are generally more subject to infection than are men's. Men, who generally do not have bleeding sex organs, are not usually exposed during intercourse because the virus, which may be present in vaginal fluids, does not seem to survive the urinary tract as do other venereal diseases.[4]

This passage perfectly illustrates the apodictic reflex characteristic of much Western AIDS reporting; and especially when one aspect of the AIDS story is declared impenetrably mysterious, reason and control must be elsewhere recuperated. Here, the numerous uncertainties that remain concerning HIV transmission are discursively suppressed by a series of seemingly simple declarative sentences that admit no possibility of doubt and at the same time unequivocally assert yet one more gerrymandered explanation of why differential risk is related to gender. This is presumably the kind of "plain speaking" called for by the author quoted above: yet these simple words can be unpacked to reveal a formidable jumble. Those familiar with the discourse of AIDS may well wonder how the "rugged vaginas" of 1985 have in 1988 evolved into "bleeding sex organs."[5] Browning's claim that "women are at greater risk" than men rests on his asymmetrical linguistic marking of gay (and presumably bisexual) men as *gay men* and straight men as simply *men*. This language obscures by needlessly gendering the correct underlying generalization: that having (unprotected) sexual contact with an infected person puts you at greater risk of becoming infected than having sexual contact with an uninfected person. Indeed, the epidemiology of AIDS in many Third World countries, where women and men are infected in equal numbers, is widely interpreted to confirm that general patterns of HIV transmission are mainly mathematical: so long as gay/bisexual men in the U.S. were the group most widely infected, the virus was most likely to infect their sexual partners—primarily gay/bisexual men but also some women;

mathematically, the group least at risk was straight men. Now that increasing infection is occurring among straight IV drug users and their partners and *their* partners, straight men are at greater risk of infection whether they develop "bleeding sex organs" or not.

By no means do such assertions exhaust the narrative repertoire of AIDS commentary. We may be thankful that Browning does not return to the "Bantu twig gatherers" and attempt to account for the equal prevalence of HIV infection in both women and men in many Third World countries. But a 1988 editorial in the *Journal of the American Medical Association,* reviewing several co-factors thought to facilitate HIV transmission (such as presence of prior sexually transmitted disease), offers this explanation: "central African heterosexual populations may be more similar to homosexual men than to most heterosexuals in the United States."[6] The sweeping nature of this statement is unwarranted, if typical of First World writing about AIDS in Africa. The "populations" implicated involve people of different countries, regions, social and political units, ages, religions, classes, and genders, whose diverse occupations, behaviors, biological and genetic characteristics, linguistic practices, sexual practices, and health histories are only beginning to be identified with respect to HIV infection and AIDS. Many studies are flawed; almost all involve small numbers of people. The only "similarity" between "African heterosexual populations" and "homosexual men" that can be claimed at this point—and even this would be disputed—is that, in the aggregate, these groups share a higher prevalence of HIV infection than some other groups. This is hardly news. What we see is American medicine's perennial quest for the magic bullet, this time in the form of that missing piece of information that will make the AIDS puzzle manageable: the magic bulletin.

Discourse about AIDS draws on widely accepted narratives of past epidemics. An underlying premise is that AIDS is a knowable biological phenomenon whose strange and seemingly contradictory aspects will ultimately prove to be illusory: decoded by experts, its mysteries will one by one be revealed as controllable material realities. Discourse about AIDS in the Third World shares but exaggerates this premise, first equating the Third World (especially Africa, "the dark continent") with the savage, the alien, or the incomprehensible, then asserting the importance and achievability of reason and control. Though these two features may initially seem to be in conflict, they exist in fact in a relationship of discursive symbiosis: the metaphors of mystery and otherness produce the desire for control, which is in turn fulfilled and justified by the metaphors of otherness and mystery.[7]

The performative work that such narrative structures do can be identified, challenged, recuperated, reassigned; it cannot be eradicated. Language about AIDS, illness, and epidemics is already informed with metaphor (*influenza* got its name because illnesses were believed to be under the *influence* of the stars; *infect* means "to contaminate," "to communicate," and "to stain or dye," a connotative web even the most vigilant housekeeping cannot sweep away). To believe that information and communication about AIDS will separate fact from fiction and reality from metaphor is to suppress the linguistic complexity of everyday life. Further, to inform is also to perform; to communicate is also to construct and interpret. Information does not simply exist, it issues from and in turn sustains a way of looking at and behaving toward the world; it shapes programmatic agendas and determines capital investments.

The Third World therefore creates some specific challenges for the process of making sense of AIDS. Efforts to meet these challenges are not always best served by the positivist "plain speaking" voice of reason that holds that accurate information and clear messages will bring about desired behavioral change. As others have noted, the seemingly simple message to "use a condom" probably raises more questions than it answers.[8] The truth is that the AIDS epidemic is unprecedentedly complex, a moving chorus that takes on new voices and produces new orchestrations wherever it goes. Nor are these always harmonious. The First World experience leaves no doubt about this. To suppose that the discursive dimensions of the epidemic are somehow less complex in the Third World is cultural imperialism indeed. Although any crisis may inevitably become a point of articulation for multiple voices and interests, the AIDS crisis in the Third World is of pressing concern for three reasons: (1) diverse interests are articulated around AIDS in ways that are socially and culturally localized and specific; (2) understanding this specificity is a necessary if not sufficient condition for effectively mobilizing resources and programs to address the epidemic in a given country or region; and (3) institutional forces and cultural precedents in the First World prevent us from hearing the story of AIDS in the Third World as a complex narrative.

To analyze the discourse of AIDS is not to evade its powerful material consequences. Far from being a detached activity restricted to an idealized realm, analyzing discursive constructions of AIDS in the Third World is a pressing practical task—as pressing as basic laboratory research, I would argue, for interpreting and influencing the everyday course of the epidemic. Especially in developing countries where AIDS/HIV education, prevention, and treatment will inevitably be labor-intensive efforts, questions of language are central to such tasks as producing effective public service announcements, employing print and electronic media, communicating to people who do not read, communicating in countries where seventy or eighty different languages are spoken, mediating between the forthright language of "safer sex" and the spiritual formulations demanded by the church leaders central to many prevention efforts, and marshalling various human resources (e.g., traditional herbal healers) for face-to-face education and counseling in rural areas.

The cultural choice in African countries between the slogans "love carefully" and "love faithfully," the effectiveness of rock music in promoting AIDS awareness, the distinction between prostitutes and "free women" as epidemiological categories, the shift from "promiscuity" to "sexual partner change" in AIDS education, the implications of thinking of condoms as "American socks," the distinction between HIV infection and AIDS—all presuppose some level of linguistic analysis.[9] Further, language is the overt subject of debate in many discussions of AIDS and its politics in the Third World. For example, the editors of *AIDS in Africa,* a 1988 collection of essays on policy, write that the "language of crisis and catastrophe has permeated the discussion of AIDS in Africa. In this book the editors and contributors have tried to curb the language while not side-stepping the real problems that HIV/AIDS poses for Africa."[10]

The close analysis of such examples and their positioning within AIDS discourse enables us to identify the key issues of that discourse—what Ernesto Laclau and Chantal Mouffe call *nodal points,* or privileged discursive points that serve in part to fix meaning and center a field of discourse—and, without automatically privileging every Third World account as somehow more authentic than accounts explicitly mediated through the West, begin to assemble and articulate a different field of discourse about AIDS in the Third World.[11]

There is a certain degree of Western cultural imperialism in believing the privilege and task of conceptualizing this crisis is ours, the question of representation ours, the need to know ours. For our benefit, African countries are rebuked for withholding facts about AIDS. Once again, Western discourse reproduces the perspective of "a development doctrine that treats Africa as a problem to be solved rather than a voice to be heard."[12] If we can find ways to circumvent the increasingly centralized and professionalized handling of the epidemic, perhaps the voices of the Third World may lead us to scrutinize the linguistic imperialism that has constructed the very terms of the question: *AIDS* and *Third World*. In that case, the voices we hear will not always and inevitably have been only our own.

"A U.S. Doctor Unmasks Truth in Haiti": Third World AIDS in First World Media

We had come near the end of a long line of anthropologists working in these remote villages . . . Coming at the end gave us certain advantages. . . . But as time passed we became aware that we had also inherited serious problems. The !Kung had been observing anthropologists for almost six years and had learned quite a bit about them. Precedents had been set that the !Kung expected us to follow.
　　　　—*Marjorie Shostak,* Nisa: The Life and Words of a !Kung Woman, *1981*[13]

The very activity of ethnographic writing—seen as inscription or textualization—enacts a redemptive Western allegory. This pervasive structure needs to be perceived and weighed against other possible emplotments for the performance of ethnography.
　　　　—*James Clifford, "On Ethnographic Allegory," 1986*[14]

Almost any account of AIDS in the Third World will serve to demonstrate problematic aspects of its linguistic and visual construction. A highly visible story was written for *Life* magazine by physician-author Richard Selzer, who visited Haiti in the mid-1980s in an effort to learn the truth about AIDS behind the government's apparent attempts to downplay its prevalence.[15] The metaphor of the article's title, "A Mask on the Face of Death," invokes the government's denials in the language of exotic tropical rituals like carnival and voodoo. The subtitle is "As AIDS Ravages Haiti, a U.S. Doctor Finds a Taboo Against Truth"; while very likely not Selzer's words, they suggest to the reader not only that official denials mask the brutality of the epidemic but also that Selzer, the expert medical observer, can perceive the reality beneath the mask. Selzer's article is in the

tradition of the privileged First World informant of conventional
ethnography and travel literature, the stranger in a strange land
whose representation of AIDS in the Third World is legitimated
by its claim to be an objective (scientific) account of phenomena
observed or experienced firsthand. As Mary Louise Pratt argues,
travel writing has provided ethnographic description with a discursive legacy, despite the ethnographer's desire to repudiate it;
both, in turn, permeate representations in other genres.[16] Thus
Selzer's article opens with the conventional arrival scene of this
dual legacy: "It is 10 o'clock at night as we drive up to the
Copacabana, a dilapidated brothel on the rue Dessalines in the
red-light district of Port-au-Prince" (p. 59). Outside the bar,
Selzer is importuned by men and women offering a variety of sexual pleasures; inside, he interviews three female prostitutes from
the Dominican Republic who describe AIDS as an economic
problem for them, not a health problem. The direct interrogation of the native informant is another staple of privileged observer accounts; in AIDS narratives, it is often prostitutes who
are interviewed, and they always seem to be wearing red. (For
the *Life* story, one of the Dominican prostitutes is glamorously
photographed, the full skirt of her red dress fanned out across a
bed; an April 1988 news account of the fear of AIDS in Mombasa, Kenya, reports an exchange between a U.S. sailor and a
prostitute, a "23-year-old Ugandan woman in red shorts"; a
Newsweek photograph of a woman in red leggings and skirt is
captioned: " 'Avoid promiscuity': Prostitute with men in
Zaire."[17]) The following day, Selzer talks with physicians and
examines a large number of patients with apparent HIV-related
illnesses for whom little in the way of treatment is available.

Selzer is carefully nonjudgmental with respect to street life
and indeed speculates that the virus may have entered Haiti as
an accidental feature of First World exploitation:

*Could it have come from the American and Canadian homosexual tour-
ists, and, yes, even some U.S. diplomats who have traveled to the island*

to have sex with impoverished Haitian men all too willing to sell them-
selves to feed their families? Throughout the international gay commu-
nity Haiti was known as a good place to go for sex. (p. 64)

Selzer pursues this characterization of Haiti as sexual victim ravaged by Western capitalists. Acting on "a private tip from an official at the Ministry of Tourism," Selzer and guide drive to a
once luxurious hotel fifty miles from Port-au-Prince that was a
prime vacation spot for gay men. Because the two French men
who own the hotel are out of the country, Selzer and his guide
are shown around by a staff member, a man of about thirty who
clearly

is desperately ill. Tottering, short of breath, he shows us about the
empty hotel. The furnishings are opulent and extreme — tiger skins on
the wall, a live leopard in the garden, a bedroom containing a giant
bathtub with gold faucets. Is it the heat of the day or the heat of my
imagination that makes these walls echo with the painful cries of
pederasty? (p. 64)

This passage reveals both the white American male, ill at ease
among the tiger skins of a hotel in Haiti, and the traditional
Western travel writer at work on Third World AIDS. Ultimately, for Selzer, AIDS in Haiti is an unambiguous mor(t)ality
tale about the evils of sexual excess: as northern homosexual
men ravaged Haitian boys, so does AIDS ravage Haiti. Nostalgia
for the observed culture's original innocence gives way to regret
at its exploitation by decadent foreigners and speculation about
the deadly effects of exotic customs and sexual practices. Selzer's
account therefore tells us something about his concrete daily activities, his heated imagination, and his strategies for transforming selected experiences into prose, but his desire to bring the
country's plight to world attention is as much about language as
about AIDS in Haiti.

The status of Selzer's article as a firsthand report of observed phenomena does not rest on our firsthand knowledge

about AIDS, the Third World, or Haiti. In certain concrete ways, just as cinematic convention represents scenes viewed through binoculars as two intersecting circles, Western AIDS discourse transforms a culture so that it ceases to recognize itself but paradoxically becomes recognizable in the West. What is needed is to sort out the multiple voices, texts, and subtexts of the AIDS epidemic—which has in part evolved, as Jan Zita Grover puts it, as a "creature of language."[18]

We may begin this process by reviewing the elements of Selzer's account of AIDS in Haiti that are now virtually obligatory in First World chronicles of Third World AIDS. First, the opening arrival scene, as I have noted, situates the First World observer in relation to the Third World culture—a culture that, in AIDS chronicles, almost always belongs to the fallen world of postcolonial development. Indeed, as I note below, the term *Third World* presupposes an analysis founded on such concepts as capitalism, colonialism, industrialization, modernity, and development. Second, the statistics provided by Haitian physicians function in part to anchor in objective fact Selzer's more personal observations about the prevalence of AIDS (I return to statistics in the next section). Third, statistics more broadly show how the First World chronicle incorporates within its own structural demands the specialized knowledge of expert native informants whose on-the-scene experience equips them to reveal the truth behind the official mask. (In Selzer's story, the inside informants assert that AIDS is more widespread than officials admit; but in other AIDS stories, insiders may function to accuse the government and the media of exaggerating the AIDS crisis for political gains.) A fourth element is provided by "the reigning American pastor," a nonnative informant whose unreliability as a cultural informant is demonstrated by his moralistic condemnation of voodoo, whose rituals are believed by some to facilitate the spread of HIV: voodoo, he tells Selzer, is "a demonic religion, a cancer on Haiti" that is "worse than AIDS" (p.

62). Though such cultural subtexts can function in AIDS narratives to prepare the ground for epidemiological hypotheses, the purpose here seems different. In positioning himself against his fellow American, "a tall, handsome Midwesterner with an ecclesiastical smile," Selzer secures his own reliability, much as ethnographers quote descriptions of a given culture by earlier travel writers to repudiate the bias of such unscientific observations. Selzer's visits to health care settings constitute a fifth element; like his discussions with Haitian physicians, they demonstrate the inadequacies of a devastated health care system, an economic fallen world that parallels his image elsewhere of Haiti as the victim of First World sexual exploitation. A sixth familiar element in AIDS stories is "the view from the street," represented by Selzer's talk with the three healthy Dominican prostitutes. Their remarks seem designed to underscore the ignorance and dangerous false security engendered by the government's official silence. One of them, Carmen, scoffs at Selzer's suggestion that prostitutes as a population are sick with AIDS:

"AIDS!" Her lips curl about the syllable. "There is no such thing. It is a false disease invented by the American government to take advantage of the poor countries. The American President hates poor people, so now he makes up AIDS to take away the little we have." The others nod vehemently. (p. 60)

The notion that AIDS is an American invention is a recurrent element of the international AIDS story, yet one not easily incorporated within a Western positivist frame, in part, perhaps, because it is political, with discursive roots in the resistance to colonialism; the Western response, accordingly, attributes it to ignorance, state propaganda, or psychological denial.[19]

Carmen's theory of AIDS invokes two other significant narratives. The first, a tale of postmodern scholarship, is about the difficulty of finding good native informants these days. As Shostak's introduction to her ethnographic study *Nisa* makes clear, native informants are quite likely to be already wise in the ways of Western inquisitors. Discussing *Nisa,* Pratt convincingly argues that Shostak is nevertheless able ultimately to transcend the "degraded" ethnographic culture of too-knowing informants and achieve a redemptive resolution for her story. Selzer's framing of Carmen accomplishes something similar, together with a second narrative, to which I have already alluded, concerning the construction of the subject in a fallen world. Pratt suggests that ethnographic characterizations of the !Kung changed in the course of foreign colonization. Precolonial ethnographers rendered them as sly, bloodthirsty, untrustworthy, appetitive, manipulative; after colonization, they came to be represented as helpful, friendly, innocent, good, and vulnerable. A parallel shift may be occurring in the course of the AIDS epidemic in the U.S. in mainstream representations of gay men, as illness and death are perceived to transform a threatening and alien community into a vulnerable and sympathetic one (a transformation challenged by many AIDS activists). In the global AIDS drama, Carmen's speech takes place at what is presented as a pivotal narrative moment, and this encourages us to hear her emphatic denial of AIDS as a prelude to tragedy—perhaps as we would hear Violetta in the first act of *La Traviata.*[20]

Selzer finally sums up:

This evening I leave Haiti. For two weeks I have fastened myself to this lovely fragile land like an ear pressed to the ground. It is a country to break a traveler's heart. . . . Perhaps one day the plague will be rendered in poetry, music, painting. But not now, not now. (p. 64)

Here the stance of physician as ethnographer is clearer, the physician's ear pressed to the body of Haiti as he might press it to the body of a patient. But though the diagnosis is grim, the language is utopian: the First World AIDS narrative has successfully repelled the threat of postmodern disruption to deliver a message of transcendent, universal human tragedy.

Visual representations are no less problematic than verbal ones. The Selzer article's facticity is buttressed by color photographs that reproduce familiar representations of the Third World and reinforce what we think we already know about AIDS in those regions: frail, wasting bodies in gloomy clinics; small children in rickety cribs; the prostitutes in red. Photographs in a 1986 *Newsweek* story on AIDS in Africa depict the "Third Worldness" of its health care system: in Tanzania, a man with AIDS lies hospitalized on a plain cot with none of the high-tech paraphernalia of U.S. representations; a widely reprinted photograph shows six "emaciated patients in a Uganda AIDS ward," two in cots, four on mats on the floor; rarely are physicians shown. A story on AIDS in Brazil carries similar nontechnological images. In contrast, African publications often run photos of African scientists and physicians, and among the photographs in a 1987 story on AIDS in the Brazilian equivalent of *Newsweek* is one of a fully equipped operating theater complete with masked and gowned physicians and nurses.[21]

A different problem occurs in a 1988 *National Geographic* story called "Uganda: Land Beyond Sorrow." The story's portrait of unrelieved despair is oddly challenged by the magazine's characteristically stunning photographs. A young woman with AIDS in a long flowing dress, for example, stands supported by her mother, who is wearing vivid pink; the caption tells us the woman, Jane Namirimu, is pregnant and already too weak to stand alone. Yet the beauty of the composition, even the adjacent photograph of her grave taken when the photographer returned three months later, transforms the text's bleak assertions into an almost utopian narrative of elegiac fatefulness in which aesthetic universality redeems individual suffering.[22]

A final problem is the literal appropriation of images. J. B. Diederich's photographs for the Selzer story were at least original for *Life;* but some AIDS photographs are familiar not simply because they invoke a familiar tradition but because precisely the same images circulate among diverse publications. In one of Diederich's photographs, a large striking study in brown and white, an emaciated Haitian woman in a white dress sits gracefully on a wooden bench and looks out at the camera. The caption reads, "Tuberculosis is but one of the wasting infections of what Haitians call *maladi-a*." Selzer's text does not define *maladi-a;* nor does it tell us whether tuberculosis is counted in Haiti as a disease that signals AIDS or is, like AIDS, simply one of many wasting diseases; nor is it clear that the woman in the photograph has actually been diagnosed with AIDS. But reproduced months later in the Canadian news magazine *Maclean's,* the identical photo, no longer ambiguous, is captioned: "Haitian AIDS victim: a former playground for holidayers."[23]

What constitutes the AIDS narrative is a layering of representational elements, narrative voices, and replicating images. Moreover, one cannot find the truth about AIDS simply by dispensing with First World mediation in favor of voices that originate in the Third World. For these voices are often in conflict as well: even the observations of trained journalists or health care professionals within a country may differ radically not only from the West's scenarios but from each other's. In central Africa, an area widely characterized in the Western media as being "devastated" by AIDS, some people believe, as Carmen does, that the disease is largely imaginary, the latest Western trick to reduce the Third World's population in the wake of failed birth control strategies in the past; others believe the disease exists, but is a "white man's disease"; still others, such as Richard C. Chirimuuta and Rosalind J. Chirimuuta, argue that most Western research on AIDS in Africa is based on racist preconceptions rather than scientific evidence, and hence the true extent of the illness is unknown.[24] Discrepancies between doomsday predictions by the Western media and official denials by Third World governments introduce another complicating factor: a state's "social imaginary"—what it dreams itself to be. As Ann Anagnost observes, a country's explicit declarations and official statistics are likely to be pervaded by the language of this implicit social dream.[25] The dream of controlling AIDS—whether of controlling the blood supply, statistical and epidemiological studies, media coverage, biotechnology, or moral and sexual behavior—may well declare itself in a Western tongue. The Brazilian photograph of a surgical operating theater, that famed invention of Western high technology, accurately documents the existence in Brazil of sophisticated medical capabilities. But as a representation of "the AIDS epidemic," it may be as bogus as the "Haitian AIDS victim." Symbiosis is self-perpetuating: while Third World representations function as icons that can be seamlessly decontextualized and appropriated by the First World narrative voice, the Third World media, dependent in varying degrees on First World sources and technology, may recontextualize these images as their own. As Edward Said argues, modern representation in the decolonized world depends increasingly on a concentration of media power in metropolitan centers; this contributes to the monolithic nature of Third World representations, which are in turn a major source of information about Third World populations not only for the "outside world" but also for those populations themselves.[26] Dependency, of course, may perpetuate dominance but it also fosters resistance. To believe otherwise is to adopt the social imaginary of the neocolonial, a dream in which shrewdly invested linguistic capital—in the form of information, communication, or consultation—earns a predictably satisfactory return.

Many people throughout the world are now pressed to make sense of AIDS, to develop a working conception that will enable them to proceed with life, including for some life with AIDS and HIV. It is increasingly clear that this goal needs to be seen for what it is—a *working* conception—and that any global effort, to work, needs to involve voices that ultimately may be neither harmonious nor reconcilable. Politically appealing as it may be to dismiss Western representations of Third World AIDS as false, we should not simply privilege as true our most trusted alternative sources in their place. Why? Because such a strategy is ultimately as paternalistic as the first, and because it fails to challenge the assumption that what is true can actually be determined. But if we relinquish the compulsion to separate true representations of AIDS from false ones and concentrate instead on the process and consequences of representation and discursive production, we can begin to sort out how particular versions of truth are produced and sustained, and what cultural work they do in given contexts. Such an approach illuminates the construction of AIDS as a complex narrative and raises questions not so much about truth as about power and representation. To understand the ways AIDS comes to be articulated within particular cultural contexts, the major problem is not determining whether a given account is true or false but identifying the underlying rules and conventions that determine whether that account is received as true or false, by whom, and with what material consequences. Richard Selzer's essay on AIDS in Haiti provides useful information: not necessarily about the true nature of AIDS in the Third World, but about the power of individual authors and Western mass print media to produce and transmit particular representations of AIDS according to certain conventions and in doing so sustain their acceptance as true.[27] Other forms of representation, drawing on different conventions, different rules, may make claims to truth in different ways. Diverse voices then represent not diverse accounts of reality we must choose among but significant points of articulation for ongoing social and cultural struggles. Once we adopt the view that reality is inevitably mediated, we become ourselves participants in the mediation process; such voices may then provide important models for challenging existing régimes of truth and disrupting their effects—in the Third World, as in the First.[28]

The Country and the City: Dreams of Third World AIDS

It is not impossible that in the future, as in the past, effective steps in the prevention of disease will be motivated by an emotional revolt against some of the inadequacies of the modern world. . . . Knowledge and power may arise from dreams as well as from facts and logic.
  —René Dubos, Mirage of Health, *1959*[29]

A régime of truth is that circular relation which truth has to the systems of power that produce and sustain it, and to the effects of power which it induces and which redirect it.
  —John Tagg, The Burden of Representation, *1988*[30]

You'd be surprised. They're all individual countries.
  —Ronald Reagan, *statement to the press after visiting Latin America*[31]

"The statistical mode of analysis," argued Raymond Williams in *The Country and the City,* was "devised in response to the impossibility of understanding contemporary society from experience." Characterizing preindustrial English society as knowable through experience (if only partially so), Williams contrasted this "knowable community" with the "new sense of the darkly unknowable" produced by urbanization and industrialization. The metaphor of darkness was routinely invoked in discussions of the rise of cities: the East End, for instance, was called "Darkest London." Statistical analysis was one of the new forms of knowledge "devised to penetrate what was rightly perceived to be to a large extent obscure."[32]

Given its historical mission, statistical analysis, not unexpectedly, is widely seen as the most powerful way to understand the latest incarnation of the "darkly unknowable": AIDS in the Third World. Statistical data, at the least, are seen as the necessary foundation for other knowledge. Further, the ability to produce statistical information is used to measure a nation's degree of development, predict its ability to cope with the AIDS crisis, and determine its eligibility for some forms of external aid. Even if a country cannot produce its own numbers internally, its ability to cope can be demonstrated as a willingness to cooperate with external studies.[33] Certainly the international discourse on AIDS and HIV infection in the Third World is shaped on a day-to-day basis by statistical findings and projections. Once numbers are generated and publicized, they take on a life of their own—one reason why AIDS estimates may sometimes be resisted. But even when specific numbers are questioned or denounced, the use of numbers as a fundamental measure of AIDS' reality is not.

Data with regard to AIDS/HIV in Third World countries are regularly generated by several sources: the World Health Organization's (WHO) Global Programme on AIDS (GPA), which includes a Surveillance, Forecasting, and Impact Assessment Unit; the U.S. Public Health Service Centers for Disease Control (CDC); the Center for International Research (CIR) of the U.S. Bureau of the Census, whose AIDS/HIV Statistics Data Base is supported in part by the U.S. Agency for International Development (USAID); and the London School of Hygiene. A number of other agencies gather more localized data, including the World Bank, the Rockefeller Foundation, the National Science Foundation, the National Institutes of Health, the Kenya Medical Research Institute (KMRI), the International Medical Research Center (Gabon), and individual hospitals and laboratories.[34] Let us briefly examine some of the numbers produced by this statistical enterprise.

Of these sources, WHO headquarters in Geneva is widely recognized and accepted as a legitimate and "politically neutral" producer, synthesizer, and interpreter of international numbers. By January 31, 1989, the number of countries reporting to the GPA was 177, of which 144 had reported one or more cases of

AIDS (up from 175 and 138 in three months): a total of 139,886 cases worldwide had been reported to WHO, an increase of close to 7,000 over the previous month; WHO considers a more realistic total of actual AIDS cases to be 250,000 to 350,000, and estimates that 5 million more are infected (with HIV) worldwide (a million or more infected in Africa alone). These totals mean that at least one new case of AIDS is being reported somewhere in the world every minute, or 60 new cases every hour and 1,440 each day. Projections about the worldwide distribution and future prospects of AIDS and HIV infection led Jonathan Mann, director of the GPA, to conclude in mid-1988 that "the global situation will get much worse before it can be brought under control."[35]

This assessment did not come readily to the World Health Organization: indeed, it was not until late 1986 that WHO officially acknowledged AIDS as a global health problem—in many countries, some five years into the epidemic. Once committed to the existence of AIDS, however, WHO's surveillance reports and seroprevalence data were sufficient, by the end of 1987, to suggest three broad global patterns of AIDS.[36] As constructed by WHO, *Pattern I* is typical of industrialized countries with large numbers of reported cases (the First World, roughly, including the United States, Canada, Western Europe, Australia, and New Zealand): HIV infection in these countries first appeared in the late 1970s and began spreading rapidly, primarily among gay, bisexual men, and IV drug users in urban coastal centers and recipients of blood products. Though infection and illness are at present slowly increasing in the heterosexual population, the male to female ratio is still between 10:1 or 15:1, perinatal transmission (from mother to infant) is not yet common, and infection in the overall population is estimated to be less than one percent (though greater than 50 percent in "some groups practicing high-risk behavior"). In *Pattern II,* characteristic of Third World countries (primarily central and eastern Africa, the Caribbean, and some Latin American countries), HIV infection appeared in the late 1970s, though was not widely identified with AIDS until 1983. Heterosexual transmission is the norm, with the male to female ratio about one to one and prenatal transmission therefore common; transmission via gay sexual contact or IV drug use appears to be low or absent. In *Pattern III,* attributed to the Second World countries of the Soviet bloc as well as North Africa, the Middle East, Asia, and most of the Pacific (excluding Australia and New Zealand), HIV is judged to have appeared in the early to mid-1980s; only small numbers of cases have so far been reported, usually in people who have traveled to and had sexual intercourse with infected persons in Pattern I or II areas, with only recent documentation of "indigenous homosexual, heterosexual and IV-drug-use transmission."[37]

What will be the material effects of the global epidemic? Again, we can identify a widely-accepted set of predictions. In developed countries like the U.S., where 13 percent of the gross national product is spent on health care, AIDS and HIV-related illnesses are already straining the health care system; in many Third World countries, where annual expenditures on health care are often less than $5 per person and totally inadequate even for current needs, future prospects are grim. Further, despite the widespread stereotype of people with AIDS as the disadvantaged of society, the twenty- to forty-year-old age group, most vulnerable worldwide, is central to the labor force, to childbearing, to caring for the dependent young and old, and, ironically, to marshalling and managing the resources for addressing the AIDS epidemic and other health problems.[38] Synthesizing a number of studies on AIDS in Africa, Miller and Rockwell spell out more specific consequences: (1) the highest risk in age group is for those between 20 and 40 (for women 25-29, for men 30-34); (2) prenatal infection threatens the health of newborn children; (3) at highest risk are city dwellers and the geographically mobile (commercial and government elites, military and paramilitary personnel, police, truckers, prostitutes); (4) under current treatment regimens, the majority of those infected will become ill (current thinking is that between 50 percent and 90 percent will show symptoms within ten years and many will die); (5) many people will become ill who won't understand their symptoms or their infectiousness and role in spreading infection; (6) the "medical care systems will be inadequate to the task of caring for the ill; (7) victims and their kinsman will embark on desperate searches for cures, with large expenditures of savings and an aggressive search for health care and ways to finance it."[39] A further point made repeatedly is that education and prevention, the major strategies at present for controlling the spread of the virus, have proved difficult enough in media-rich Western countries; the task of communicating complex health messages to the diverse populations and geographical sites of Third World countries is formidable.

A global AIDS/HIV epidemic has now been documented and its existence widely authorized as true.[40] Despite the reluctance of some nations to acknowledge it, many others have now taken formal steps to address the crisis by endorsing WHO's global AIDS statement and policy and the United Nations statement, distributing information for travelers, and attending national and international conferences and summits. International assessments by the World Bank and others have reinforced a sense of global urgency by identifying the multiple adverse economic effects of AIDS on Third World—and First World—countries; in Africa, such effects are now considered to be unavoidable. The 1988 International AIDS Conference in Stockholm closed with the plea that the rich developed countries help developing nations fight AIDS and that international support be given to WHO. Halfdan Mahler, the director-general of WHO, rebuked rich countries for "self congratulation" in anti-AIDS drives based on blood screening, technology, and expensive educational campaigns far beyond the reach of the African countries, emphasizing that national self-sufficiency in an infectious pandemic is an illusion: "AIDS cannot be stopped in any country, until it is stopped in all countries."[41]

The power and centrality of numbers to these constructions of AIDS are obvious. Without the power and authority of statistical methods, the epidemic as a global issue could not have been articulated. Yet while the First World chronicle of global AIDS may appear to be unfolding smoothly as our knowledge grows, in fact this knowledge is problematic in several ways. Indeed, even the most fundamental meaning of the narrative remains contested. Consider the following judgments about the epidemic in Africa, all published in 1988:

(1) "The continent hardest hit by the AIDS pandemic is Africa where all three infection patterns can be found." (WHO)

(2) "Medical experts consider the epidemic an accelerating catastrophe that, in the words of one, 'will make the Ethiopian famine look like a picnic.'" (Congressional Research Service)

(3) In many of the urban centers of central Africa, "from 5 to 20 percent of the sexually active age-group has already been infected with HIV. Rates of infection among some prostitute groups range from 27 percent in Kinshasa, Zaire, to 66 percent in Nairobi, Kenya, and 88 percent in Butare, Rwanda. Close to half of all patients in the medical wards of hospitals in those cities are currently infected with HIV. So are from 10 to 25 percent of the women of childbearing age, and that will mean an increase in child mortality by at least 25 percent; the gains achieved with difficulty by child-survival programs over the past two decades may be nullified. By the early 1990s the total adult mortality rate in these urban areas will have been doubled or tripled by AIDS." (WHO)

(4) "A *Newsweek* cover story claimed one Rakai village [in Uganda] had seven discos and 'sex orgies.' In reality it has 20 mud huts, a handful of fishing boats, and no electricity." *(The Guardian)*

(5) "The tale of AIDS in Africa is not one of widespread devastation and the collapse of nations. There are 53 countries in Africa and AIDS exists substantially in only a few of them." (*Washington Post*)

(6) "Like the tenacious theories put forward as explanations for the heterosexual spread of HIV in Africa, the whole AIDS pandemic is shrouded in mystery and uncertainty. There is no reliable information on AIDS and by the time one message has percolated its way down to the general population, it is out of date and a new one is already on its way to replace it." (*West Africa*)[42]

Some sources of confusion and contradiction are recognized and articulated by epidemiologists and social scientists. Estimates of infection and actual cases of AIDS for entire populations may be derived from inadequate data: too few studies, studies of too small a sample size, nonrepresentative samples, and so on. In Africa, "underreporting" is taken for granted and estimates corrected upwards; at the same time, the number of positive cases actually diagnosed may be too high or too low, depending on the procedure used. Many studies presented at conferences never become available for scrutiny in published form; and many published papers do not report important data about how the study was conducted. Finally, observations by experienced medical experts in Africa, which tend to make lower estimates of cases than WHO, are discounted as clinical and experiential rather than scientific and technical.[43] Though increased international scientific dialogue about the global AIDS and HIV situation has answered some questions, it has confirmed the difficulty of answering others. A 1988 book edited by the virologist Jay A. Levy, for example, includes detailed review chapters on AIDS in Haiti and AIDS in Africa. Both demonstrate the diverse and very different clinical manifestations of HIV infection in those settings and emphasize the need for revised diagnostic and reporting systems. Treated at length in the

Haiti chapter are the complex interaction of HIV infection with tuberculosis (alluded to by Selzer), while the Africa chapter reviews the controversial origin questions and challenges the various dubious explanations for the high rate of heterosexual transmission; both chapters emphasize remaining questions and the need for continuing investigation.[44]

The provisional nature of science is difficult for policy and funding agencies to live with; indeed, it is hard for science to live with. Rather, there is pressure to produce a coherent narrative in which qualifications and ambiguities, if they must be mentioned, become simply routinized features of the story, to be quickly forgotten; problems of data are perceived to be mere temporary impediments to a refined and comprehensive analysis. Yet AIDS continually escapes the boundaries placed on it by positivist medical science, and its meanings mutate on a parallel with the virus itself. Added to the medical, epidemiological, social, economic, and educational challenges of the AIDS crisis is its inevitably political subtext. AIDS is not a precious national resource; it is something nobody wants. Wherever it appears, AIDS quickly becomes political, and in the discourses of each Third World country where the question of AIDS (even if not yet AIDS itself) has become an increasingly pressing problem, we find AIDS living a dual life. While the dominant international narrative picks up pieces of the local setting and incorporates them into the demands of its format, that narrative is itself being disassembled and grafted onto discursive structures and issues already at work in those cultures. These processes are disguised, however, when AIDS is treated as an unmediated biological and epidemiological phenomenon in which cultural differences (differences in sexual practices, for example) can simply be factored into a universal transcultural equation. Thus it may be useful to draw back from the power of numbers and explore other forms of knowledge produced about and by the AIDS epidemic.

A different kind of knowledge involves the interaction of

AIDS discourse with local concerns. In Africa, analysis of AIDS must inevitably confront questions of decolonization, urbanization, modernization, poverty, endemic disease, development, and racism: in Uganda, for example, the legacy of civil war is rarely ignored in assessments of the AIDS situation nor the influence of the church in discussions of health education; in Kenya, for the independent press at any rate, AIDS is used as an ongoing test of the central government's ability to acknowledge and resolve conflict; in many countries the lack of resources to address the AIDS crisis simply confirms for a global audience the widespread failure of development policies and the deepening poverty they are believed to have produced.[45] In France, as Jamie Feldman found in interviews with French AIDS researchers, the AIDS narrative forms a kind of bridge between the First World and the Third: on the one hand, the early appearance in French hospitals of African patients with AIDS prevented its characterization as a "gay disease"; on the other hand, one French physician who met his American counterpart at the Third International AIDS Conference in Washington reported that "He treated me like an African." Feldman writes that this story

constructs Americans as condescending, perceiving the French and other Europeans as backward "Third Worlders." On a deeper level, French attitudes towards Africans emerge out of this story — the American treated the Frenchman as the Frenchman might treat an African. The narrative also reveals the impact that France's colonial past and present African immigration have on French life.[46]

In his ethnographic study of AIDS in urban Brazil, Richard Parker suggests that the epidemic needs to be linked to "the social and cultural construction of sexual ideology," or what he calls the "cultural grammar" of the Brazilian sexual universe.[47] In both the United States and Great Britain, AIDS intensifies stress on health care systems already in crisis. In South Africa, apartheid reproduces itself in the government's public health campaign: in billboards targeted at the white community, the slogan "AIDS is Now in South Africa" appears as graffiti on a wall; in billboards for the black community, the slogan appears as a bold banner over a picture of a black family huddled around a grave "as if," writes David Seftel, "it were a new brand of burial casket."[48] Such conceptualizations have consequences, of course: a survey of black attitudes in the Johannesburg area revealed total confusion. Many believed that there were "two totally different kinds of AIDS. The one that only affected blacks was acquired through sexual and ritual contact with baboons in central Africa. The other was acquired by sexual contact with homosexuals—white AIDS" (p. 22). Such a conception, as Seftel notes, is reinforced by the material realities of apartheid: in 1986, black patients were treated at the state hospital in Johannesburg for $19 per day while care for white patients cost $88 per day at the private hospital (p. 18). In Cuba, mandatory HIV testing of the general population has identified a small number of infected people who have been placed, for the good of the state, under permanent quarantine. For incarceration in an AIDS sanitorium, they are compensated with air conditioning and color television, capitalist amenities not available to the rest of the population.[49]

The reproduction in AIDS discourse of existing social divisions appears to be virtually universal, whether it is white or black AIDS, gay or straight AIDS, European or African AIDS, wet or hot AIDS, central African or West African AIDS, guilty or innocent AIDS.[50] A First World/Third World dichotomy manifests itself in diverse ways. In Africa, some people simply invert the figure of the Bantu twig gatherers and characterize African people with AIDS as having sexual practices as strange as those of gay white men in San Francisco.[51] In Japan, transfusion-related HIV infection among Japanese is nonexistent thanks to the longstanding practice of sequestering the national blood supply from foreign influences; the Japanese/foreign divi-

sion is an animating feature of AIDS discourse and policy measures in Japan, with suggestions that visas will be denied to
HIV-positive foreigners judged "likely to spread the virus to
many people in Japan."[52] Great Britain's announcement that
HIV-positive applicants for visas from high-risk countries would
be denied entry provoked accusations of racial imperialism when
central African countries were classified as "high-risk" but the
United States was not.[53] In Brazil, officials until recently sought
to treat AIDS like other blood-born endemic diseases, but this
position was challenged when prominent sociologist Herbert de
Souza announced in September 1987 that he and his two brothers were HIV positive, all infected through the blood product
used to treat hemophilia; Souza went public to urge that, no
matter what the cause of AIDS in a given case, the powerful
stigma associated with homosexuality and drug addiction makes
it a special condition that must "be viewed as a social issue and
not an individual [medical] problem."[54] Parker identifies a related dichotomy involving the Brazilian medical community's
transition from conceptualizing AIDS as a "foreign import" to
accepting it (from 1985 on) as a disease that has "taken root."[55]

Does our knowledge of such divisions in discourse add to
our understanding of AIDS? These divisions are, at least in part,
produced by what Dubos (cited above) calls the inadequacies of
the modern world—that is, by a set of historically produced social arrangements. If we keep in mind the multiple meanings of
infect, we can see that the AIDS crisis, like certain other infectious diseases in human history, at once infects the individual
human body with disease and functions like a dye or tissue stain
to illuminate the social body as a whole. A sustained crisis,
moreover, compels us to look at the image thus produced and to
keep looking at it. When AIDS in Africa or Brazil is termed "a
disease of development," it is precisely the intractable social to-
pography of recent history that is invoked, the problematic contours of development—environmental devastation, malnutrition,

war, social upheaval, poverty, debt, endemic disease—now unavoidably illuminated and scrutinized in the international light of the AIDS crisis. As Rudolph Virchow wrote in 1948, "Epidemics correspond to large signs of warning which tell the true statesman that a disturbance has occurred in the development of his people which even a policy of unconcern can no longer overlook."[56]

Dubos also suggested that preventive disease measures can grow out of *revolt*. The production of differences is a persistent phenomenon among human beings, no doubt as pervasive as the production of similarities or the production of metaphors—and as resistant to termination by decree. Indeed, the identification and articulation of differences and divisions may be as crucial to resistance and revolution as the desire to erase them. Hence the fact that specific divisions resist dissolution may signal their significant role in the social formation and thus their potential as a site for conceptual transformation, cultural resistance, or social change.

If we focus on a single issue in international AIDS discourse, like condoms, we can see examples of this phenomenon. I said earlier that the seemingly simple message to "use a condom" is in fact very complicated and may raise more questions than it answers. Already the condom drama has returned to the world stage such familiar characters as the Ugly American who, in the guise of USAID, distributes in central Africa condoms that are too small and inelastic.[57] While we may legitimately see this as a literal enactment of the dependency relationship the First World desires (i.e., having the Third World by the balls), the larger point is that, as Brooke Grundfest Schoepf and her colleagues in Project CONAISSIDA argue, the adoption of condoms involves "much more than a simple transfer of material culture."[58] Describing the project's experience in Zaire, Schoepf demonstrates in detail the myriad ways the condom question puts stress on the entire fabric of social relations. She points out, for example, that multiple partner relationships appear to be increasing in response to a continuing economic crisis that affects men and women somewhat differently: women may take up prostitution as a means of survival because their husbands, under current economic conditions, can no longer support traditional plural households. Women's groups with whom CONAISSIDA has contact express interest in information about AIDS, and about condoms; but they also articulate resistance to the view that information and condoms offer a total solution, emphasizing the role of deepening poverty and the need for income-generating activities for women to provide alternatives to multiple-partner sex.

The important role in Africa of nongovernmental organizations (NGOs) and private voluntary organizations (PVOs) shows another dimension of the condom issue and the question of differences. Many NGOs, though reluctant to shift their agendas to include AIDS (and thus ally already fragile causes with a more stigmatized one), are well organized with excellent international and community networks. One organization that has taken up the AIDS issue is the International Planned Parenthood Association, which has prepared and distributed *Preventing a Crisis,* a well-received manual on AIDS for local as well as national use; such efforts are likely to bring about increased U.S. aid for family planning.[59] But as Schoepf and her colleagues point out,

Ideological issues also need to be addressed. In Zaire nationalist senti-ment currently links contraception and condom use to western popula-tion control strategies, which are viewed as a form of imperialism. Some husbands also view contraception as an encouragement for wives' extra-marital sexual relations. . . . These considerations suggest that it may be preferable to separate AIDS prevention from birth control efforts, rather than to place responsibility for AIDS interventions within family planning programs. (p. 219)

One alternative is to *emphasize* division, to distinguish explicitly between *contraception,* "a barrier against conception," and what might be called *contrasepsis,* "a barrier against disease," carefully articulating the specific purposes of the latter. (A similar distinction was created between *birth control* and *birth spacing,* the latter emphasizing voluntariness and degree.) A second strategy, being widely pursued by women's groups and family planning organizations in a number of Latin American countries, is to use the pressing nature of the AIDS epidemic to modify men's attitudes and the Catholic Church's policy toward controlled fertility. Resistance to unprotected sex depends on reinforcing rather than collapsing the division between contraception and contrasepsis. A third strategy is to explore alternatives to condoms as methods of contrasepsis. Spermicides, for example, could potentially be developed that would provide protection against HIV and could be put in place by women themselves, thus avoiding the multiple social tensions created by the condom drama. Here disease prevention depends on resisting male attitudes toward condoms, the equation of male and female sexuality the condom solution implies, and the penis fixation on which it seems to depend.[60]

But acknowledgment of difference is not accomplished by formula. To take one final example with implications for condom use, the system of sexual classification that dominates discussions of AIDS internationally—heterosexual, homosexual, bisexual—is neither stable nor universal. Criticisms of this system applied to AIDS discourse in Western industrialized countries are all the more valid in other cultures; for not only is sexuality complicated for individuals, with no fixed relationship between official definition, sexual desire, actual practice, and self-perceived identity, but it is culturally complicated as well. Richard Parker argues that the hetero/homo/bi classification is seriously, conceptually, at odds with "the fluidity of sexual desire" in contemporary Brazil.[61] While the medical model's distinctions clearly exist in Brazilian society and are increasingly familiar as a result of media dissemination, they remain largely part of an elite discourse introduced to Brazil in the mid-twentieth century. An older, more pervasive classification system relates sexual practices to gender *roles,* with both gender and sex constructed by a fundamental division between a masculine *atividade* (activity) and a feminine *passividade* (passivity). Two males engaged in anal intercourse would be distinguished by who was the active masculine penetrator, who the passive feminine penetrated. Neither would necessarily perceive their activity as "homosexual," nor would everyday language readily furnish them with the lexicon to do so. As Parker suggests, the potential implications of this for standard "risk group" identification and "safer sex" education are obvious and dismaying.[62]

Parker's work, like other projects noted here, demonstrates the contributions by observers whose goal is to analyze what the members of a culture find meaningful in relation to AIDS. A significant feature of such knowledge is that these meanings must be produced by or in cooperation with those who have authentically experienced that culture and are committed to its interests. This knowledge is neither better nor less mediated than statistical knowledge or other kinds of "objective" ways of knowing a culture, but it is different and produces insights different from those available through the statistical procedures and epidemiological categories developed and formalized by Western medical science. And it is a difference that can be used to articulate alternative narratives. Western medical science is conceived in international AIDS discourse as a transhistorical, transcultural model of reality; when cultural differences among human communities are taken into account, they tend to be enlisted in the service of this reality and their status remains utilitarian. This utilization may effectively accomplish specific goals: it is reported that some native practitioners (e.g., of voodoo) have successfully overcome men's traditional resistance to the use of condoms by describing AIDS as the work of an evil spirit who uses sexual desire and the virus as secret weapons; condoms provide a means to trick the spirit and escape his lethal designs.[63] One can certainly support a global anti-AIDS strategy that mobilizes the scientific model of AIDS in culturally-specific ways, yet acknowledge imperialist aspects of a strategy that valorizes itself as universal rather than culturally produced. As the foregoing examples suggest, experience within a cultural unit produces a unique kind of knowledge. Indeed, the term *experience* is linked to the term *expert,* an etymological connection that encourages a dissolution of the conventional division between *expert knowledge* and *experience.* Experience of a particular culture, however, does not merely mean representing it or being able to testify to its activities; experience entails observation, awareness, analysis: the self-conscious development of expertise. As Victor Turner puts it, experience entails both "living through" and "looking back."[64] Experiential expertise is thus not in the least incompatible with theoretical sophistication.

But experiential expertise of this kind is not the currency of the First World/Third World transaction. Experts are trained professionals, often American and European (but being born in a culture is no guarantee of experiential expertise), trained to do expert advising of the Third World. Expert advising is now a major Third World industry: more than half of the $7 to 8 billion spent yearly on aid to Africa goes to European and North American expert advisers.[65] Gathering information, reporting facts, advising the Third World are also mediated activities, permeated by history and convention. In *Blaming Others,* the Panos Institute's immensely useful 1988 sequel to and self-critique of its indispensable 1986 dossier *AIDS and the Third World,* Renee Sabatier observes how ironic it is that in the information age, information should be such an elusive resource, particularly with respect to a disease where it is so crucial.[66] But a second irony explains the first. What is elusive is not, precisely, the obtaining and disseminating of "information" but rather the acknowledging of what information entails: that language is embedded in culture, that stories contradict each other, that narratives perform as well as inform, that information constructs reality. Cultural analysts in many fields are acknowledging the inevitability and indeed the necessity of such multiple and contradictory stories. Yet having recognized the theoretical complexity of communication, we are pressing communication into a purely pragmatic role that subordinates complication and contradiction to unequivocal assertion and scientific harmony—precisely the kind of circular relation Michel Foucault called a régime of truth.[67]

Tracing the historical relationship between the "country" and the "city" and their evolution in English literature and social thought, Raymond Williams argues that in the course of nineteenth-century imperialism, these two ideas became a model for the world, dividing not only the rural from the urban within a single state but the undeveloped world from the developed one. Underlying this model is the notion of universal industrialization, underdeveloped countries always on their way toward becoming developed, just as the poor man is always assumed to be striving to become rich. "All the 'country' will become 'city': that is the logic of its development."[68] Though this linear progression is largely the social imaginary of late capitalism, that does not impede its deployment as an agenda item for the Third World. For the new possibilities arising out of the AIDS epidemic, the "country" is a very fertile field. As of 1986, according to a reference work called *Emerging AIDS Markets,* 1,119 companies and other organizations are involved in AIDS-related activities: only 20 to 30 of them are based in Third World countries but at least 200 of them are engaged in research on AIDS in Africa and other projects likely to entail the use of Third World populations as trial subjects in the development of diagnostic products and vaccines.[69] Recent reports about vaccine trials make explicit the need for test populations that are "pharmacologically virgin" and, further, are still becoming infected at high rates. Gay men and IV drug users in the First World do not fulfill these criteria, not only because infection is leveling off in the first group and pharmacological virginity is not characteristic of the second, but also because *any* First World population is too educated, too exposed to the media, and too likely to take steps (including alternative treatments) to avoid infection or reduce clinical illness.[70] In the mind of the city, only the country can furnish the unspoiled virgin material that the market needs, the naive informant still too ignorant to contradict instructions.

But there is always another story, and a continuing one in the AIDS epidemic involves the untrustworthiness of other stories—their sources, motives, data, presuppositions, methodologies, and conclusions. If statistical analysis arose as a form of inquiry precisely as the instrument of the developed world, it followed that experience was left as the only form of knowledge the developing world itself was capable of. But we can reject this logic. Williams concluded that "we can overcome division only by refusing to be divided."[71] One strategy for challenging the dominant statistical narrative is to amplify destabilizing counter-narratives. To paraphrase Williams for the nineties, we can overcome contradiction only by demanding to be contradicted.

First and Third World Chronicles

History is a legend, an invention of the present.
    —*V. Y. Mudimbe,* The Invention of Africa[72]

The ethnographer's trials in working to know another people now become the reader's trials in making sense of the text.
    —*Mary Louise Pratt, "Fieldwork in Common Places"*[73]

Resisting the temptation to conclude on the epigrammatic note that Williams offers, I will instead suggest that to demand contradiction is, in practice, to acknowledge that the international AIDS archive is neither complete nor fully accessible. The present invents the past but the present itself has not yet been invented: hence this is a narrative necessarily *in fieri*. I suggested initially that a crisis serves as a point of articulation for multiple voices and interests, and that the AIDS crisis in the Third World is no different. My goal has been to demonstrate that, as in the First World, (1) diverse interests are articulated around AIDS in ways that are socially and culturally localized and specific; (2) understanding this specificity is a necessary if not sufficient condition for effectively mobilizing resources and programs to address the epidemic in a given country or region; and (3) institutional forces and cultural precedents in the First World prevent us from hearing the story of AIDS in the Third World as a complex narrative.

To guarantee that one will hear contradictions requires, that one forsake the coherent AIDS narrative of the professional and technological agencies and obtain access to multiple sources about and within the Third World—which means, at the very least, multiple sources about and within a single country. Publications about AIDS in Kenya exemplify this argument. In January 1985, the Nairobi *Standard* publicly reported the presence of AIDS in Kenya for the first time in stories headlined "Killer disease in Kenya" and "Horror sex disease in Kakamenga."[74] Subsequent accounts in state-owned newspapers repudiated the report, claiming the deaths were from skin cancer rather than AIDS, but Western press accounts speculated increasingly on the frightening implications of the presence of AIDS in central Africa. Then in November 1985, Lawrence K. Altman's multi-part series on AIDS in Africa in the *New York Times* reported not only that the epidemic was spreading rapidly in Africa but also that prominent U.S. researchers were convinced the disease started there. Altman's opening sentence dramatically presented the thesis that was to become most controversial: "Tantalizing but sketchy clues pointing to Africa as the origin of AIDS have unleashed one of the bitterest disputes in the recent annals of medicine."[75] Altman went on to say that these "sketchy clues," including blood samples, *have led to what has now emerged as the prevailing thesis in American and European medical circles that the worldwide spread of acquired immune deficiency syndrome began in Central Africa, the home of several other recently recognized diseases.*

But not everyone accepts this designation of the virus' homeland:

The Africans vigorously disagree, and there is some criticism of the validity of the studies on which the theories are predicated. Indeed, controversial new results point both to and against AIDS originating in Africa, a fact that is fueling the international furor.[76]

Much of the "furor" was caused by criticisms of the studies, some of which I have noted above. Rates estimated for all Africans were often based on small studies in urban areas; rates estimated for prostitutes were often derived from problematic assumptions (for example, some studies identify all sexually active single women as prostitutes); serious problems were also raised by claims not based on studies at all but simply on rumor, armchair speculation, anthropological reports taken out of context, ideological conviction, and morality tales. These included claims that Africans had sexual contact with African green monkeys, or ate them, or kept dead monkeys as children's toys; that Africans practiced strange sexual customs and that African women's bodies were radically different from those of Western women; and that various other cultural practices or medical conditions or environmental factors were responsible for the spread of HIV and AIDS. In each case, cultural practices were taken out of context, exaggerated, and presented as the magic bulletin that would explain AIDS. Further, the challenging voices coming from Africa were ignored. These myths did nothing to dispel controversies over AIDS about and within Africa.[77]

A major effect of the *Times* series on the Western press was to place Africa firmly on the national agenda for AIDS media coverage, culminating in the journalistic frenzy of late 1986 that represented Africa as "devastated" by AIDS and AIDS-related illnesses.[78] In Africa, the effect was different. When Altman's series began to run in the *International Herald Tribune* in November 1985, for example, outraged Kenyan officials confiscated the entire shipment. The African offensive against the "African origin" theory was launched with an editorial in *Medicus,* the official publication of the Kenya Medical Association, which hypothesized that tourists from around the world had introduced AIDS into Africa.[79]

At this point the Kenyan news magazine, the *Weekly Review,* published and edited in Nairobi by Hilary Ng'weno and widely considered one of the best news magazines in Africa, took on the responsibility of keeping the public informed about AIDS reports in the African and international press. In the face of increasingly vocal controversy and government silence, the magazine's general position was that developing adequate public health measures was more important than countering Western propaganda. The *Weekly Review* continues to summarize material printed in the West, cite the numbers of AIDS patients reported in Zaire, Rwanda, Uganda, and Kenya, and provide fairly detailed analysis of scientific and press reports. Although itself often critical of the Kenyan government's mode of responding to the AIDS epidemic, the *Weekly Review* is also critical of Western reporting. What Africa needs, Ng'weno told the Panos Institute, is concrete assistance, not "a never ending siren recounting a litany of disasters about to engulf the continent."[80]

An insightful analysis of the AIDS situation in Kenya and the *Weekly Review*'s contributions is provided by the political scientist Alfred J. Fortin in "The Politics of AIDS in Kenya." Although Fortin criticizes the actions of the Kenyan government, he is primarily critical of the "development establishment," a position he has made repeatedly clear in other papers. In "AIDS and the Third World: The Politics of International Discourse," for example, he writes that the "current discursive framing of AIDS in the Third World is a highly depoliticized one" and argues that while this way of seeing AIDS may be technically necessary to get the job done, it fails to acknowledge important power relations. Given its "aggressive bureaucratic and careerist politics," the "development establishment" must remain under fire or its forces will reproduce the power relations of dominance and dependency already in place.[81] In the Kenya paper, Fortin argues that the dominance-dependency relationship guarantees English as the international language of AIDS discourse, a language that is necessarily "blind to the African world of meaning." He concludes that despite Kenya's "comparatively well-developed medical infrastructure and working coterie of Western scientists, its efforts have fallen short of even the minimum requirements suggested by its statistics."[82]

However much the *Weekly Review* may itself be skeptical of the "development establishment" as well as Kenya's response to the AIDS epidemic, it does not buy Fortin's position either. Calling his paper "a hard-hitting and indictive, if lopsided, criticism of the Kenyan government, the ministry of health and the local press," the editor goes on to contest a number of points of Fortin's analysis.[83] An interesting and complex discussion centers around language:

[Fortin's] paper questions the language of discourse at discussions on AIDS in Africa. It argues that Africans have chosen to use the Western language when talking about the disease and since the language is transplanted, Africa is dependent on the West for its meaning and its continued development. Since the language is not indigenous to Africa, Fortin says, hence it is "blind to the African world of meaning."

Students of African history have long argued that most of the diseases prevalent in Africa today were first witnessed with the advent of the foreigners on the continent and most of the terminology used by the medical practitioners in Africa are also borrowed from the developed world.

African governments and researchers have also been emphatic that the AIDS virus was first diagnosed in the United States and, therefore, it would follow automatically that the language used in ref-

erence to the disease should be that developed by those who diagnosed it first. (pp. 12-13)

Fortin's argument about discourse is intended to challenge—as Parker's is with regard to Brazil—the entire discursive formation of international AIDS discussions applied unthinkingly and hence in some sense imperialistically to diverse cultures; it is a position most discourse analysts would share. Ng'weno, however, rejects the corollary implication of this view: that English is somehow "foreign" to Kenya and Kenyan leaders. Though English is indeed a colonial legacy, it plays many roles in Kenyan activities today. (Zairean philosopher V. Y. Mudimbe argues that Western discourse has contributed to but not monopolized what he calls "the invention of Africa"; rather, the objects of that discourse are also subjects who have produced an intricate interweaving of European and African commentary, rendering the notion of a "purely African discourse" an impossible dream."[84]) At the same time, Ng'weno makes the political point that language marks nationality and origin: to use English with regard to AIDS helps sustain its identity as a Western disease. This resistance to adopting AIDS, to giving it—in the words of the Altman story—a home, is reflected elsewhere in the *Weekly Review,* where supposedly indigenous African terms for AIDS and AIDS-related terms (like "slim disease" and "AIDS belt") are placed in quotation marks and often explicitly rejected; the term *magada,* cited by Fortin as the name for AIDS in Swahili, is never used in the *Review.* (This is not to say that many African publications do not translate AIDS terms into their own language; for example, one acronym, UKIMWI, appears in a number of Kenyan and Tanzanian newspapers.)

The juxtaposition of these two complex and interlocking analyses makes clear that the chronicle of AIDS in the Third World cannot be understood monolithically. Not only must it be understood in terms of the "rich history and complex political chemistry" of each affected country, but also as a heteroglossic series of conflicted, shifting, and contradictory positions that exist within systems of cultural stereotypes and hegemonic power relations.[85] And we may ask, at last, whether the title of this chronicle should not be interrogated as well. What is AIDS? What is the Third World? We are talking about an epidemic disease with more than forty distinct clinical manifestations, some of which consist of the absence of manifestation, some of which are unique to particular regions in the world, and some of which apparently have nothing to do with a deficiency of the immune system.[86] When we talk about the Third World, we are talking about more than 100 countries of the world. When we talk about Africa, we are talking about a continent four times as large as the United States, which has more than 50 countries, 900 ethnic groups, and 300 language families (Zambia alone has 74 languages). As Miller and Rockwell argue, it is absurd to talk about "the AIDS problem in Africa" except for specific and well-defined purposes. As for "the Third World," we may turn to Carl E. Pletsch's discussion of the evolution of the concept of the Third World, which opens with this quotation from Alexis de Tocqueville:

The Deity does not regard the human race collectively [but] surveys at one glance and severally all the beings of whom mankind is composed; and he discerns in each man the resemblances that assimilate him to all his fellows, and the differences that distinguish him from them.[87]

Pletsch's own analysis suggests that the term "Third World" is totally bogus. "With the possible exception of the political categories of left and right," Pletsch writes, "the scheme of three worlds is perhaps the most primitive system of classification in our social scientific discourse" (p. 566). This highly authoritative conceptual framework has had a major influence on the organization of social scientific labor for the last three decades; yet as a framework for genuine scientific investigation, it yields studies in which the societies outside of Western civilization (societies, that is, belonging to the Second and Third Worlds) become, in Pletsch's words, "almost pure fantasies" (p. 566). Bad enough that in the mundane scheme of things, the three-worlds concept perpetuates a self-serving innovation by postwar social scientists to revamp modernization theory for the Cold War era. In the large scheme of things, it enables us to continue to avoid doing what we—in contrast to the Deity—seem to find so difficult: to regard human beings simultaneously both "collectively" and "severally," in multiple ways both same and different.

To hear the story "AIDS in the Third World" requires us to confront familiar problems in the human sciences: How do we know what we know? What cultural work will we ask our knowledge to perform? What are our own stakes in the success or failure of that performance? In the course of this essay, I have identified several analytic strategies through which we may explore these questions and tried to suggest areas of discourse where better understandings may be particularly valuable: the conventions of mass media stories, the discursive traditions and modes of representation that figure in the AIDS narrative told by the sciences and social sciences (including tropes, stereotypes, linguistic structures, and pervasive metaphors); the emergence of a dominant international AIDS narrative and its role in the linguistic and professional management of the epidemic; the exclusion or silencing of alternative narratives, including those originating in the "Third World," in part because they do not tell the story in a "First World" way; the processes through which AIDS is conceptualized within given institutions for everyday use; and the very terms through which we identify what chronicle it is we think we are telling. The checks and balances provided by the warring voices at each of these multiple discursive points helps render it impossible to refuse contradiction—impossible, that is, to argue that any single unchallenged account of AIDS exists in the Third World, anymore than it does in the First. If I have succeeded in discrediting the phrase "AIDS in the Third World," I will have begun to achieve my aim, one directed toward dismantling the First World chronicle about Third World AIDS: a chronicle designed in part to strengthen or disrupt (as the case may be) specific First World discursive chains and in doing so rearrange without redistributing the material benefits that depend on them. It is also a chronicle that must be allowed to exist precisely so that it can be discredited and resisted.

Notes

Research for this essay was supported in part by grants from the National Council of Teachers of English and the University of Illinois at Urbana-Champaign Graduate College Research Board and by a fellowship at the Society for the Humanities, Cornell University. I thank Cary Nelson for critical comments and continuing assistance. I am also indebted to Barbara Kruger and Phil Mariani, to Gayatri Spivak, to Simon Watney, and to members of the feminist theory seminar at the University of Illinois in spring 1988. For research assistance, I thank Anne Balsamo and University of Illinois librarians John Littlewood (Documents) and Yvette Scheven (Africana).

The term *AIDS* in this essay refers to the AIDS epidemic as a broad social and cultural crisis; the compound phrase *AIDS and HIV infection* refers to the broad clinical spectrum of HIV-related conditions from asymptomatic infection to the specific diseases presently used to define "AIDS" (I use *AIDS* to mean the medical condition only if this more restricted sense is clear in context). I have elsewhere discussed the status of these signifiers as "real" and "true" and will not do so here; see "AIDS, Homophobia, and Biomedical Discourse: An Epidemic of Signification," in *AIDS: Cultural Analysis/Cultural Activism,* ed. Douglas Crimp (Cambridge, Mass.: MIT Press, 1988), pp. 31-70.

1. See Philip Babcock Gove, ed., *Webster's Third New International Dictionary of the English Language* (Springfield, Mass.: Merriam, 1971), and James A. Murray, ed., *Oxford English Dictionary,* 1874-1928, compact ed. (Oxford: Oxford University Press, 1971).

2. Frank Browning, "AIDS: The Mythology of Plague," *Tikkun* 3, no. 2 (March-April 1988): 70. Review of Randy Shilts, *And the Band Played On: Politics, People, and the AIDS Epidemic* (New York: St. Martin's Press, 1987).

3. Judith Wilson Ross, "Ethics and the Language of AIDS," in *AIDS, Ethics, and Public Policy,* ed. Christine Pierce and Donald VandeVeer (Belmont, Calif.:

Wadsworth, 1988), p. 47. See also Susan Sontag, *AIDS and Its Metaphors* (New York: Farrar Straus & Giroux, 1989). This positivist position is contrasted by Allan M. Brandt with the position that disease is socially constructed in "Toward the Social Meaning of Epidemic Disease," *Social Research* 55, no. 3 (Autumn 1988): 413-432; Brandt also specifically addresses Sontag's position as articulated in *Illness as Metaphor* (New York: Vintage Books, 1975).

4. Browning, "Mythology of Plague," p. 70.

5. For discussion of the "rugged vagina"/"vulnerable rectum" dichotomy and related permutations, see my "AIDS, Homophobia, and Biomedical Discourse: An Epidemic of Signification," in *AIDS: Cultural Analysis/Cultural Activism,* ed. Douglas Crimp (Cambridge, Mass.: MIT Press, 1988), pp. 31-70, and "AIDS, Gender, and Biomedical Discourse: Current Contests for Meaning," in *AIDS: The Burdens of History,* ed. Elizabeth Fee and Daniel M. Fox (Berkeley: University of California Press, 1988), pp. 190-266.

6. H. Hunter Handsfield, "Heterosexual Transmission of Human Immunodeficiency Virus," *Journal of the American Medical Association* 260, no. 13 (October 1988): 1943.

7. Cf. Homi Bhabha, "The Other Question—The Stereotype and Colonial Discourse," *Screen* 24 (November-December 1983), and Chandra Talpade Mohanty, "Under Western Eyes: Feminist Scholarship and Colonial Discourses," *Boundary 2* 12, no. 3 (Spring 1984), and 13, no. 1 (Fall 1984).

8. Advice to "use a condom," like many other seemingly unproblematic educational programs, can create unforeseen and very complex problems. For discussion of the nature and use of culturally-specific AIDS information as well as specific examples of problems in Third World contexts, see Panos Institute, *AIDS and the Third World* (London: Panos Institute, in association with Norwegian Red Cross, 1989), Renee Sabatier, *Blaming Others: Prejudice, Race, and Worldwide AIDS* (Washington: Panos Institute, 1988), and Cindy Patton, *Sex and Germs: The Politics of AIDS* (Boston: South End Press, 1985).

9. Details of these and other examples are readily available in such publications as the weekly *News and Features Bulletin* of the *All Africa Press Service,* the Panos Institute studies, and U.S. government reports.

10. Norman Miller and Richard C. Rockwell, eds., *AIDS in Africa: The Social and Policy Impact* (Lewiston, N.Y.: Edwin Mellen, 1988), p. xxxi.

11. Ernesto Laclau and Chantal Mouffe, *Hegemony and Socialist Strategy: Towards a Radical Democratic Politics,* trans. Winston Moore and Paul Cammack (London: Verso, 1985).

12. Kenneth Prewitt, "AIDS in Africa: The Triple Disaster," in *AIDS in Africa,* ed. Miller and Rockwell, pp. xi-xii.

13. Marjorie Shostak, *Nisa: The Life and Words of a !Kung Woman* (New York: Vintage Books, 1983), p. 26.

14. James Clifford, "On Ethnographic Allegory," in *Writing Culture,* ed. James

Clifford and George E. Marcus (Berkeley: University of California Press, 1986), p. 99.

15. Richard Selzer, "A Mask on the Face of Death: As AIDS Ravages Haiti, a U.S. Doctor Finds a Taboo Against Truth," *Life* 10 (August 1987): 58-64. Hereafter documented internally by page number.

16. Mary Louise Pratt, "Fieldwork in Common Places," in *Writing Culture,* ed. Clifford and Marcus, pp. 27-50; see pp. 33-45 for discussion of arrival scenes. The Clifford and Marcus collection offers an extended reflection on relationships between anthropology, ethnography, and travel writing.

17. Photograph of "Mercedes" by J. B. Diederich for *Life* 10 (August 1987): 60; story on Mombasa by Tom Masland, "AIDS Threat Turns Shore Leave into Naval Exercise in Caution," *Chicago Tribune,* April 1988; *Newsweek* photo of prostitute in Rod Nordland, with Ray Wilkinson and Ruth Marshall, "Africa in the Plague Years," *Newsweek,* November 24, 1986, p. 46.

18. Jan Zita Grover, "A Matter of Life and Death," *Women's Review of Books* 5, no. 6 (March 1988): 3.

19. Conspiracy theories of AIDS are reviewed by Robert Lederer, "Origin and Spread of AIDS: Is the West Responsible?" *CovertAction,* no. 28 (1987): 43-54, and no. 29 (1988): 52-67, and are reported regularly in the New York *Native.*

20. The ubiquitous interpretation of the AIDS drama as inevitably tragic and the person with AIDS as dying victim is one challenged by gay activist groups like ACT UP; see Douglas Crimp, "How to Have Promiscuity in an Epidemic," in *AIDS: Cultural Analysis/Cultural Activism,* ed. Crimp, pp. 237-271, and Michael Callan, *Surviving and Thriving with AIDS: Collected Wisdom,* 2 vols. (New York: People With AIDS Coalition, 1987-1988). Pratt, "Fieldwork in Common Places," pp. 44-50, discusses redemptive endings, made all the more imperative by the ethnographic commonplace that the innocent Other often becomes worldly-wise through contact with "modern civilization" in the guise of ethnographers themselves. In Selzer's encounter, a further irony is that he pays the prostitutes to talk to him, again paralleling ethnographic research where the privileged investigator enters into a commodity exchange with the native informant—an exchange which, as Pratt puts it, turns the "anthropologist preserver-of-the-culture" into the "interventionist corrupter-of-the-culture."

21. See photographs in Nordland et al., "Africa in the Plague Years," and Kenneth M. Pierce, "Nowhere to Run, Nowhere to Hide," *Time,* September 1, 1986. Brazilian magazines' high-tech medical images were described to me by Elisabeth Santos, M.D., personal communication. Odd linkages among photographs, captions, and text do not only occur in Third World contexts, of course. A story on AIDS in the Canadian journal *Maclean's,* for example, includes a photograph of pedestrians on a crowded Toronto city street; shot from behind so that the pedestrians are moving away from the camera, the photo appears to illus-

trate the caption: "Toronto sidewalk traffic: growing fear as AIDS virus spreads to general public," August 24, 1987, p. 31.

22. Robert Caputo, "Uganda: Land Beyond Sorrow," *National Geographic* 173, no. 4 (April 1988): 468-474; the Caputo photo of Jane Namirimu and her mother is on p. 470. Pratt, "Fieldwork in Common Places," pp. 40 and 45, discusses respectively the fallen postcolonial world of ethnographic writing and the trope of utopian universality.

23. Selzer, "Mask on the Face of Death," p. 63. The Diederich photograph is reprinted in *Maclean's,* August 31, 1987, p. 37. To take another example, the *Newsweek* photographs accompanying Nordland, "Africa in the Plague Years," have been widely reprinted. One (p. 44) shows an emaciated woman framed in a doorway, holding a thin baby in her lap. The *Newsweek* print is captioned "Two victims: Uganda barmaid and son," and credited to Ed Hooper—Picture Search. Appearing on the cover of the May 24, 1988 issue of the *Washington Post*'s weekly journal *Health* is a photograph of the identical woman shot at a slightly different angle; accompanying Philip J. Hilts's featured story, "Out of Africa," pp. 12-17, the photograph is now captioned as follows: "In the Ugandan village of Kinyiga, Florence Masaka, 22, and her 2-month-old daughter have both tested positive for the AIDS virus." The credit line accompanying the story reads "Photos by Al Hooper." Hilts's article and the photographs were reprinted in *Africa Report* (November-December 1988): 26-31, as "Dispelling Myths about AIDS in Africa"; the photos were captioned only with text from the story. The Hooper photographs (Al or Ed) also accompanied Catharine Watson's "Africa's AIDS Time Bomb: Region Scrambles to Fight Epidemic," *The Guardian,* June 17, 1987, pp. 10-11; and the *Weekly Review* (Nairobi) of June 24, 1988, p. 18, reprinted the mother and child photograph with the caption "Ugandan AIDS victims" and no picture credit. For a general discussion of the documentary use of photographs and how "original meanings" may be lost, see Eric Margolis, "Mining Photographs: Unearthing the Meanings of Historical Photos," *Radical History Review* 40 (1988): 33-48.

24. Sabatier, *Blaming Others,* p. 96, quotes a Nigerian prostitute named Juliet as follows: "Although white clients generally pay better than their African counterparts, I will never go to bed with a white man unless he wears a condom. As far as I am concerned, AIDS is a white man's disease." Richard C. Chirimuuta and Rosalind J. Chirimuuta, *AIDS, Africa, and Racism* (Bretby, Darbyshire: R. C. Chirimuuta, 1987; London: Free Association Books, 1987).

25. Ann S. Anagnost, "Magical Practice, Birth Policy, and Women's Health in Post-Mao China," Unit for Criticism and Interpretive Theory Colloquium, University of Illinois at Urbana, December 7, 1988.

26. Edward Said, "In the Shadow of the West," *wedge,* no. 7-8 (Winter-Spring 1985): 5.

27. Jean William Pape, a leading AIDS researcher in Haiti and one of the phy-

sicians Selzer consulted, expresses disenchantment with the Western press for consistently ignoring "the efforts of the Haitian people to fight, with almost no resources, the most devastating disease of this century." He told the Panos Institute: "I have given over 60 interviews to American and other reporters about AIDS in Haiti. It is very time-consuming and exhausting, and takes energy I would like to put into my work. Of all those interviews there are only one or two that recorded what I said, and the context in which I said it, accurately. The others often painted a picture of AIDS in Haiti that was unrecognisable to me." Quoted in Sabatier, *Blaming Others,* p. 90. (Selzer consulted Pape too, but I have no evidence that Pape found his report objectionable.) But negative reactions to Western media reports do not necessarily disrupt the cycle of representation. Some African governments, for example, angry at what they believed to be inflations of their statistics or simply wishing to deflect focus on the AIDS problem, prohibited AIDS researchers and physicians from giving interviews to the Western press. "One result of such attempts at control," said James Brooke, the *New York Times* West Africa correspondent in an interview with the Panos Institute in November 1987, "has been to force foreign reporters to rely more heavily on foreign researchers working in those countries, making it more difficult than before to convey an authentically African point of view." Quoted in Sabatier, *Blaming Others,* p. 95. Chirimuuta and Chirimuuta, *AIDS, Africa, and Racism,* go further in providing instances where the "authentically African point of view" is equally powerless to challenge prevailing conceptions. (Anecdotes from the U.S. gay community describe numerous instances of journalists refusing to photograph particular people with AIDS because they "don't look sick enough.")

28. "Régime of truth" is Michel Foucault's term. See "The Political Function of the Intellectual," *Radical Philosophy,* no. 17 (1977): 13-14. See also Treichler, "AIDS, Homophobia, and Biomedical Discourse."

29. René Dubos, *Mirage of Health: Utopias, Progress, and Biological Change* (1959; New Brunswick, N.J.: Rutgers University Press, 1987), pp. 218, 219.

30. John Tagg, using Foucault to analyze the function of photographs in representing "the true" in *The Burden of Representation* (Amherst: University of Massachusetts Press, 1988), p. 94.

31. Ronald Reagan, at a press conference after returning from a Latin American trip, December 15, 1987.

32. Raymond Williams, *Politics and Letters: Interviews with New Left Review* (London: New Left Review Editions, 1981), pp. 164-165; Williams here refers to his earlier analysis in *The Country and the City* of experience and statistical analysis as different ways of producing knowledge (London: Chatto and Windus, 1973), especially pp. 215-232.

33. See, for example, the testimony of Bradshaw Langmaid, Bureau of Science and Technology, USAID, on funding criteria for AIDS aid to African countries,

in *AIDS and the Third World: The Impact on Development,* Hearing before the Select Committee on Hunger, U.S. House of Representatives, 100th Congress, 2nd Session held in Washington D.C., June 30, 1988, Serial no. 100-29 (Washington, D.C.: U.S. Government Printing Office, 1988), pp. 33-34.

34. Most studies depend on some degree of cooperation between the First and the Third World, and are thus influenced by the scientific and political commitments of given agencies and their ability to find common grounds of inquiry as well as resources. In Africa, for example, scarce resources have created wide variation in scientific research, yet much more research goes on than stereotypes about Africa suggest. Some facilities, like the Kenya Medical Research Institute, have sustained fairly continuous research programs throughout the period of decolonization and independence. Although the respected biomedical research programs of Makarere University and of the East African Virus Institute in Uganda were seriously disrupted under Idi Amin, ironically Amin's paranoia about viruses saved the physical facilities from destruction; these programs are now being rebuilt. Research contributions of the International Medical Research Center in Franceville, Gabon, in central Africa, are described by James Brooke, "Virus Discoveries Help an African Outpost of AIDS Research Gain Notice," *New York Times,* February 28, 1988. Needless to say, African attitudes toward cooperation with Western scientists are also highly variable, reflecting in some respects the ideological commitments of the state as a whole. Sabatier's Panos Institute study, *Blaming Others,* pp. 108-109, distinguishes between the many long-term collaborative projects that predate AIDS and what African commentators call "parachute research," in which foreign researchers drop in "to collect blood samples, data or clinical observations, and just as quickly [take] off again, to write up their findings for a (Western) scientific journal." Chirimuuta and Chirimuuta, *AIDS, Africa, and Racism,* provide a well-documented analysis and critique of First World versus Third World research on Third World AIDS; they also note, p. 85, the contradictory tendency of American and European "Third Worldists" (including the Panos Institute) to simultaneously criticize and cite the findings of such "hit-and-run" research.

35. Jonathan M. Mann, James Chin, Peter Piot, and Thomas Quinn, "The International Epidemiology of AIDS," *Scientific American,* October 1988, p. 82. See also Peter Piot, F. A. Plummer, F. S. Mhalu, J.-L. Lamboray, James Chin, and Jonathan M. Mann, "AIDS: An International Perspective," *Science* 239 (1988): 573-579. Monthly statistical updates are available from the PanAmerican Health Organization in Washington, WHO's regional health office for the Americas.

36. Mann et al., "International Epidemiology of AIDS," p. 84, and Piot et al., "AIDS: An International Perspective," p. 576.

37. Mann et al., "International Epidemiology of AIDS," p. 84. The Soviet Union did not report its first official "indigenous" death from AIDS until September 1988—a pregnant Leningrad prostitute named Olga Gaeevskaya; "Epi-

demiologists were incensed that the woman's doctors failed to diagnose AIDS before she died," *Edmonton Journal,* October 11, 1988. More mysterious is a recent "outbreak" of HIV infection (the headline says "AIDS") among twenty-seven babies and five of their mothers in a hospital in Elista, capital of a region along the Caspian Sea. Some authorities blame unsterilized needles for the babies' infection and suggest that the mothers' infection was contracted while breast-feeding the infected babies (I have not seen the baby-to-mother explanation anywhere else). John F. Burns, "Outbreak of AIDS Triples Testing in a Soviet City," *New York Times,* February 5, 1989.

38. For a multinational assessment of the impact of AIDS on the Third World, see *AIDS Prevention and Control: Invited Presentations and Papers from the World Summit of Ministers of Health on Programmes for AIDS Prevention* (Geneva: World Health Organization; Oxford: Pergamon Press, 1988). Assessments centered in the First World include *AIDS and the Third World: The Impact on Development;* R. M. Anderson, R. M. May, and A. R. McLean, "Possible Demographic Consequences of AIDS in Developing Countries," *Nature* 332 (1988): 228-234; Institute of Medicine/National Academy of Sciences, *Confronting AIDS: Update 1988* (Washington, D.C.: National Academy Press, 1988). Discussions of Africa include Robert J. Biggar, "Overview: Africa, AIDS, and Epidemiology," in *AIDS in Africa,* ed. Miller and Rockwell, pp. 1-8; Raymond W. Copson, *AIDS in Africa: Background/Issues for U.S. Policy* (Washington, D.C.: Congressional Research Service, Library of Congress, 1987); Christine Hawkins, "AIDS Expected to Slow Population Growth," *New Africa* 251 (August 1988): 25; Charles W. Hunt, "Africa and AIDS," *Monthly Review* 39, no. 9 (February 1988): 10-22; Nancy Krieger, "The Epidemiology of AIDS in Africa," *Science for the People* 19, no.1 (January-February 1987): 18-21; Miller and Rockwell, eds., *AIDS in Africa;* M. Over, S. Bertozzi, James Chin, B. N'Galy, and K. Nyamuryekung'e, "The Direct and Indirect Costs of HIV Infection in Developing Countries: The Cases of Zaire and Tanzania," paper presented at the International Conference on the Global Impact of AIDS, London, March 8-10, 1988; Panos Institute, *AIDS and the Third World;* Kenneth Prewitt, "AIDS in Africa: The Triple Disaster," in *AIDS in Africa,* ed. Miller and Rockwell, pp. ix-xv; Sabatier, *Blaming Others;* Jane Perlez, "Africans Weigh Threat of AIDS to Economies," *New York Times,* September 22, 1988, p. 16; Al J. Venter, "AIDS: Its Strategic Consequences in Black Africa," *International Defense Review* 21 (April 1988): 357-359; Watson, "Africa's AIDS Time Bomb."

39. Miller and Rockwell, "Introduction," in *AIDS in Africa,* pp. xiv-xxiv.

40. The progressive visibility and reality of the AIDS epidemic are illustrated in Lawrence K. Altman, "New Support from Africa as WHO Plans Effort on AIDS," *New York Times,* December 22, 1985; Erik Eckholm, "AIDS, an Unknown Disease Before 1981, Grows into a Worldwide Scourge," *New York Times,* March 16, 1987; Thomas W. Netter, "AIDS Spurs Countries to Act as Cases Rise

Around World," *New York Times,* March 22, 1987; Steven V. Roberts, "Politicians Awaken to the Threat of a Global Epidemic," *New York Times,* June 7, 1987; "AIDS Now Is A Global Public Health Crisis, Harvard MD Stresses," *American Medical News,* June 12, 1987, p. 19.

41. Quoted in Marilyn Chase, "Rich Nations Urged to Help Poor Lands Fight AIDS by Backing WHO Program," *Wall Street Journal,* June 17, 1988. On international cooperation, see Simon Watney, "Our Rights and Our Dignity," *Gay Times* (March 1988): 32-34; Sabatier, *Blaming Others;* Amadou Traore, "Meeting Point: Dr. Gottlieb Monekosso, WHO Regional Director for Africa," *The Courier* (Africa-Caribbean-Pacific-European Community) 105 (September-October 1987): 2-5. A cooperative international policy is outlined in the document *Concerning a Common European Public Health Policy to Fight the Acquired Immunodeficiency Syndrome (AIDS),* Council of Europe Committee of Ministers Recommendation No. R (87) 25, adopted at the 81st session, November 26, 1987. Jonathan Mann, director of the Global AIDS Program, advocates aggressive, activist strategies to achieve global cooperation; in an "AIDS Monitor" column on the January 1988 global summit, *New Scientist,* February 4, 1988, p. 32, Mann states that the international declaration reached at the summit represents "an extraordinary consensus."

42. (1) Mann et al., "International Epidemiology of AIDS," p. 84; (2) Copson, *AIDS in Africa,* p. 9; (3) Mann et al., "International Epidemiology of AIDS," p. 84; (4) Watson, "Africa's AIDS Time Bomb," p. 10; (5) Hilts, "Out of Africa," p. 12; (6) Mary Harper, "AIDS in Africa—Plague or Propaganda?" *West Africa,* November 7-13, 1988, p. 2072.

43. Chirimuuta and Chirimuuta, *AIDS, Africa, and Racism,* suggest that "underreporting" is no more a problem than "overdiagnosing." See also Cynthia Haq, "Data on AIDS in Africa: An Assessment," in *AIDS in Africa,* ed. Miller and Rockwell, pp. 9-29; Barbara Boyle Torrey, Peter O. Way, and Patricia Rowe, "Epidemiology of HIV and AIDS in Africa: Emerging Issues and Social Implications," in *AIDS in Africa,* ed. Miller and Rockwell, pp. 31-54. A general critique of African AIDS studies is provided by Margaret Cerullo and Evelynn Hammonds, "AIDS in Africa: The Western Imagination and the Dark Continent," *Radical America* 21, no. 2-3 (March-April 1987): 17-23; and Krieger, "The Epidemiology of AIDS in Africa." An attempt to place AIDS statistics within a broader political and economic perspective is presented in Carol Barker and Meredeth Turshen, "Briefings: AIDS in Africa," *Review of African Political Economy* 27 (January-March 1986): 51-54. An unexpectedly skeptical assessment of the value of current theoretical analysis and statistical projections for the purposes of strategic decision making in the private sector is provided by Manny Ratafia and Frederick I. Scott, Jr., "AIDS: A Glimpse of Its Impact," *American Clinical Products Review* (May 1987): 26-29; this article also suggests the size and diversity of the "AIDS market" for the development of clinical products.

44. Nathan Clumeck, "AIDS in Africa" in *AIDS: Pathogenesis and Treatment,* ed. Jay A. Levy (New York: Marcel Dekker, 1989), pp. 37-63. Clumeck, Hilts, "Out of Africa," and Torrey et al., "Epidemiology of HIV and AIDS in Africa" summarize existing studies. On the clinical manifestations of AIDS in Haiti, see Warren D. Johnson, Jr., and Jean W. Pape, "AIDS in Haiti," in *AIDS,* ed. Levy, pp. 65-78; interactions of AIDS with tuberculosis are discussed on pp. 72-77.

45. Caputo, "Uganda: Land Beyond Sorrow"; Hilary Ng'weno, *Weekly Review* (Nairobi); Lloyd Timberlake, *Africa in Crisis: The Causes, the Cures of Environmental Bankruptcy,* ed. Jon Tinker (Philadelphia: New Society/Earthscan, 1986).

46. Jamie Feldman, "Identity, Illness, and the Process of Giving Meaning: French Medical Discourse on AIDS," unpublished manuscript, University of Illinois at Urbana-Champaign, July 1988. See also Michael Pollack, *AIDS and Culture in France* (forthcoming).

47. Richard Parker, "Acquired Immunodeficiency Syndrome in Brazil," *Medical Anthropology Quarterly* 1, no. 2 (1987): 158, 159.

48. David Seftel, "AIDS and Apartheid: Double Trouble," *Africa Report* (November-December 1988): 21.

49. Nicholas Wade, "Cuba's Quarantine for AIDS: A Police State's Health Experiment," *New York Times,* editorial, February 6, 1989; Richard Goldstein, "AIDS Arrest: The Cuban Solution," *Village Voice,* February 14, 1989, p. 18.

50. Though these dichotomies are primarily social, the differentiation among types of AIDS is also a scientific and clinical question. For example, Clumeck, "AIDS in Africa," p. 43, states that American, European, and African isolates of the virus are quite similar; the greater polymorphism of the African strains may suggest (according to Clumeck) a longer period of evolution and the problem of developing a vaccine. The wet/hot dichotomy reported by Clumeck, p. 52, characterizes the breakdown of cases in Zaire, where 80 percent of patients in one study were diagnosed with "wet AIDS" (weight loss with diarrhea), 14 percent with "hot AIDS" (weight loss with fever), and 6 percent with Kaposi's Sarcoma; Clumeck argues that these clinical expressions make a new case definition badly needed for AIDS in Africa. At least two related but different types of virus have now been isolated in African patients; labeled HIV-1 and HIV-2, both are considered to produce AIDS-like immune deficiencies, though only HIV-1 is currently believed to produce the more serious syndrome that leads to AIDS. In addition, there are distinct strains of HIV-1 that, to some extent, can be used to trace different geographical routes of transmission, not only through the countries but also the virology laboratories the virus has inhabited. Viral relationships are evaluated according to the degree to which the genetic structures perfectly match.

51. Hilts, "Out of Africa," p. 12, notes the incredulity that greeted the appearance of AIDS in Africa. He quotes a pulmonary specialist in Uganda who first

saw AIDS there in 1983: "It looked like the new American disease. But none of us could believe it." Many scientists and reporters in Africa worked to counter the "African connection" theory so readily adopted in the West (Chirimuuta and Chirimuuta, *AIDS, Africa, and Racism,* pp. 121-126, document this response); but others in Africa began to place the blame for AIDS on the loose morals of African people—always those in other countries, classes, or ethnic groups. Thus an editorial in the *Kenya Times* (Nairobi), May 26, 1987, blamed Uganda for lax sexual behavior, noting that "nature has its own law of retribution." See discussion in Sabatier, *Blaming Others,* p. 105.

52. Clyde Haberman, "Japan Plans to Deny Visas Over AIDS," *New York Times,* April 1, 1987. According to a report in the *Independent* (London), February 14, 1987, when the death of a Japanese prostitute in Kobe was attributed to AIDS, the immediate conclusion was that she had been infected by sexual contact with a foreigner; as one Japanese newspaper put it, "Her death was the result of an infatuation with Europe." Sabatier, *Blaming Others,* p. 114, notes that "in the red light district of Tokyo warning signs suddenly appeared: '*Gaijin* [foreigners] off limits.'"

53. Chirimuuta and Chirimuuta, *AIDS, Africa, and Racism,* pp. 124-125; Sabatier, *Blaming Others,* pp. 106-107. See also Robert Pear, "U.S. Seeks to Bar Aliens with AIDS," *New York Times,* March 27, 1988, and Serge Schmemann, "Calls of 'Hi Sailor' Get the Heave-Ho," *New York Times,* May 14, 1988.

54. Alan Riding, "AIDS in Brazil: Taboo of Silence Ends," *New York Times,* October 28, 1987. Blood is a pressing problem in Brazil. Whereas blood transfusion cases represent 2 to 3 percent of the total AIDS cases in the U.S., France, and the U.K., they account for 14 percent of the cases in Brazil (18 percent in Rio de Janeiro). "Some senior health officials have fed the controversy by arguing that AIDS is less of a priority than other diseases that affect millions of people here—say, malaria, leprosy, and Chagas's disease, a chronic wasting disease caused by a parasite carried by insects."

55. Parker, "Acquired Immunodeficiency Syndrome in Brazil," p. 157.

56. Dubos, *Mirage of Health,* p. 218; many researchers characterize AIDS as a "disease of development," among them Marc H. Dawson, "AIDS in Africa: Historical Roots," in *AIDS in Africa,* ed. Miller and Rockwell, pp. 58-69. Virchow is cited in Paul Epstein and Randall Packard, "Ecology and Immunology," *Science for the People* 19, no.1 (January-February 1987): 10-17, who also discuss AIDS and development.

57. Brooke Grundfest Schoepf, Rukarangira wa Nkara, Claude Schoepf, Walu Engundu, and Payanzo Ntsomo, "AIDS and Society in Central Africa: A View from Zaire," in *AIDS in Africa,* ed. Miller and Rockwell, p. 218.

58. Ibid., p. 228; the authors make the observation (not obvious, apparently, to USAID) that condoms "which hurt their wearer or break during normal use

may limit the effectiveness of AIDS prevention efforts."

59. Gill Gordon and Tony Klouda, *Preventing a Crisis* (London: IPPF, 1988). Reviewed by Harper, "AIDS in Africa—Plague or Propaganda?"

60. I am indebted to Emily Martin for pointing out the mysterious failure of most safer sex education campaigns for women to advocate or even explore the use of spermicides, except in conjunction with condoms, despite their proven effectiveness against HIV.

61. Parker, "Acquired Immunodeficiency Syndrome in Brazil," p. 161.

62. Ibid., pp. 160-163. I have greatly oversimplified Parker's intricate representation of Brazilian sexuality that, as he emphasizes, is not the mere overlay of a Western ethnographer but permeates language, slang, informal discussion, and ongoing open debate about sexuality as an essential aspect of cultural identity: "Brazilianness." But the penetrator/recipient and other distinctions that construct masculinity/femininity between same-sex partners occur elsewhere, including the U.S. See Charles F. Turner, Heather G. Miller, and Lincoln E. Moses, eds., *AIDS: Sexual Behavior and Intravenous Drug Use* (Washington, D.C.: National Academy Press, 1989), pp. 73-185, for an illuminating review of recent research on "same-gender sexual behaviors" in several cultural settings. An analysis of sexuality from a very different perspective, but one potentially helpful in articulating women's concerns, are the conclusions and recommendations "adopted by the group of experts" at a UNESCO conference in Madrid, March 12-21, 1986: "UNESCO: On Prostitution and Strategies Against Promiscuity and Sexual Exploitation of Women," *Echo* (Newsletter of the Association of African Women for Research Development) 1, no. 2-3 (1986): 16-17.

63. Sabatier, *Blaming Others,* p. 134.

64. Victor Turner, *From Ritual to Theater: The Human Seriousness of Play* (New York: PAJ Publications, 1982), p. 18.

65. Timberlake, *Africa in Crisis,* p. 8.

66. Sabatier, *Blaming Others,* p. 4.

67. Foucault, "Political Function of the Intellectual."

68. Williams, *The Country and the City,* p. 284.

69. *Emerging AIDS Markets: A Worldwide Study of Drugs, Vaccines, and Diagnostics* (New Haven: Technology Management Group, August 1986). See also Vicki Glaser, "AIDS Crisis Spurs Hunt for New Tests," *High Technology Business,* January 1988.

70. See Gina Kolata, "Africa is Favored for AIDS Testing," *New York Times,* February 19, 1988, the "AIDS Monitor" column in the *New Scientist,* February 18, 1988, p. 36, and Jane Perlez, "Scientists from Western Countries Pressing for AIDS Studies in Africa," *New York Times,* September 18, 1988. Perlez, reporting various vaccine discussions at a conference in Tanzania on AIDS and Africa, writes:

In Africa, unlike the United States, the virus is most commonly spread through heterosexual contact. Officials believe that, despite warnings to use condoms and avoid multiple partners, further spread of the virus is inevitable. . . .

Because of behavioral changes brought about by extensive education about AIDS, the spread of the infection among gay men in the United States has slowed. Thus, there would be few new infections in a study group, whether or not its members took the vaccine, the scientists said.

The scientists said they regarded intravenous drug users, a group that continues to have a high incidence of AIDS in the United States, as unreliable for the necessary follow-up that is needed for a study group.

A WHO committee developing guidelines for vaccine testing said the decision to go ahead should be made by three groups: scientists developing the vaccine, scientists knowledgable about vaccine development but with no academic or commercial stakes in it, and "government officials and their scientific advisers from the population where the vaccine is to be tried." No representatives of the population to be tested are mentioned.

71. Williams, *The Country and the City,* p. 306.

72. V. Y. Mudimbe, *The Invention of Africa: Gnosis, Philosophy, and the Order of Knowledge* (Bloomington: Indiana University Press, 1988), p. 195.

73. Pratt, "Fieldwork in Common Places," p. 42.

74. Nairobi *Standard,* January 15 and 18, 1985. For the development of research on AIDS in Africa, see Ruth Kulstad, ed., *AIDS: Papers from Science, 1982-1985* (Washington, D.C.: American Association for the Advancement of Science, 1986). Chirimuuta and Chirimuuta, *AIDS, Africa, and Racism,* describe this same history from an African perspective, noting how African challenges and counterevidence were repeatedly brushed aside.

75. Lawrence K. Altman, "Linking AIDS to Africa Provokes Bitter Debate," *New York Times,* November 21, 1985.

76. On the "international furor" see especially Chirimuuta and Chirimuuta, *AIDS, Africa, and Racism:* at the end of a symposium in Brussels in November 1985, for example, the African representatives issued a statement repudiating virtually all the assumptions made by European and American scientists and government officials (p. 122). See also Richard C. Chirimuuta, Rosalind Harrison, and Davis Gazi, "AIDS: The Spread of Racism," *West Africa,* February 9, 1987, pp. 261-262; and Gloria Waite, "The Politics of Disease: The AIDS Virus and Africa," in *AIDS in Africa,* ed. Miller and Rockwell, pp. 145-164.

77. The most publicized study of prostitutes is Joan K. Kreiss, Davy Koech, Francis A. Plummer et al., "AIDS Virus Infection in Nairobi Prostitutes: Spread of the Epidemic to East Africa," *New England Journal of Medicine* 314, no. 7 (February 13, 1986): 414-418. On myths and their refutation, see Sabatier, *Blaming*

Others, Clumeck, "AIDS in Africa," and Chirimuuta and Chirimuuta, *AIDS, Africa, and Racism.*

78. In the Western media, AIDS in the Third World is used to draw conclusions about the West. Thus Selzer's view that Haiti is "devastated" is intended to serve as a cautionary lesson about gay excess. Stories about Africa may likewise serve to warn Western readers about themselves. "FUTURE SHOCK," proclaimed the cover of *Newsweek* in December 1986, citing new worrisome projections of AIDS increases in the U.S.; a related cover headline was titled "AFRICA: THE FUTURE IS NOW." On AIDS and the media in general, see James Dearing and Everett M. Rogers, "The Agenda-Setting Process for the Issue of AIDS," paper presented at the International Communication Association, May 28-June 2, 1988.

79. Alfred J. Fortin, "The Politics of AIDS in Kenya," *Third World Quarterly* 9, no. 3 (July 1987): 907.

80. Quoted by Sabatier, *Blaming Others,* p. 97.

81. Alfred J. Fortin, "AIDS and the Third World: The Politics of International Discourse," paper presented at the 14th World Congress of the International Political Science Association, August 28-September 1, 1988, Washington, D.C.

82. Fortin, "The Politics of AIDS in Kenya," p. 907.

83. Hilary Ng'weno, "The Politics of AIDS in Kenya," *Weekly Review,* September 4, 1987, pp. 11-13. Another perspective on this debate is provided by Waite, "The Politics of Disease."

84. Mudimbe, *The Invention of Africa.*

85. Miller and Rockwell, eds., *AIDS in Africa,* p. xxiii.

86. See Levy, ed., *AIDS: Pathogenesis and Treatment.*

87. Carl E. Pletsch, "The Three Worlds, or the Division of Social Scientific Labor, circa 1950 to 1975," *Comparative Studies in Society and History* 23, no. 4 (October 1981): 565.

Cornel West

BLACK CULTURE AND POSTMODERNISM

We live now forty-four years after the age of Europe—that is, an unprecedented world-transforming historical period (1492-1945) in which those countries that reside between the Ural Mountains and Atlantic Ocean discovered new lands, subjugated those peoples on these lands, degraded the identities and cultures of non-European peoples (Africans, Asians, Latin Americans, and indigenous peoples), and exploited laborers of both European and non-European descent. We live now seventeen years after the heyday of American world hegemony—namely, a brief yet pacesetting historical interlude (1945-72) in which the U.S.A. emerged as the supreme military and economic power in the world upon the eclipse of European domination and in the wake of European devastation and decline. Lastly and most importantly, we live now in the midst of the second stage of the decolonization of the Third World—specifically, a rather paralytic moment in that world-historical process in which those subjugated and oppressed, degraded and exploited peoples bring power and pressure to bear against the status quos in Third World neocolonial nations, North Atlantic and Eastern European societies. These three fundamental historical coordinates—the aftermath and legacy of the age of Europe, the precarious yet still prominent power of the United States, and the protracted opposition of Third World peoples (here and abroad)—circumscribe the discursive space wherein "postmodernism" is constituted as an object of investigation.

The current "postmodernism" debate is first and foremost a product of significant First World reflections upon the decentering of Europe that take such forms as the demystification of European cultural predominance and the deconstruction of European philosophical edifices. With the emergence of the United States as the world center for military arms, political direction, and cultural production *and* the advent of Third World politically independent nations, the making of a new world order seemed quite likely. Ironically, most First World reflections on "postmodernism" remain rather parochial and provincial—that is, narrowly Eurocentric. For example, Jean-François Lyotard's well-known characterization of the postmodern condition, with its increasing incredulity toward master (or meta) narratives, a rejection of representation, and a demand for radical artistic experimentation, is an interesting but insulated Eurocentric view: a kind of European navel-gazing in which postmodernism becomes a recurring moment within the modern that is performative in character and aesthetic in content. The major sources from which Lyotard borrows—Kant's notion of the sublime and Wittgenstein's idea of language games—are deployed to promote and encourage certain kinds of modernist practices: namely, nonrepresentational, experimental techniques and outlooks that shun and shatter quests for totality. Similar Eurocentric frameworks and modernist loyalties can be detected in Jacques Derrida's deconstructive version of poststructuralism, and even in Michel Foucault's archeological and genealogical investigations into premodern and modern modes of constituting subjects. Derrida's own marginal status as Algerian (a special kind of French colonial subject) and a Jew may indeed lead him to highlight the transgressive and disruptive aspects of Nietzsche and Heidegger, Mallarmé and Artaud. Yet his project remains a thoroughly Eurocentric and modernist one. It could signify the absence and silence of those viewed as other, alien, marginal—Third World peoples, women, gays, lesbians—as well as their relative political impotence in creatively transforming the legacy of the age of Europe. Foucault provides more concrete social and historical ana-

lytical substance to a discourse of otherness and marginality in
his focus on the fundamental role and function of the insane and
the incarcerated. But even the "others" Foucault investigates remain within European boundaries, and his heroes, like Derrida's
remain transgressive modernists such as Nietzsche and Georges
Bataille. Needless to say, the two prominent opponents of postmodernism, Hilton Kramer from the far right and Jürgen
Habermas from the not-too-far left, do so in the name of the
highbrow achievements and intellectual "seriousness" of a
European/Anglo-American modernism and the social and political accomplishments and potentialities of a European Enlightenment project.

Significant attempts to focus the postmodernism debate on
post-World War II American cultural practices and artifacts (for
example, in architecture and painting) can be seen in the early
work of William Spanos and Paul Bové. In their illuminating
neo-Heideggerian readings of American poets like Robert
Creeley and Charles Olson, postmodern notions of temporality,
difference, and heterogeneity loomed large, yet still it remained
at the level of philosophic outlook and artistic enactment. This
observation also holds for the pioneering work of Rosalind
Krauss and Susan Sontag, who view postmodernism as either a
complex set of sensibilities and styles, or as ideological beliefs.

Fredric Jameson, Hal Foster, and to a certain extent, An-
dreas Huyssen have brought a particular debate "down to earth"
(as it were) by situating it in relation to larger developments in
society and history. In short, Jameson and Huyssen try to lay
bare the contours of the forest that goes beyond the useful
though limited squirrel work done by other postmodern critics.
They do this by positing postmodernism as a social category—a
dominant yet diverse set of structural and institutional processes
wherein certain sensibilities, styles, and outlooks are understood
as reactions and responses to new societal conditions and historical circumstances.

The important point here is neither whether one agrees with Jameson's laundry lists of postmodern features (e.g., depthlessness, persuasiveness of the image and simulacrum, weakening of historicity, emotional intensities, and schizo-phrenic subjects), nor whether one approves of his treatments of individual cultural artifacts. Rather what is crucial is that First World reflections on postmodernism have become more con-sciously historical, social, political, and ideological. For too long, the postmodernism debate has remained inscribed within nar-row disciplinary boundaries, insulated artistic practices, and vague formulations of men and women of letters. The time has come for this debate to be moved more forthrightly into social theory and historiography. To do so is to raise methodological questions about historical periodization, demarcation of cultural practices and archives, and issues of politics and ideology.

For instance, every conception of postmodernism presup-poses some idea of the modern — when it began, when it peaked, when it declined, when it ended. And any such idea of the mod-ern bears directly and indirectly upon how one conceives of change in the present. Secondly, different cultural practices have generally agreed upon uses of the term "modern" that require a recognition of the diverse logics within specific disciplinary practices. For example, philosophers view the advent of the modern as a seventeenth-century affair and shun the term "modernist" as a description of philosophical rhetorical strat-egies, whereas literary critics view nineteenth-century works as major examples of "the modern" and make much of the break between modern and modernist literary texts. Architects under-stand modernist works as those that valorize reason, technique, instrumentality, and functionality in thoroughgoing utopian terms. On the other hand, literary critics view modernist texts as those that dismiss rationality, instrumentality, and func-tionality in favor of myth, montage, simultaneity, and play in deeply anti-utopian terms. Adequate conceptions of historical periodization must keep track of these complex convergences and divergences of different cultural traditions, yet still not lose sight of the larger social and historical forces at work at any particular moment. This means that the very historical periodizations and cultural demarcations we make are, in part, ideological constructs shot through with political presuppositions, prejudgments, prejudices. Intellectual honesty requires that one make them crystal clear and give reasons as to why one holds them.

From my own viewpoint, I remain quite suspicious of the term "postmodernism" for two basic reasons. First, because the precursor term "modern" itself has not simply been used to devalue the cultures of oppressed and exploited peoples, but also has failed to deeply illumine the internal complexities of these cultures. Under the circumstances, there is little reason to hold out hope for the new term "postmodernism" as applied to the practices of oppressed peoples. Second, the sheer facticity of black people in the United States historically embodies and enacts the "postmodern" themes of degraded otherness and subaltern marginality. Black resistances have attacked notions of exclusionary identity, dominating heterogeneity, and universality—or, in more blunt language, white supremacy. Yet the historical experience of black people in North America, as well as Latinos, women, workers, gays, and lesbians, always requires that one examine the relation of any Eurocentric (patriarchal, homophobic) discourse to black resistance. The issue here is not simply some sophomoric, moralistic test that surveys the racial biases of the interlocutors in a debate. Rather the point is to engage in a structural and institutional analysis to see *where* the debate is taking place, *why* at this historical moment, and *how* this debate enables or disenables oppressed peoples to exercise their opposition to the hierarchies of power. For example, does the postmodernism debate seriously acknowledge the distinctive cultural and political practices of oppressed peoples, e.g., African-Americans? Or does this debate highlight notions of difference,

91

marginality, and otherness in such a way that it further marginalizes actual people of difference and otherness, e.g., African-Americans, Latinos, women, etc.? My point here is not a crude instrumental one, that is, I am not calling for some "vulgar" populist discourse for mobilizing oppressed peoples. Rather, I am asking whether postmodernism debates can cast some significant light on cultural practices of oppressed peoples.

My own hunch is that oppositional black intellectuals must be conversant with and, to a degree, participants in the debate. Yet until the complex relations between race, class, and gender are more adequately theorized, more fully delineated in specific historiographical studies, and more fused in our concrete ideological and political practices, the postmodernism debate, though at times illuminating, will remain rather blind to the plight and predicament of black America. Therefore I do not displace myself from the postmodernism debate, I simply try to keep my distance from its parochialism and view it as a symptom of our present cultural crisis.

When one turns to African-American cultural practices and products during the historical moment in which the postmodernism debate begins, it is undeniable that U.S. mass culture is disproportionately influenced by black people. This is so especially in popular music, linguistic innovation, and athletics. Owing to both a particular African heritage and specific forms of Euro-American oppression, black American cultural production has focused primarily on performance and pageantry, style and spectacle in music, sermons, and certain sports. The music and sermons are rooted in black religious practices; the sports, in black male-bonding networks that flaunt *machismo,* promote camaraderie, and, in some cases, lead to financial success. Black religious practices — the indigenous cradle of African-American culture — principally attempt to provide hope and sustain sanity in light of the difficult position of black Americans and the ab-

surdity of transplanted European moderns casting America in
the role of the promised land. The black religious ideological response was often to recast America as Egypt; and the concrete,
everyday response to institutionalized terrorism—slavery or Jim-
Crowism—was to deploy weapons of kinetic orality, passionate
physicality, and combative spirituality to survive and dream of
freedom.

By kinetic orality, I mean dynamic repetitive and energetic
rhetorical styles that form communities, e.g., antiphonal styles
and linguistic innovations that accent fluid, improvisational identities and that promote survival at almost any cost. By passionate
physicality, I mean bodily stylizations of the world, syncopations
and polyrhythms that assert one's somebodiness in a society in
which one's body has no public worth, only economic value as a
laboring metabolism. And by combative spirituality, I mean a
sense of historical patience, subversive joy, and daily per-
severance in an apparently hopeless and meaningless historical
situation. Black cultural practices emerge out of an acknowledgment of a reality they cannot *not know*—the ragged edges of the
real, of necessity; a reality historically constructed by white supremacist practices in North America during the age of Europe.
These ragged edges—of not being able to eat, not to have shelter, not to have health care—all this is infused into the strategies
and styles of black cultural practices. Of course, all peoples have
undergone some form of social misery, yet peoples of African
descent in the United States have done so in the midst of the
most prosperous and wealthy country in the world.

A distinctive feature of these black styles is a certain projection of the self—more a *persona*—in performance. This is not
simply a self-investment and self-involvement in musical, rhetorical, and athletic enactments; it also acknowledges radical con-
tingency and even solicits challenge and danger. In short, it is a
spectacular form of risk-ridden execution that is self-imposed—
be it a Charlie Parker solo, a Sarah Vaughan rendition, Muham-

mad Ali footwork, a Martin Luther King, Jr., sermon, a James Brown dancing act, a Julius Erving dunk shot, or a Kathleen Battle interpretation of Handel. This feature not only results from what some anthropologists have called the African deification of accident—the sense of perennially being on a slippery tightrope; it also comes from the highly precarious historical situations in which black people have found themselves. And with political and economic avenues usually blocked, specific cultural arenas become the space wherein black resistance is channeled.

Ironically, black American culture has surfaced with power and potency in our own time principally owing to three basic reasons. First, upon the emergence of the United States as a world power, it was quite clear that black music—spirituals, gospels, blues, jazz, soul—was the most unique cultural product created by Americans of any hue. So as the globalization of American culture escalated, black music was given vast international exposure. Second, as the consumption cycle of advanced multinational corporate capitalism was sped up in order to sustain the production of luxury goods, cultural production became more and more mass-commodity production. The stress here is not simply on the new and fashionable but also on the exotic and primitive. Black cultural products have historically served as a major source for European and Euro-American exotic interests—interests that issue from a healthy critique of the mechanistic, puritanical, utilitarian, and productivist aspects of modern life.

Yet as black cultural products become the commodified possession of Euro-Americans, they play a very different role in U.S. society. For example, they speak less of the black sense of absurdity in America and more of the "universal" values of love. Needless to say, the sheer size of the white consumer market provides material incentives to black artists to be "crossover artists," i.e., more attuned to white tastes and sensibilities. There indeed are some cases where artistic and cultural integrity is preserved by crossover artists (Sly Stone in the sixties, Luther Vandross and Anita Baker in the eighties). Yet the temptation to de-Africanize one's style and dilute one's black cultural content for commercial reasons is often irresistible.

The third reason black culture has recently become so salient is that it became identified with the first mass youth culture, an ever-growing world consumer market since the fifties. This culture responded to the eclipse of First World utopian energies and waning alternative political options by associating modes of transcendence with music and sexual liberation. Given the European and Euro-American identification of Africans and African-Americans with sexual licentiousness, libertinism, and liberation, black music became both a symbol and facilitator of white sexual freedom. And with the vast sexualization of the advertising industry, which now specializes in recycling black music hits of the recent past, much of black popular music has become thoroughly accepted by not simply rebellious white youth (as of old), but also the cultural mainstream.

What then is the oppositional potential of black cultural practices in our time? And to what extent is it legitimate to designate some of them "postmodern"? Of the three major forms of black cultural products — musical, sermonic, and athletic practices — certainly the latter is the most incorporated and co-opted of the three. Sermonic practices, still far removed from most white observation and consumption, are limited owing to ecclesiastical and denominational constituencies that make it difficult for ecumenical figures to emerge who can remain rooted in black institutional life, yet attract peoples from outside their own constituencies. Yet when such figures do emerge — Martin Luther King, Jr., Malcolm X, Jesse Jackson — they can generate tremendous oppositional energy due to the paucity of articulate and charismatic spokespersons on the American left and the potentially positive role charismatic leaders can play in empowering people to believe in themselves and act in unity against the powers that be.

Black musical practices—packaged via radio or video, records or live performances—are oppositional principally in the weak sense that they keep alive some sense of the agency and creativity of oppressed peoples. Yet this sense is so vague and far removed from organized political resistance that one must conclude that most of black music here and abroad has simply become a major means by which U.S. record companies have colonized the leisure time of eager consumers (including myself). Yet since black music is so integral to black life in America, it is difficult to imagine a black resistance movement in which black music does not play an important role.

But what of literary artists, visual artists, and other black intellectuals in general? Have I not unduly neglected them? Are they not the possible candidates for producers of postmodern products—which thereby makes the term partly relevant to black life? Granted, I have spent most of my time on black mass culture. This is so because my interest in black resistance in the form of social movements leads me to look for the possible motion and momentum of black people who suffer, work, and long for social freedom. But much more serious reflection must be done in regards to this crucial matter. This essay is but a mere gesture toward constructing possible critical positions for blacks both in and around popular culture, the ways in which these positions can be viewed as sites of a potentially enabling yet resisting postmodernism.

Michele Wallace

READING 1968 AND

THE GREAT AMERICAN WHITEWASH

After 1968, none of the "other" groups in struggle—
neither women nor racial "minorities" nor sexual "minorities" nor the handicapped nor the "ecologists" (those
who refused the acceptance, unquestioningly, of the imperatives of increased global production)—would ever
again accept the legitimacy of "waiting" upon some other
revolution.
—Immanuel Wallerstein, "1968, Revolution in the World
System: Theses and Queries," 1988

We must become more radically historical than is envisioned by the Marxist tradition. By becoming more "radically historical" I mean confronting more candidly the
myriad of effects and consequences (intended and unin-
tended, conscious and unconscious) of power-laden and
conflict-ridden social practice—e.g., the complex con-
fluence of human bodies, traditions and institutions.
—Cornel West, "Race and Social Theory: Toward a
Genealogical Materialist Analysis," 1987

You who understand the dehumanization of forced
removal-relocation-reeducation-redefinition, the humiliation of having to falsify your own reality, your voice—
you know. And often cannot say it. You try and keep on
trying to unsay it, for if you don't they will not fail to fill
in the blanks on your behalf, and you will be said.
—Trinh T. Minh-ha, "Difference: A Special Third World
Women Issue," 1988

I recently participated in a conference called "1968 in Global Retrospective," which was built around a twenty-seven page paper by Immanuel Wallerstein about 1968 as "one of the great formative events in the history of our modern world-system, the kind we call watershed events." My job was to talk about "The Key Role of 'Minority' Revolutions," and to chair a panel on "Representations of 1968: Invention and Use of Symbols," which included 1968 historians Todd Gitlin, David Caute, Jim Hoberman, and James Miller. I was eager to do this because so many people had criticized my book *Black Macho and the Myth of the Superwoman* as inaccurate and overly harsh in my judgments of the failures of black leadership and black female complicity in that failure in the 1960s.

Minority Revolutions in a Major Key

As I observe the emerging patterns of codification and interpretation of U.S. and global 1960s history, I am beginning to understand how Afro-American intellectual history, despite the publication of Harold Cruse's *The Crisis of the Negro Intellectual* in 1967, continues to fail to exist at the level of most white scholarship and commentary. Therefore, it continues to hold only marginal interest for those who would reflect upon the fate of "minority revolutions." Yet it is precisely the caliber of Afro-American intellectual reflection about itself, the New Left, and other "minority" revolutions that needs to be considered here. Without doing so, first theory, then history helps to consolidate at the level of collective memory the very segregation 1960s youth were once so determined to undo.

Such Afro-Americanists as Cornel West, Manning Marable, Hortense Spillers, Henry Louis Gates, Houston Baker, Hazel Carby, Paula Giddings, and Bell Hooks have become instrumental in revealing an underlying coherence in Afro-American intellectual and cultural development. Collectively, such efforts begin to reveal the degree to which people of African descent have demonstrated in writing and speaking a historical consciousness that connects Phillis Wheatley, Frederick Douglass, and Frances Harper to Ida B. Wells, W. E. B. DuBois, and Zora Neale Hurston, to C. L. R. James, James Baldwin, and Lorraine Hansberry, to Stuart Hall, Amiri Baraka, and Toni Morrison.

Historical consciousness is no less true of the black intellectual grasp of 1968. At the time, such figures as Angela Davis, Stokely Carmichael, Nikki Giovanni, Martin Luther King, Sonia Sanchez, Amiri Baraka, Ron Karenga, and Harold Cruse were crucial to how the period imagined its goals. Now, in retrospect, the impact and significance of such figures is made to seem slight indeed, unless, of course, the project becomes to write a *black* history of 1968, but then that would still be "minor" and "minority" history. My intention here is to point out the tendency for "history" in the major sense to corroborate a racist, phallocentric hegemony by always marginalizing, trivializing, and decentering the black subject, even as its specific historical object may involve an apparent focus upon issues of ethnicity, or racism, or, as in this case, "minority revolutions." To put it another way, somehow, ultimately, black subjectivity always seems irrelevant to any serious academic or political discussion of a "black," "ethnic," or "minority" object. For instance, Daniel Patrick Moynihan once used the scholarship of E. Franklin Frazier to verify the distinction between margin (the black family) and center (the white family). I want to decenter our present discussion of "minority" revolutions in favor of a discussion of "black subjectivity." This habit of leaving the black subject out always seems to coincide with a preference for global or synthetic views, and should continue no longer.

Therefore, my role here is to contest the notion of a "world system" as yet another attempt to universalize white male intellectual authority over the voiceless masses. However, I don't for a moment believe that high-minded collections of oral history, which allow "the people to speak for themselves," or that autonomous insular black intellectual debate will fill the gap. I have no objection to the notion of "world systems," in and of themselves, especially since I understand that in this case it carries the more practical purpose of addressing the problem of an increasingly global economic arrangement that stifles substantive change and resistance at the local or the national level, or at the level of a specific issue such as ethnicity, class, or sexuality. I understand that most of the people of color in the world are getting screwed as a function of a world system, so it makes sense that amelioration would propose a global approach at some point.

Moreover, regarding the idea that there may be repetitions and parallels in events around the globe, I have noticed certain patterns, conscious and unconscious, in contemporary black cultural and intellectual reflections on the limits of 1960s black male political leadership "style," in terms of its failure to recognize or accommodate the question of sexual difference. Particularly in black film and literature from the U.S. and England, there has developed not only a conventional feminist critique of inequality within the Black Liberation Movement, but also a trend toward subverting the male/female gender duality in favor of multiple sexualities, including homosexuality and lesbianism, as well as an increasing focus on the inadequacies of a rigid and inflexible concept of masculinity. Besides the considerable literature that explores such approaches (novels and poetry by black feminist writers Ntozake Shange, Alice Walker, Toni Morrison, Toni Cade Bambara, Lucille Clifton, Audre Lorde, and black male writers Ishmael Reed, Charles Johnson, John Edgar Wideman, Ralph Ellison), I see Spike Lee's *School Daze* (1988), Isaac Julien and Maureen Blackwood's *The Passion of Remembrance* (1986), and Sarah Maldoror's *Sambizanga* (about the struggle for liberation in Angola [1972]) all as films in which there is a related concern about the loss of a unitary concept of "the black (male) leader."

For instance, in *School Daze* (at a level that is perhaps unconscious to director Spike Lee), Dap's leadership (and his role as protagonist) is constantly questioned and challenged, not only by the college administration, but also by "women" and by his friends, as well as by the continuous flow of dance, song, style, and sexual spectacle that seems to be saying that this film has more important business to attend to than the telling of a linear (phallic) narrative.

In *Passion of Remembrance,* which more candidly embraces a critique of sixties male leadership, and its knee-jerk heterosexism, the combination of carnivalesque spectacle, political commentary, and archival footage is, finally, much more satisfying than the English film that is most often lauded for these attributes, *Sammy and Rosie Get Laid* (1987). While I admire the films of Stephen Frears and Hanif Kureishi, it seems more problematic that Third Worldism becomes an excuse for excessive cynicism about the possibility for fundamental world change coupled with an implicit hierarchizing of a literate and prosperous "Third World" (Indian) and an illiterate and impoverished "Third World" (poor blacks) in England. From the first scene in *Sammy and Rosie,* it is blacks who occupy the film's most desperate and precarious social, sexual, and economic positions.

In *Sambizanga,* while the critique seems thoroughly unconsious on the director's part, the black male "leader" is both figuratively and literally slain from the beginning of the film. It is the crying of the women and their context in culture, and the men who can relate to them, who will carry on.

In real life in the U.S. — if you can call *The Morton Downey Show* real life — this critique of past black male leadership takes the form of Roy Innis and Al Sharpton's fistfight at Harlem's Apollo Theater ostensibly over the case of Tawana Brawley.

Meanwhile, Brawley is a fifteen-year-old black teenager whose rape is somehow unimaginable and unspeakable to present black political discourse, as the debate rages over whether Sharpton is a "fake." Black male leadership seems no better prepared to fathom the black teenager's psychological, social, economic, and educational plight now than in 1968. And no better prepared to cast out the Sharptons. At the same time, we should not dismiss too quickly the inherent dangers that even progressive "world systems" present. This is the danger of neocolonialism or neo-imperialism in intellectual form and what makes it so is that mostly only white males are empowered to engage in that discourse. The problem then becomes, as Trinh Minh-ha points out, "they work toward your erasure while urging you to keep your way of life and ethnic values within the border of your homelands. This is called the policy of 'separate development' in apartheid language."

Somewhere Over the Rainbow

Thirdly, no desirable transformation of the capitalist world-economy is possible in the absence of trans-zonal political cooperation by anti-systemic movements. This trans-zonal cooperation would have to be both strategic and tactical. It might be easier (albeit still not easy) to establish the bases of tactical cooperation. But strategic? It is probable that strategic collaboration can only be on the basis of a profound rad-icalization of the objectives.
—Immanuel Wallerstein, 1988

I am not concerned to question here the nature of this proposal. Rather, my focus is upon "a profound radicalization of objectives," which is perhaps least accessible through the theorizing of "world systems." This theorizing, after all, in no way subverts or transforms white male academic authority and, therefore, confirms our present unsatisfactory arrangements of cultural hegemony. The only door through which "change" at a critical level can enter is by altering the composition of that community that considers the problems of "objectives." White men have to stop thinking that it is their place alone to determine the course of our lives.

So I am not proposing that if Wallerstein were black, everything would be fine. I am not a nationalist nor a postnationalist, nor does "racial pride" make a lot of sense to me as a political goal (though I have my fair share). Rather, I am proposing that if the experiences of race, ethnicity, gender, and sexuality were made central to future considerations of "world systems" the process would be a lot more convincing in terms of locating a "profound radicalization of objectives." Moreover, this blindspot to ethnicity and sexuality transcends the problem of "minorities" as "women and blacks," who are not, after all, global minorities, but who are simply minor in the sphere of knowledge production. Not only is there a failure to consider the question of world systems or global perspectives from the view of the racial or sexual "other." There is also a failure to consider the other that may ultimately be at the center of even a so-called majority white male existence, the other of ethnicity, religion, sexuality, rationality, the other of homelessness, both geographical and existential, which may be the driving force behind this compulsive white male Western insistence upon majority and dominance.

So the question for me is not even whether or not Wallerstein is right or wrong. Such a question cannot even be addressed until we have contended with the discrepancy in that perspective itself, the view from which the history of 1968 is first recollected that obliterates the possibility of black subjectivity.

Perhaps the clearest occasion upon which this occurs is in Wallerstein's Thesis 4: "Counterculture was part of the revolutionary euphoria, but was not politically central to 1968." The subsequent explanation of this thesis goes on to define the "counterculture" in a way that not only precludes its historical relationship to Afro-American culture, but also renders 1960s

Afro-American culture, including the Civil Rights Movement and Black Power, entirely invisible. Afro-American cultural production then becomes an incidental and minor aspect of U.S. and European counterculture or, in this case, a nonentity. The historical relationship is first reversed; counterculture no longer comes out of Afro-American culture—as in rock 'n' roll coming out of rhythm 'n' blues, the beat aesthetic coming out of a performance style and belief structures of bebop and black jazz musicians, and American youth street culture coming out of a kind of Afro-American existentialism of the streets, as Norman Mailer proposed in *The White Negro*.

Then, in the most preemptive move, in the move that makes history irrecoverable by turning it into myth, the counterculture is defined as that which is gratuitous, which belongs to no one, which is not culture at all, but *counter-to-culture* or against culture. "We generally mean by counterculture," Wallerstein writes, "behavior in daily life (sexuality, drugs, dress) and in the arts that is unconventional, non 'bourgeois,' and Dionysiac." There is never any doubt in this statement that there is a more useful, mainstream, conventional, bourgeois, and Apollonian culture that will counteract the countercultural. The countercultural is then perceived as entirely peripheral to profound change. Still, I would like to claim this degraded form of culture as the true location for a revolutionary potential in Afro-American culture.

Afro-American culture has long been the starting point for white self-criticism in the U.S. Mid-twentieth-century white youth and black youth observed the resilience and versatility of Afro-American culture—its working mothers employed as domestics with husbands who could not find work; its poor elderly black men who had labored for a pittance all their lives yet could invent songs of indescribable beauty in which they accurately weighed the material and psychological complexity of their world; its tradition of black religious music, which seemed to turn the hypocrisy of conventional white Protestantism inside

out; its churchgoing blacks who would lay their bodies down before waterhoses, dogs, and white Southern racism and then get
up and fight for the Mississippi Freedom Party and against U.S.
military involvement in the Vietnam War.

The recognition of that culture, or the weight of that culture, or the price that had been paid for that culture, was a
prime motivating factor in the 1968 sense that U.S. dominance
and world hegemony were unconscionable and parasitic, and
that the "Old Left" lacked the sensitivity to grapple with real
people in a real world of cultural diversity. Afro-American culture has been crucial in forming the aspirations of the New Left,
as well as minority revolutions—not so much by its considerable
political activism—but precisely by its counterculture. While
this "minor" culture may sometimes be difficult to explicate as
protest, it was always clearly formed in the spirit of subverting a
majority culture that tried to choke it at the root. Precisely by
its sex, drugs, dance, dress, music, and style, it kept the record
of its discontents accurately and well. Perhaps this counterculture is the level at which mainstream culture is still most
forcefully challenged, even as "revolutions" come and go.

Maybe there are many "countercultures," not just one. For
instance, today black youth resist total white hegemonic control
over everyday life, often by means considered counter to culture,
by drug use and the life of the streets, by their unwillingness to
go to school and their inclination to have babies. Clearly, such
developments are socially constructed and economically predestined. I am not claiming this culture of demoralization for
political radicalism. I am saying that what they are doing is connected, by influence and osmosis, to countercultural developments, white and black, in the 1950s and 1960s.

As for those decades, I am certain of a deliberate and self-
conscious black counterculture because my parents—my father
who was a jazz musician, my mother who was an artist, and my
stepfather who was their close friend—were part of it. When
the 1960s came, my father, Earl Wallace, who was divorced from

my mother and who was not a successful musician, was dead of a heroin overdose. In 1965, the summer he died, my mother, Faith Ringgold, my sister, and I took classes at Amiri Baraka's newly inaugurated School of Black Arts. A public high school teacher then, Faith became a 1960s radical, taking an active role in the black struggle against the United Federation of Teachers over "decentralization" of the public schools.

In those years, the hardest thing to figure out was culture, how our everyday lives would bear the mark of our political commitment. In 1963, Faith had also begun to produce a series of paintings called "American People," in which she tried to capture the drama and historical significance of the Civil Rights Movement, as we then viewed it on our television screens, as it affected race relations in the North, as it was written about by James Baldwin in *The Fire Next Time* (1963) and Amiri Baraka (LeRoi Jones) in *Dutchman* (1964). In 1970, when I became a student at the City College of New York, I was already struck by how many politically active black students were getting involved in heavy drug use, and dying.

1968 Revisited

"Where is tomorrow's avant-garde in art and entertainment to take on the racial bias of the snowblind, the sexual politics of the frigid, and the class anxieties of the perennially upper crust?" When I asked this question a few months ago, I was trying to make light of something that is not light at all. As ridiculous as it may seem, a white cultural avant-garde, here and abroad, has always believed it possible to make an oppositional art without fundamentally challenging hegemonic notions of race, sexuality, and even class.

Of course, when I was a kid, we didn't call it "white cultural hegemony." We called it the "Great American White-wash." I had the great good fortune to be raised in a family of artists (my stepfather Burdette Ringgold was not an artist, but worked at GM to finance our creativity) in which resistance to the old truism, "If you're white, you're alright; if you're brown, stick around; and if you're black, stay back," was viewed not only as paramount to making art, but basic to one's psychological survival. I still find it astonishing when white people consistently conceptualize resistance in ways that minimize the importance of race, or the vital contribution black artists and intellectuals have made to the discussion of that issue.

But I was first struck by the true dimension of this problem in 1970 when Faith and I attended a guerrilla art action protest against Art Strike, which was, itself, a protest against "racism, sexism, war, and repression." A group of famous white male artists led by Robert Morris decided to withdraw their work from the Venice Biennale, a prestigious international exhibition, in order to protest U.S. military involvement in Vietnam. Although the protest was supposed to be against "racism, sexism, and repression," Art Strike then expected to mount a counter-Biennale in New York without altering the all-white male composition of the show. This seems to be the key to understanding the intrinsic limits of Western cultural avant-gardism: while it can no longer deny its own white male supremacist presuppositions, it cannot be rid of them either.

In the first years of our feminism, working through an organization that we founded called Women Students and Artists for Black Art Liberation (WSABAL), Faith and others succeeded in opening this exhibition to women and people of color. WSABAL was also influential in the subsequent development of Ad Hoc Women Artists, led by Lucy Lippard. This group repeated WSABAL's 50 percent women demand in their protest against the Whitney Biennial, which was in the habit of including white male artists almost exclusively. Specifically because of Faith's research and support of Ad Hoc, black women artists Barbara Chase and Betye Saar were included in the next Whitney Biennial.

Of course, Faith's activism against the museums had not begun in 1970. It really began in 1968, the year of Martin Luther King's assassination, when every black artist and cultural worker in the country was galvanized into action. Only sixteen years old at the time, I accompanied Faith to the first demonstration of black artists against the Whitney Museum and then to a series of free-for-all (Art Workers' Coalition) demonstrations against the Museum of Modern Art. The museums were still reluctant to call in the police at that point. Yet, since the Civil Rights Movement, Black Power, and the riots, it was no longer tolerable to just "picket" in an orderly fashion, and these demonstrations were very exciting and unpredictable, full of street theater and creative mayhem, very countercultural.

In one case, I can remember museum administrators and security guards standing helplessly by as Faith led a walking tour through MoMA's first-floor galleries during which she lectured on the influence of African art and the art of the African Diaspora on the so-called modern art displayed there. The manner in which academic and critical expertise and the museum's curatorial staff conspired to render the importance of that influence either invisible, trivial, or instrumental shaped the force of her remarks. When we finally came to a room in which the works of a black artist were displayed—perhaps two or three gouaches from Jacob Lawrence's 1930s "Black Migration Series"—Faith designated it the location for the Martin Luther King Wing, which was then the principal demand of the Art Workers' Coalition demonstrations at MoMA. This wing was supposed to serve as an exhibition space that would revolve around a cultural education center, which would train blacks, Puerto Ricans, and Native Americans in art history and museum administration. This would not only lead to the canonization of some black artists and the hiring of nonwhite curators, but it was intended to promote an increase in the number of young people of color who would be drawn to careers in art and art education, to foster a different relationship to museums and "high culture" for the throngs of nonwhite public school children who were obliged to visit the museums every year.

For many, the Civil Rights Movement was their first exposure to the power of Rainbow Coalitions. My first exposure came during those years of involvement with the Art Workers' Coalition. But the lesson was a hard one: there would be no wing, no cultural center, only retrospectives for black artists Romare Bearden and Richard Hunt, which made them (no doubt because they were men) even more famous than Barbara Chase and Betye Saar.

The resulting tokenism of a few museum shows for a few black artists, or women artists, did not really change the intrinsic elitism of the art world. Visual art is still perceived by many as the exclusive entertainment of the rich, as though the rest of us didn't need something to look at. At the time, the important thing seemed to be that my mother was an activist whose work as an artist was consistent with her politics, although I pointedly failed to mention any such thing in my own recollection of the 1960s in *Black Macho*. This was perhaps my greatest and most unfortunate oversight, since her politics were my politics in the 1960s and even for much of the 1970s. Now, however, the important thing has become that as recollections of the 1960s mount up—Todd Gitlin's *The Sixties: Years of Hope, Days of Rage,* James Miller's *"Democracy Is in the Streets": From Port Huron to the Siege of Chicago,* David Caute's *The Year of the Barricades: A Journey Through 1968,* Sara Evans' *Personal Politics: The Roots of Women's Liberation in the Civil Rights Movement and the New Left,* and the forthcoming *Daring to Be Bad: A History of the Radical Feminist Movement, 1967-1975* by Alice Echols—again we are facing the Great American Whitewash in which the true breadth of the Afro-American cultural presence and contribution either ceases to exist, or becomes so small and trivial, we can hardly see it.

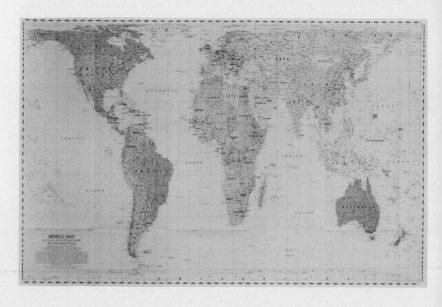

World map in equal area representation (Peters Projection). Copyright © by Akademische Verlagsanstalt; English version by Oxford Cartographers Ltd., Oxford, U.K.

Janet Abu-Lughod

ON THE REMAKING OF HISTORY:

HOW TO REINVENT THE PAST

It seems ironic that as recently as 1987 a second edition of a book entitled *The European Miracle* was published. Ironic because, in the face of stock market "corrections" that were still seeking bottom and of growing protectionism against what has been called the "Asian miracle" of Japan and the newly industrializing countries of the Pacific rim, we sense that the great self-congratulatory literature of the Rise of the West, which for so long shaped our view of the past, should be reevaluated, may need to be "remade." Depending on one's point of view, this process of revision may prove to be a blessing: if indeed the power accumulated by Europe from the sixteenth century onward and then inherited by the United States did not emanate from a unique genius, perhaps the "fall of the West" need not be attributed to a decline in Western "virtue." Indeed, factors other than inherent capacity and intelligence may account for the rise and fall of nations in the world system. Perhaps we need to construct a new *storia* (the Italian term is much more honest than its English counterpart).

To anyone concerned with issues of race and gender, the creation of alternative histories is nothing new, and in fact, a necessary and vital component of many disciplines. But to the traditional historian, the suggestion that historical writing is a construction, perhaps as imaginative as any literary creation, is a heresy. (Do we really make up history? For if we do, then we can certainly remake it.) But what may be heresy to a historian is an ordinary working assumption to a sociologist. Scholarly interpretations of historical events are subject to many of the same biases and distortions sociologists must guard against when they research contemporary events, whether through participant observation, the collection of narratives from participants, or via surveys of knowledge and attitudes. The meta-methodological difficulties are at least of three kinds.

First, what sociologists take as a truism—namely, that accounts of social events are "constructions" rather than descriptions isomorphic with some "objective reality"—has yet to be fully assimilated into historical methodology. Just as is the case when studying ongoing social life, in historical reconstruction there is no archimedean point *outside* the system from which to view historic "reality." The only antidote to this dilemma is the same one used in sociological research, namely, triangulation. We assume that *somewhere* between the accounts given, duly discounted for "distortions" due to partial perspectives and vested interests, one can "find" an approximation of social reality that *might have been constructed* by an unbiased and virtually omniscient narrator, had such an observer been possible. The lesson for historical investigation is clear. Any history of "the other" or of a "world system" written from the perspective of only one actor or society can be only a partial telling of the *storia,* regardless of its erudition. (This is the point behind Edward Said's *Orientalism* [1978] and the work of the Indian historians who call themselves the "subalterns.")

Second, we know from sociological work that all accounts are not only constructed but, what is worse, are constructed *backwards.* That is, it is only "after the fact" that narratives are built, especially narratives that seek to explain. A divorce occurs. One tries to explain "why." One does not then construct the equally plausible (and equally selective) account of how happy the marriage was. Freud perceptively acknowledged that diagnosis always precedes the etiological account. In history also, it is only after events have run their course that we build the narrative that appears to make them inevitable. How to avoid these self-fulfilling hypotheses? Counterfactuals are one way to guard against this, but they have an inauthentic ring. It is far better, I think, to stop along the way, assessing relative conditions at successive points in time and then trying to analyze how these various states could have come about. If, indeed, the end point inescapably determines the account, then we need to take a series of end points, in the same way we need to triangulate among accounts.

This is all the more important because interests determine *where* any narrator will begin his/her account, which is our third point. Think of an argument that escalates. Interviewing the participants, one notices that their narratives start at very different points. Each begins at the moment when a wrong *to them* is perceived; their own acts are all "retaliatory." Any prior provocation they may have given is left out of the account since it "predates" the narrative. Similarly, in accounting for a successful outcome, the false starts and early defeats will usually be ignored, unless they have a twist. Consider the new heavyweight champion of the world, asked to what he attributes his success. An answer that begins with "I was a very sickly baby" would be bizarre—unless it introduces a statement about how he overcame this. Similarly, a response such as "my opponent was suffering from indigestion and an abscessed tooth" is highly unlikely, since it clearly detracts from the accomplishment that is enhanced not by the weakness of the defeated but only by the strength of the victor.

What does all of this have to do with remaking history? Here, I want to relate some of the findings of a project that has occupied my attention for the past few years, now published as a book entitled *Before Europe's Hegemony*. In it, I analyze the complexly reticulated system of world production and trade (organized on capitalist and state capitalist lines) that, in the century between AD 1250 to AD 1350 (e.g., the late thirteenth and early fourteenth centuries, a period identified by Western historians as "the commercial revolution"), integrated the economies of an "archipelago of towns" located along several long-distance land and sea routes that stretched all the way from China to northwestern Europe. In this world system—whose core lay in near and farther Asia—Europe was but a recent and still marginal participant. It was not, then, a time of *general* revolution; it was merely a time when *Europe* underwent enormous changes as it became more integrated into the preexistent world system.

This is certainly an anomalous finding since, as every one conversant with the Miracle of the West knows, Europe was unique in forging capitalism out of feudalism. Furthermore, *the* modern world system came into being in the long sixteenth century when Europe achieved hegemony. According to this orthodoxy, Europe's leap into modernity was achieved solely by its own strengths and virtues. My book seeks to refute all of these accepted dogmas. But before offering a "re-*storia,*" we must ask how such a history got written in the first place.

One can see the operation of the mechanisms described earlier as soon as one examines critically the chief problematic of many Western historical sociologists. The present hegemony of the West is assumed, that is, the outcome is determined, the "diagnosis" is complete. The task remains to *account for why this outcome occurred.* In short, the question is, "Why did the West rise to hegemony?" Past historical events are then interrogated selectively to answer this question. Two biases immediately follow.

First, the narrative is begun just at the point when the outcome—not foreordained earlier—becomes relatively inevitable. Consider the time periods taken as the starting points for such histories. The year 1400 is almost always the earliest marker we find. The voluminous and dazzling multi-volumes of the corpus of Fernand Braudel's works begin with that year. Even Eric Wolf's otherwise nonethnocentric work, *Europe and*

the People Without History (1982), takes this as the starting point.
Most writers, however, begin even later with the sixteenth century. Thus, Max Weber, whose first dissertation had, in fact,
dealt with business practices in medieval Europe, then shifted
his focus to the later period. In the introduction to his essays on
the Protestant ethic (1904-1905), for example, he went to great
lengths (using an often involuted and, to my mind, suspect logic)
to distinguish between a preexisting but "spurious" spirit of
(Oriental) capitalism, which he dismisses as mere "avarice," and
a "true" (i.e., European) spirit of modern capitalism whose
source he traces to the religious reformation of the sixteenth
century. Immanuel Wallerstein's account, *The Modern World-
System,* shares this ambivalence. While the narrative starts about
1450, it is not until the sixteenth century that the process of European domination is shown to be established. Even Marx wa-
vered, originally seeing the origins of Western capitalism in the
thirteenth century but later revising his view by insisting on the
sixteenth century.

As I argue on the basis of my own research, 1400 is the
earliest moment at which a "rise of the West" to world
hegemony could have been predicted with any probability, and
the early decades of the sixteenth century (the 1500s) constitute
the first moment when European hegemony had become virtually inevitable. The late fourteenth century saw the collapse of
the Yuan dynasty in China and a subsequent Ming retrenchment,
the mid-fifteenth century marked the Ottoman spread to Constantinople, the late fifteenth century witnessed the "discoveries"
of Columbus and Vasco da Gama, while circa 1510 marked the
decisive defeat in the Arabian Sea of the Egyptian-Indian Muslim
fleet by Portuguese men-of-war. Everything followed from these
events.

If instead of starting the narrative at these points, however,
one looked at the impressive world system as it had evolved by
the late thirteenth and early fourteenth centuries, one would, I

The North: 18.9 mill.sq.miles

The South: 38.6 mill.sq.miles

argue, have been more likely to predict the continuation and increased reticulation of an Asian-based world system, focused on the Indian Ocean and China, than to have foreseen a shift to the Eurocentered one. My problematic, then, was different. I wanted to know not why the West rose but why the East fell, for fall it did at the time when, and perhaps even before, the Portuguese men-of-war entered their waters, and certainly before Luther tacked his bill of particulars to the door of All Saints Church in Wittenberg in 1517.

Western scholars not only begin the narrative "too late" but they take only partial testimony, thereby biasing the reconstructed account. In making this judgment one ought not to be harsh. Given the challenge of making up a credible story about the past, there has been a natural and necessary division of labor among historians. At the minimum, "making up" history requires at least two types of persons working together, the archivists and the synthesizers, at various levels.

The producers of the primary raw materials are engaged in the laborious task of "new" historical research; it is they who must spend years learning arcane languages and then sift

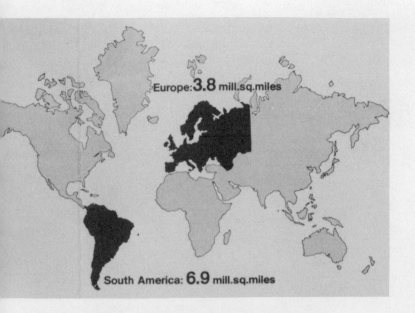

through dusty archives in search of a hitherto undiscovered document, meticulously piecing together the accidental sample of surviving fragments to make modest statements, qualified within narrow parameters of time and space. In the last analysis, these workers become the informants, respondents if you will, for the synthesizers who write the larger "fictive" accounts of "what happened" and why it was significant.

Synthesis takes place at two different levels. First, there are those who compose the socio-economic or intellectual histories of given societies or regions, and then there are the rarer synthesizers who attempt to construct global accounts covering wider regions over longer cycles. Perhaps William McNeill (whose *Rise of the West,* published in 1963, gave us the "name" for our problematic) and the late Fernand Braudel are today's masters of this genre, as Arnold Toynbee was for the last generation.

Comparative historical sociologists, including Max Weber and Wallerstein, work at an even higher level of generality. They are thus dependent upon both the raw materials harvested by archivists and the semi-processed goods prepared by regionally and temporally specialized glossers whose "prejudices" go un-recognized, at least for a while. Furthermore, they cannot help but be deeply influenced by the grand syntheses produced by the globalists (as Wallerstein certainly was by Braudel). With each higher level of generality, there are reduced options for recon-ceptualization. That is why I believe it is absolutely essential, if we are to get away from Eurocentric views of the universe, to "pick our respondents" carefully and broadly.

This is not as easy as it sounds. Hegemony is not merely political and economic; it is intellectual as well. If history is written by the victor, then it must, almost by definition, "de-form" the history of the others (to adopt the term used by J. C. van Leur to describe this defect in Southeast Asian studies). Scholars work best in their own languages and are able to access works in cognate languages more easily than those in very "for-eign" tongues. Available in translation are accidental arrays of documents that *someone* thought worthy of dissemination. Fur-thermore, in seeking explanations from the plethora of data about the past, we naturally select out "relevant" facts—their relevance having been determined by our working hypotheses drawn from partial and global glossers. These are dangerous methods.

If someone presented us with what purported to be an ac-count of a football game, based on interviews with only one team's supporters, we would be justifiably skeptical of the con-clusions. And yet this is what much historical sociological writ-ing does. It is only by following the rules of triangulation that we can escape the tautological process of confirming basic as-sumptions. Non-Western histories and sources must be included among the "respondents" if bias is not to reconfirm itself.

Finally, we must take seriously what we know to be true of human behavior. Change is a complex process that involves an organism with potential for evolution, a perception of an en-vironment and the opportunities it offers, an "objective" environment that hinders or helps such development, a capacity for action, and a set of interacting others who may facilitate or block one's growth. If we grant this, then the "rise of the West" cannot have been due exclusively or even predominantly to forces "immanent" in Western culture.

I am amused by the contrast between Western accounts of the "fall of Rome" and parallel accounts of the "rise of the West." In the former, the prior existence of internal decadence is always, albeit reluctantly, acknowledged, but the actual "fall" is always overwhelmingly attributed to Rome's inability to defend itself against barbarian incursions. How different, however, are the variables used to explain the "rise of the West." Examined critically, most literature on this subject has a smug, self-congratulatory ring. It answers the question, crudely put: "What was so special about the West that it won the world?" And even when that question is inverted—to ask "what were the weaknesses of the East that allowed it to be overcome and subordinated so readily in the opening decades of the sixteenth century?"—the variables turn out to be mirror images of those used to prove Western superiority. The West was technologically advanced; the East was "backward." The West was institutionally developed in business techniques; the East was "irrational" and "particularistic" in its commercial and industrial practices. The West had laissez-faire capitalism; the East was monopolistic and statist. And so on.

In fact, had all these things been true, there would have been no Asian-centered world system for the West to attach itself to in the twelfth and thirteenth centuries, nor would the conquest of Asia have yielded so rich a prize. Had the East been as underdeveloped as these accounts would lead us to believe, it would not have been worth despoiling. To the contrary, every shred of historical evidence points to the exact opposite conclusion.

Take technology, for example. By the eleventh and twelfth

centuries, the Chinese were already producing complex iron and even steel by highly advanced coal-powered techniques of metallurgy; Europe would not reach a comparable level of technological competence until many centuries later. By the eleventh century Chinese ships were navigated by the compass, a piece of equipment that would not diffuse to the Italians until the second half of the thirteenth century. Chinese war ships as early as the twelfth or early thirteenth century were equipped with cannons that used gunpowder to propel missiles, long before such defenses were available on European vessels. Middle Eastern textiles, the real "bread and butter" of medieval long-distance trade, were of a quality so much higher than what was produced in Europe that, at least through the thirteenth century, Europe was a net exporter of primary products and a net importer of finished goods. European silver and gold continued to flow into India throughout the fourteenth century, and possibly later, to counterbalance the imports of Indian textiles and other items of trade.

In the areas of investment acumen and business institutions, Westerners also had many lessons to learn from their Eastern trading partners. Checks, investment partnerships and *commenda* agreements, credit, double-entry bookkeeping, bills of exchange, and even paper money issued as legal tender by the state were all widely used in the East long before they were "invented" in twelfth- to fourteenth-century Italy (as claimed by Tawney, 1926). Checks were used in Sassanid Persia by the fifth and sixth centuries. *Commenda* agreements were the usual way of conducting the Arabian caravan trade even before the seventh century, when Islam codified and regularized these practices with respect to credit and the apportioning of profits and risks. Bills of exchange and credit transfers were routine ways of conducting long-distance trade in the advanced economies of the Orient. Merchant bankers formed investment partnerships with industrial producers and wholesale traders, served as money assayers and changers, and kept careful records of debits and credits for their customers. Paper script, backed by the government, was legal tender in twelfth-century Sung China many centuries before Europe would finally devise this system.

And finally, Max Weber and Marx notwithstanding, it is very hard to find evidence in most cities of medieval Europe for their model of the emergence of an independent bourgeoisie engaged in laissez-faire capitalism, unencumbered by feudal lords with rural bases of power. At least in the important towns of France and Flanders, which provide two of the twelve "cases" in my book, one finds clear evidence of "statism," alliances (marital and otherwise) between feudal and urban elites, state monopolies, and even state capitalism. (In Venice, for example, the state even owned the basic means of production used by the marine mercantilist city—namely, the galleys.) These systems were really not very different from those found in the larger, more centralized imperial centers of, for example, Egypt and China. The major difference was scale, not the *sui generis* difference Weber posited between the "true city" and the Oriental city or Marx posited between the Asiatic and Occidental capitalist modes of production.

If these allegations are indeed correct, then clearly we must reformulate our questions. The rise and fall of empires and even of hegemonic powers within world systems have occurred before in history, just as the process can now be observed in the rise of Japan and the Newly Industrializing Countries—NICs—of Asia. It is not legitimate "science" to seek explanations exclusively in variables internal to the societies that rise and fall. Nor is the opposite approach, which takes historic cycles as "natural" events governed by their own logic, any more illuminating. Only a more fine-grained contextual analysis of historic change that pays attention to both extrinsic world-system transformations and developments of more internal origin can satisfy the minimum requirements of credibility.

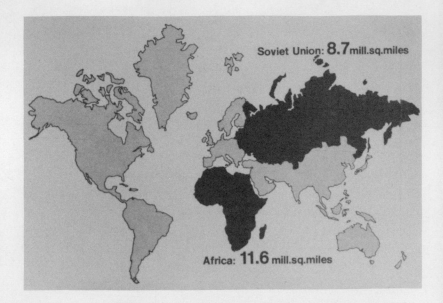

Applying this kind of contextual analysis in my own study of global economic systems, I have found that at least two "world systems" predated the one whose sixteenth-century evolutionary beginnings have been so cogently described by Wallerstein (1974) and whose end now seems imminent: (1) the Hellenic-Roman-Middle Eastern-Indian Ocean partial system, around the beginning of the Christian era, and (2) the wider-ranging eastern Mediterranean to China system from the ninth century onward. While the first had aborted before full flowering, the second was still operating over extensive regions when, at the end of the eleventh century, Western Europe attached itself to it through the First Crusade.

This initiated a period of efflorescence of urban, commercial, and industrial growth in northwestern Europe, clearly related to its radically expanded access to new raw and processed materials. While at first this drained the European economy of precious metals and some primary products—chiefly salt, timber, and slaves—eventually the imbalance of trade stimulated industrial production, largely of textiles in Flanders, which became the first part of Europe to undergo an industrial revolution—all

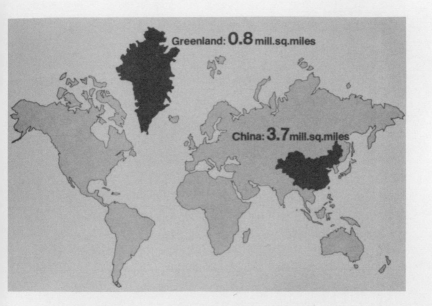

Greenland: 0.8 mill.sq.miles

China: 3.7 mill.sq.miles

this by the late thirteenth and early fourteenth centuries.

The heightened trade encouraged the inhabitants of a few city-states in Italy to assume the banking and transport functions for the continent during this same period. Through the Italian intermediaries, Europe was firmly connected to Oriental lines of supplies that terminated at three points along the eastern Mediterranean: at Constantinople, which led to the Black Sea and Central Asia; at ports on the Palestinian coast, which connected through Mesopotamia to the Persian Gulf and then by sea to India and even China; and at Alexandria, which led to Cairo and then the Red Sea and Indian Ocean beyond.

Thus, during the second half of the thirteenth century, which I consider to be a critical turning point, there was rapid articulation and reticulation of a true "world system" that, at its height—around 1290-1300—had drawn Western Europe, China, and intermediate points into a production and exchange system far more elaborate and extensive than the world had ever before known. It seemed probable that this process would continue and that all parts of the system would either remain roughly balanced (which they appear to have been at the time, each of the

major contenders dominant in its own region) or that the
"heavyweights" would continue to be found mostly south and
east of the Mediterranean.

This situation, however, proved unstable. Shortly after it
had been set up, it began to unravel. It was to prove an aborted
effort. As early as the 1330s, there were signs of strain, by the
1340s contractions were evident at many points, and by the
1350s only remnants—albeit still healthy—were left. The lines
of communication and trade that had broadened and grown
more complex and interwoven during the second half of the
thirteenth century were fraying and snapping. By the second half
of the fourteenth century, the trifold heartland system had been
stripped down to a single strand that connected Venice with
Egypt—the former dominating the European subsystem, the latter monopolizing access to the Indian Ocean trade.

The chief question is why. Any explanation that depends
upon long-term and deep-seated "cultural" traits cannot account
for so rapid a cycle of rise and devolution; nor was the devolution greatest in the Orient, the region where it would have been
predicted by Eurocentric theory. Indeed, the long cycles of Indian Ocean trade seem to have neither mirrored nor paralleled
those identified for Europe. In fact, it was not until the final
withdrawal of the powerful Chinese fleet from that zone after
1435 (and its subsequent attrition through port rot) that the Indian Ocean cycle entered its downswing.

Of one thing I am certain: monocausal explanations are
completely inadequate. There was no single overriding fact that,
like some *deus ex machina,* accounted generally for the breakup.
Rather, there was a concatenation of trends that, when they
combined, shifted the vector of change.

Some of these trends were major—like the dissolution of
the Pax Mongolica that eventually split apart the circuit of trade
that had connected the land route across Central Asia with the
sea trade through southern Chinese ports, or like the end of the

Crusader state at Acre, which thus blocked Europe's land link between the Mediterranean and the Persian Gulf. Some were minor—like the conversion to Islam of the Ghazanids of Iraq, which reduced their tensions with the Mamluks of Egypt, thus permitting the reopening of the land route between Mesopotamia and Egypt.

Some of these trends were dramatically precipitant—such as the Black Death, which decimated populations from Central Asia to the Mediterranean shores. The resultant labor shortage caused transformations in business practices in Europe (the introduction of resident overseas "factors") and shook the bases of class structure in many regions. In China, the devastations of disease weakened the power of the Mongol Yuan state, soon afterwards overthrown by the Ming.

Some changes were slower but in ways more insidious, such as decisions to export raw materials that had previously fed local industries or to retain for local production raw materials formerly exported to others. This appeared in two critical parts of the world system in the early fourteenth century. First, the Flemish textile industry was put into a permanent tailspin by English embargos on the export of high quality wool, needed to produce the expensive cloth for which Flanders was famous. In a reverse development, Italian merchants began to buy up the raw cotton and sugar that had formerly been processed in Syria and Egypt, thus undermining the industrial base of these societies.

In *Before Europe's Hegemony,* I have studied the alterations within and between the eight interlocking and overlapping subsystems that I believe cumulated synergistically to create the near-global world system of the early fourteenth century, in order to understand why that system did not continue to grow. Through a more fine-grained historical inquiry than sociologists usually employ and through a much closer attention to the geopolitical context within which these historical events occurred, I have attempted to unpack the complex events that precipitated the abortion of this developed system and that allowed the West, in the early sixteenth century, to gain hegemonic control over the next "world system" through a drastic reshaping of the subsystems and the connections among them.

What I am proposing is a rethinking of why the West was able to "rise" in the sixteenth century. The basic argument is that the Eastern system was already in severe decline by the mid-fifteenth century and that, therefore, an enormous vacuum of power already existed in the Indian Ocean arena by the time that Portuguese men-of-war entered that zone. It was the unpreparedness of the East, even more than the strength of the West, that was responsible for the ultimate outcome, the "rise of the West." Of perhaps even greater significance was the shift from the Mediterranean to the Atlantic, which changed the location of the center of gravity of the world system, hence to the greater power of the countries of the Atlantic rim. To some extent, this shift was a temporary deviation from the usual focus of trade from time immemorial, namely between the Mediterranean Sea and the Indian Ocean.

We may now be seeing a third shift in world geopolitics, this time to the Pacific, with a new enhancement of the position of flanking countries and a new backward linkage to the Indian Ocean. Associated with this shift is the increased hegemony of Asian powers and, inevitably, of the west coast American ports that flank that ocean. We might ask whether the world system is now undergoing a crucial restructuring as significant as the one that led to almost five hundred years of "Western" hegemony. The first partial world system focused on the Mediterranean, ruled by Rome. The second world system moved to the Indian Ocean. The third, beginning roughly in the 1500s, centered on the Atlantic. The new one appears to be shifting to the Pacific.

This brings us to our final point. While it is true that we "make up" history, we do not have full and arbitrary latitude to make it up as we please. The line by Marx, to the effect that people make their history but not as they choose, may be the most relevant note on which to end. Something real is going on out there, and a knowledge of the past may be helpful to us in our efforts to "read" it, interpret it, and possibly even to deal with it.

Selected Bibliography

(Includes only works cited or representing ideas alluded to in the text.)

Abu-Lughod, Janet. *Before Europe's Hegemony: The World System, A.D. 1250-1350.* New York and London: Oxford University Press, 1989.

Aston, T. H., and C. H. E. Philpin, eds. *The Brenner Debate: Agrarian Class Structure and Economic Development in Pre-Industrial Europe.* Cambridge: Cambridge University Press, 1985.

Balazs, Étienne. "The Birth of Capitalism in China." In his *Chinese Civilization and Bureaucracy: Variations on a Theme.* Trans. H. M. Wright. London and New Haven: Yale University Press, 1964.

Braudel, Fernand. *Capitalism and Material Life: 1400-1800.* Trans. Miriam Kochan. London: Weidenfeld and Nicolson, 1973.

Braudel, Fernand. *Civilization and Capitalism, 15th-18th Century.* 3 vols. Trans. Siân Reynolds. New York: Harper & Row, 1981-1984.

Bretschneider, E. V., ed. and trans. *Mediaeval Researches from Eastern Asiatic Sources: Fragments Towards the Knowledge of the Geography and History of Central and Western Asia from the 13th to the 17th Century.* 2 vols. London: K. Paul, Trench and Trubner, 1910.

Chao Ju-Kua. *Chau Ju-Kua: His Work on the Chinese and Arab Trade in the Twelfth and Thirteenth Centuries.* St. Petersburg: Imperial Academy of Sciences, 1911.

Chaudhuri, K. N. *Trade and Civilisation in the Indian Ocean.* Cambridge: Cambridge University Press, 1985.

Chirot, Daniel. "The Rise of the West." *American Sociological Review* 50 (April 1985): 181-195.

Chou, Chin Sheng. "An Economic History of China." Western Washington State College, 1974, manuscript.

Curtin, Philip D. *Cross-Cultural Trade in World History.* Cambridge: Cambridge University Press, 1984.

De Roover, Raymond A. *Money, Banking and Credit in Mediaeval Bruges: Italian Merchant Bankers, Lombards and Money-Changers.* Cambridge, Mass.: Mediaeval Academy of America, 1948.

Goitein, Solomon. *A Mediterranean Society: The Jewish Communities of the Arab World.* 4 vols. Berkeley: University of California Press, 1967-1983. (See especially Vol. 1: *Economic Foundations.*)

Hartwell, Robert. "A Cycle of Economic Change in Imperial China: Coal and Iron in Northeast China, 750-1350." *Journal of the Economic and Social History of the Orient* 10, no. 1 (July 1967): 102-159.

Hartwell, Robert. "Markets, Technology, and the Structure of Enterprise in the Development of the Eleventh-Century Iron and Steel Industry." *Journal of Economic History* 26, no. 1 (March 1966): 29-58.

Hohenberg, Paul M., and Lynn Hollen Lees. *The Making of Urban Europe, 1000-1950.* Cambridge, Mass.: Harvard University Press, 1985.

Hourani, G. H. *Arab Seafaring in the Indian Ocean in Ancient and Early Medieval Times.* Princeton: Princeton University Press, 1951.

Lestocquoy, Jean. *Aux origines de la bourgeoisie: Les villes de Flandre et d'Italie sous le gouvernement des patriciens.* Paris: Presses universitaires de France, 1952.

Leur, J. C. van. *Indonesian Trade and Society: Essays in Asian Social and Economic History.* Trans. James S. Holmes and A. van Marle. The Hague: W. Van Hoeve, 1955.

Levenson, Joseph R., ed. *European Expansion and the Counter-Example of Asia.* Englewood Cliffs, N.J.: Prentice-Hall, 1967.

Li Guohao, Zheng Mengwen, and Cao Tianqin, eds. *Explorations in the History of Science and Technology in China.* Shanghai: Shanghai Chinese Classics Publishing House, 1982.

Lo, Jung-Pang. "The Emergence of China as a Sea Power during the Late Sung and Early Yuan Periods." *Far Eastern Quarterly* (1954-1955): 489-503.

Lo, Jung-Pang. "The Decline of the Early Ming Navy." *Oriens Extremis* 5 (1958): 149-168.

Lopez, Robert S. *The Commercial Revolution of the Middle Ages, 950-1350.* Cambridge: Cambridge University Press, 1976.

McNeill, William H. *Plagues and Peoples.* Garden City, N.Y.: Doubleday, 1976.

McNeill, William H. *The Pursuit of Power.* Chicago: University of Chicago Press, 1982.

McNeill, William H. *The Rise of the West.* Chicago: University of Chicago Press, 1963.

McNeill, William H. *Venice: The Hinge of Europe, 1081-1797.* Chicago: University of Chicago Press, 1974.

Needham, Joseph. *Clerks and Craftsmen in China and the West: Lectures and Addresses on the History of Science and Technology.* Cambridge: Cambridge University Press, 1970.

Needham, Joseph. *Science and Civilisation in China.* 6 vols. Cambridge: Cambridge University Press, 1954-1985.

Richards, D. S., ed. *Islam and the Trade of Asia.* Philadelphia: University of Pennsylvania Press, 1970.

Rockhill, W. W. "Notes on the Relations and Trade of China with the Eastern Archipelago and the Coast of the Indian Ocean During the Fourteenth Century." *T'oung Pao* 15 (1914), entire issue.

Shiba, Yoshinobu. *Commerce and Society in Sung China.* Ann Arbor: Asian Center, 1970.

Tawney, R. H. *Religion and the Rise of Capitalism.* New York: Harcourt, Brace and Company, 1926.

Tibbetts, G. R., ed. and trans. *Arab Navigation in the Indian Ocean before the Coming of the Portuguese.* London: Royal Asiatic Society of Great Britain and Ireland, 1971 (reprint).

Toussaint, Auguste. *The History of the Indian Ocean.* Trans. June Guicharnaud. London: Routledge & Kegan Paul, 1966.

Udovitch, Abraham L. *Partnership and Profit in Medieval Islam.* Princeton: Princeton University Press, 1970.

Wallerstein, Immanuel. *The Modern World-System.* 2 vols. New York: Academic Press, 1974-1980.

Weber, Max. *The City.* Trans. Don Martindale and Gertrud Neuwirth. Glencoe, Ill.: Free Press, 1958.

Weber, Max. *The Protestant Ethic and the Spirit of Capitalism* (1904-1905). Trans. Talcott Parsons. New York: Free Press, 1958.

Weber, Max. "Premodern Capitalism" and "Modern Capitalism." In *Max Weber on Charisma and Institution Building.* Ed. S. N. Eisenstadt. Chicago: University of Chicago Press, 1968, pp. 129-165.

Wolf, Eric R. *Europe and the People Without History.* Berkeley: University of California Press, 1982.

Wolters, O. W. *The Fall of Srivijaya in Malay History.* Ithaca: Cornell University Press, 1970.

Yang, Lien-Sheng. *Money and Credit in China: A Short History.* Cambridge, Mass.: Harvard University Press, 1952.

Yule, Henry, trans. and ed. *Cathay and the Way Thither, Being a Collection of Medieval Notices of China.* 4 vols. London: Hakluyt Society, 1913-1926.

Homi K. Bhabha

REMEMBERING FANON: SELF, PSYCHE,

AND THE COLONIAL CONDITION

> O my body, make of me always a man who questions!
> —Frantz Fanon

The mention of Frantz Fanon in left circles stirs a dim, deceiving echo. *Black Skin, White Masks, The Wretched of the Earth, Toward the African Revolution*—these memorable titles reverberate in the self-righteous rhetoric of "resistance" whenever the left gathers to deplore the immiseration of the colonized world. Repeatedly used as the idioms of simple moral outrage, Fanon's titles emptily echo a political spirit that is far from his own; they sound the troubled conscience of a socialist vision that extends, in the main, from an ethnocentric provincialism to large trade union internationalism. When that laborist line of vision is challenged by the "autonomous" struggles of the politics of race and gender, or threatened by problems of human psychology or cultural representation, it can only make an empty gesture of solidarity. Whenever questions of race and sexuality make their own organizational and theoretical demands on the primacy of "class," "state," and "party," the language of traditional socialism is quick to describe those urgent, "other" questions as symptoms of petty-bourgeois deviation, signs of the bad faith of socialist intellectuals. The ritual respect accorded to the name of Fanon, the currency of his titles in the common language of liberation, are part of the ceremony of a polite refusal.

Memories of Fanon tend to the mythical. He is either revered as the prophetic spirit of Third World Liberation or reviled as an exterminating angel, the inspiration to violence in the Black Power movement. Despite his historic participation in the Algerian revolution and the influence of his ideas on the race politics of the 1960s and 1970s, Fanon's work will not be possessed by one political moment or movement, nor can it be easily placed in a seamless narrative of liberationist history. Fanon refuses to be so completely claimed by events or eventualities. It is the sustaining irony of his work that his severe commitment to the political task in hand never restricted the restless, inquiring movement of his thought.

It is not for the finitude of philosophical thinking nor for the finality of a political direction that we turn to Fanon. Heir to the ingenuity and artistry of Toussaint and Senghor, as well as the iconoclasm of Nietzsche, Freud, and Sartre, Fanon is the purveyor of the transgressive and transitional truth. He may yearn for the total transformation of Man and Society, but he speaks most effectively from the uncertain interstices of historical change: from the area of ambivalence between race and sexuality; out of an unresolved contradiction between culture and class; from deep within the struggle of psychic representation and social reality.

To read Fanon is to experience the sense of division that prefigures—and fissures—the emergence of a truly radical thought that never dawns without casting an uncertain dark. His voice is most clearly heard in the subversive turn of a familiar term, in the silence of a sudden rupture: *"The Negro is not. Any more than the white man."* The awkward division that breaks his line of thought keeps alive the dramatic and enigmatic sense of the process of change. That familiar alignment of colonial subjects—black/white, Self/Other—is disturbed with one brief pause and the traditional grounds of racial identity are dispersed, whenever they are found to rest in the narcissistic myths of *négritude* or white cultural supremacy. It is this palpable pressure of division and displacement that pushes Fanon's writing to the edge of things; the cutting edge that reveals no ultimate radiance but, in his words, "exposes an utterly naked declivity where an authentic upheaval can be born."

The psychiatric hospital at Blida-Joinville is one such place where, in the divided world of French Algeria, Fanon discovered the impossibility of his mission as a colonial psychiatrist:

If psychiatry is the medical technique that aims to enable man no longer to be a stranger to his environment, I owe it to myself to affirm that the Arab, permanently an alien in his own country, lives in a state of absolute depersonalization . . . The social structure existing in Algeria was hostile to any attempt to put the individual back where he belonged. [1]

The extremity of this colonial alienation of the person—this end of the "idea" of the individual—produces a restless urgency in Fanon's search for a conceptual form appropriate to the social antagonism of the colonial relation. The body of his work splits between a Hegelian-Marxist dialectic, a phenomenological affirmation of Self and Other, and the psychoanalytic ambivalence of the Unconscious, its turning from love to hate, mastery to servitude. In his desperate, doomed search for a dialectic of deliverance, Fanon explores the edge of these modes for thought: his Hegelianism restores hope to history; his existentialist evocation of the "I" restores the presence of the marginalized; and his psychoanalytic framework illuminates the "madness" of racism, the pleasure of pain, the agonistic fantasy of political power.

As Fanon attempts such audacious, often impossible, transformations of truth and value, the jagged testimony of colonial dislocation, its displacement of time and person, its defilement of culture and territory, refuses the ambition of any "total" theory of colonial oppression. The Antillean *évolué* cut to the quick by the glancing look of a frightened, confused white child; the stereotype of the native fixed at the shifting boundaries between

barbarism and civility; the insatiable fear and desire for the
Negro: "Our women are at the mercy of Negroes . . . God
knows how they make love"; the deep cultural fear of the black
figured in the psychic trembling of Western sexuality—it is
these signs and symptoms of the colonial condition that drive
Fanon from one conceptual scheme to another, while the colonial relation takes shape in the gaps between them, articulated
in the intrepid engagements of his style. As Fanon's text unfolds,
the "scientific" fact comes to be aggressed by the experience of
the street; sociological observations are intercut with literary artifacts, and the poetry of liberation is brought up short against
the leaden, deadening prose of the colonized world.

What is this distinctive *force* of Fanon's vision that has been
forming even as I write about the division, the displacement, the
cutting edge of his thought? It comes, I believe, from the tradition of the oppressed, as Walter Benjamin suggests; it is the language of a revolutionary awareness that "the state of emergency
in which we live is not the exception but the rule. We must at-
tain to a concept of history that is in keeping with this insight."
And the state of emergency is also always a state of *emergence*.
The struggle against colonial oppression changes not only the direction of Western history, but challenges its historicist "idea"
of time as a progressive, ordered whole. The analysis of colonial
depersonalization alienates not only the Enlightenment idea of
"Man," but challenges the transparency of social reality, as a
pregiven image of human knowledge. If the order of Western
historicism is disturbed in the colonial state of emergency, even
more deeply disturbed is the social and psychic representation
of the human subject. For the very nature of humanity becomes
estranged in the colonial condition and from that "naked declivity" it emerges, not as an assertion of will nor as an evocation of freedom, but as an enigmatic questioning. With a
question that echoes Freud's *what does woman want?*, Fanon turns
to confront the colonized world. "What does a man want?" he

asks, in the introduction to *Black Skin, White Masks,* "What does the black man want?"

To this loaded question where cultural alienation bears down on the ambivalence of psychic identification, Fanon responds with an agonizing performance of self-images:

I had to meet the white man's eyes. An unfamiliar weight burdened me. In the white world the man of color encounters difficulties in the development of his bodily schema . . . I was battered down by tom-toms, cannibalism, intellectual deficiency, racial defects . . . I took myself far off from my own presence . . . What else could it be for me but an amputation, an excision, a hemorrhage that spattered my whole body with black blood?

From within the metaphor of vision complicit with a Western metaphysic of Man emerges the displacement of the colonial relation. The black presence ruins the representative narrative of Western personhood: its past tethered to treacherous stereotypes of primitivism and degeneracy will not produce a history of civil progress, a space for the *Socius;* its present, dismembered and dislocated, will not contain the image of identity that is questioned in the dialectic of mind/body and resolved in the epistemology of "appearance and reality." The white man's eyes break up the black man's body and in that act of epistemic violence its own frame of reference is transgressed, its field of vision disturbed.

"What does the black man *want?*" Fanon insists and in privileging the psychic dimension, he changes not only what we understand by a *political* demand but transforms the very means by which we recognize and identify its *human agency.* Fanon is not principally posing the question of political oppression as the violation of a human "essence," although he lapses into such a lament in his more existential moments. He is not raising the question of colonial man in the universalist terms of the liberal-humanist ("How does colonialism deny the Rights of Man?");

nor is he posing an ontological question about Man's being ("*Who* is the alienated colonial man?"). Fanon's question is not addressed to such a unified notion of history nor such a unitary concept of Man. It is one of the original and disturbing qualities of *Black Skin, White Masks* that it rarely historicizes the colonial experience. There is no master narrative or realist perspective that provide a background of social and historical facts against which emerge the problems of the individual or collective psyche. Such a traditional sociological alignment of Self and Society or History and Psyche is rendered questionable in Fanon's identification of the colonial subject, who is historicized as it comes to be heterogeneously inscribed in the texts of history, literature, science, myth. The colonial subject is always "over-determined from without," Fanon writes. It is through image and fantasy—those orders that figure transgressively on the borders of history and the unconscious—that Fanon most profoundly evokes the colonial condition.

In articulating the problem of colonial cultural alienation in the psychoanalytic language of demand and desire, Fanon radically questions the formation of both individual and social authority as they come to be developed in the discourse of Social Sovereignty. The social virtues of historical rationality, cultural cohesion, the autonomy of individual consciousness assume an immediate, utopian identity with the subjects upon whom they confer a civil status. The civil state is the ultimate expression of the innate ethical and rational bent of the human mind; the social instinct is the progressive destiny of human nature, the necessary transition from Nature to Culture. The direct access from individual interests to social authority is objectified in the representative structure of a General Will—Law or Culture—where Psyche and Society mirror each other, transparently translating their difference, without loss, into a historical totality. Forms of social and psychic alienation and aggression—madness, self-hate, treason, violence—can never be acknowledged as determinate

and constitutive conditions of civil authority, or as the ambivalent effects of the social instinct itself. They are always explained away as alien presences, occlusions of historical progress,
the ultimate misrecognition of Man.

For Fanon such a myth of Man and Society is fundamentally undermined in the colonial situation, where everyday life
exhibits a "constellation of delirium" that mediates the normal
social relations of its subjects: "The Negro enslaved by his in-
feriority, the white man enslaved by his superiority alike behave
in accordance with a neurotic orientation." Fanon's demand for
a psychoanalytic explanation emerges from the perverse reflections of "civil virtue" in the alienating acts of colonial gover-
nance: the visibility of cultural "mummification" in the
colonizer's avowed ambition to civilize or modernize the native,
which results in "archaic inert institutions [that function] under
the oppressor's supervision like a caricature of formerly fertile
institutions"; or the validity of violence in the very definition of
the colonial social space; or the viability of the febrile, phantasmatic images of racial hatred that come to be absorbed and acted
out in the wisdom of the West. These interpositions, indeed col-
laborations of political and psychic violence *within* civic virtue,
alienation within identity, drive Fanon to describe the splitting
of the colonial space of consciousness and society as marked by
a "Manichean delirium."

The representative figure of such a perversion, I want to
suggest, is the image of post-Enlightenment man tethered to, *not*
confronted by, his dark reflection, the shadow of colonized man,
that splits his presence, distorts his outline, breaches his boundaries, repeats his action at a distance, disturbs and divides the
very time of his being. This ambivalent identification of the racist world—moving on two planes without being in the least
embarrassed by it, as Sartre says of the anti-Semitic consciousness—turns on the idea of Man *as* his alienated image, not Self
and Other but the "Otherness" of the Self inscribed in the per-

verse palimpsest of colonial identity. And it is that bizarre figure of desire, which splits along the axis on which it turns, that compels Fanon to put the psychoanalytic question of the desire of the subject to the historic condition of colonial man.

"What is often called the black soul is a white man's artifact," Fanon writes. This transference, I've argued, speaks otherwise. It reveals the deep psychic uncertainty of the colonial relation itself; its split representations stage the division of "body" and "soul" that enacts the artifice of "identity"; a division that cuts across the fragile skin—black and white—of individual and social authority. What emerges from the figurative language I have used to make such an argument, are three conditions that underlie an understanding of the *process of identification* in the analytic of desire.

First: to exist is to be called into being in relation to an Otherness, its look or locus. It is a demand that reaches outward to an external object and, as Jacqueline Rose writes, "it is the relation of this demand to the place of the object it claims that becomes the basis for identification." This process is visible in that exchange of looks between native and settler that structures their psychic relation in the paranoid fantasy of boundless possession and its familiar language of reversal: "when their glances meet he [the settler] ascertains bitterly, always on the defensive, 'They want to take our place.' It is true for there is no native who does not dream at least once a day of setting himself up in the settler's place." It is always in relation to the place of the Other that colonial desire is articulated: that is, in part, the phantasmatic space of "possession" that no one subject can singly occupy that permits the dream of the inversion of roles.

Second: the very place of identification, caught in the tension of demand and desire, is a space of splitting. The fantasy of the native is precisely to occupy the master's place while keeping his place in the slave's *avenging* anger. "Black skins, white masks" is not, for example, a neat division; it is a doubling, dissembling

image of being in at least two places at once that makes it impossible for the devalued, insatiable *évolué* (an abandonment neurotic, Fanon claims) to accept the colonizer's invitation to
identity: "You're a doctor, a writer, a student, you're *different,*
you're one of *us.*" It is precisely in that ambivalent use of
"different"—to be different from those that are different makes
you the same—that the Unconscious speaks of the form of Otherness, the tethered shadow of deferral and displacement. It is
not the Colonialist Self or the Colonized Other, but the disturbing distance in between that constitutes the figure of colonial
Otherness—the white man's artifice inscribed on the black
man's body. It is in relation to this impossible object that
emerges the liminal problem of colonial identity and its
vicissitudes.

Finally, as has already been disclosed by the rhetorical figures of my account of desire and Otherness, the question of
identification is never the affirmation of a pregiven identity,
never a self-fulfilling prophecy—it is always the production of an
"image" of identity and the transformation of the subject in assuming that image. The demand of identification—that is, to be
for an Other—entails the representation of the subject in the
differentiating order of Otherness. Identification, as we inferred
from the illustrations above, is always the return of an image of
identity that bears the mark of splitting in that "Other" place
from which it comes. For Fanon, like Lacan, the primary moments of such a repetition of the self lie in the desire of the look
and the limits of language. The "atmosphere of certain uncertainty" that surrounds the body certifies its existence and
threatens its dismemberment.

Look a Negro . . . Mama, see the Negro! I'm frightened . . . I could no
longer laugh, because I already know there were legends, stories, history
and above all historicity *. . . Then assailed at various points, the cor-*
poral schema crumbled, its place taken by a racial epidermal schema
. . . It was no longer a question of being aware of my body in the

*third person but in a triple person . . . I was responsible for my body,
for my race, for my ancestors.*

In reading *Black Skin, White Masks,* it is crucial to respect the
difference between "personal identity" as an intimation of reality, or an intuition of being, and the psychoanalytic problem of
identification that, in a sense, always begs the question of the
subject—"What does a man want?" The emergence of the human subject as socially and psychically authenticated depends
upon the *negation* of an originary narrative of fulfillment or an
imaginary coincidence between individual interest or instinct
and the General Will. Such binary, two-part identities function
in a kind of narcissistic reflection of the One in the Other that is
confronted in the language of desire by the psychoanalytic process of identification. For identification, identity is never an
a priori, nor a finished product; it is only ever the problematic
process of access to an "image" of totality. The discursive conditions of this psychic image of identification will be clarified if we
think of the perilous perspective of the concept of the image itself. For the image—as point of identification—marks the site of
an ambivalence. Its representation is always spatially split—it
makes *present* something that is *absent*—and temporarily
deferred—it is the representation of a time that is always elsewhere, a repetition. The image is only ever an *appurtenance* to
authority and identity; it must never be read mimetically as the
"appearance" of a "reality." The access to the image of identity
is only ever possible in the *negation* of any sense of originality or
plenitude, through the principle of displacement and differentiation (absence/presence; representation/repetition) that always
renders it a liminal reality. The image is at once a metaphoric
substitution, an illusion of presence and by that same token a
metonym, a sign of its absence and loss. It is precisely from this
edge of meaning and being, from this shifting boundary of otherness within identity, that Fanon asks: "What does a *black* man
want?"

When it encounters resistance from the other, self-consciousness under-
goes the experience of desire . . . As soon as I desire I ask to be consid-
ered. I am not merely here and now, sealed into thingness. I am for
somewhere else and for something else. I demand that notice be taken
of my negating activity in so far as I pursue something other than life
. . . I occupied space. I moved towards the other . . . and the evanescent
other, hostile but not opaque, transparent, not there, disappeared.
Nausea.

From that overwhelming emptiness of nausea, Fanon makes his
answer: the black man wants the objectifying confrontation with
otherness; in the colonial psyche there is an unconscious disavowal of the negating, splitting moment of desire. The place of
the Other must not be imaged as Fanon sometimes suggests as a
fixed phenomenological point, opposed to the self, that represents a culturally alien consciousness. The Other must be seen as
the necessary negation of a primordial identity—cultural or
psychic—that introduces the system of differentiation that enables the "cultural" to be signified as a linguistic, symbolic, historic reality. If, as I have suggested, the subject of desire is never
simply a Myself, then the Other is never simply an *It-self,* a font
of identity, truth, or misrecognition.

As a principle of identification, the Other bestows a degree
of objectivity but its representation—be it the social process of
the law or the psychic process of the Oedipus—is always ambivalent, disclosing a lack. For instance, the common, conversational distinction between "the letter and spirit" of the Law
displays the otherness of Law itself; the ambiguous grey area between "Justice" and judicial procedure is, quite literally, a conflict of judgment. In the language of psychoanalysis, the Law of
the Father or the paternal metaphor, again, cannot be taken at
its word. It is a process of substitution and exchange that in-
scribes a normative, normalizing place for the subject; but that
metaphoric access to identity is exactly the place of prohibition
and repression, precisely a conflict of authority. Identification, as

it is spoken in the *desire of the Other,* is always a question of interpretation, for it is the elusive assignation of myself with a one-self, the elision of person and place.

If the differentiating force of the Other is the process of the subject's signification in language and society's objectification in Law, then how can the Other disappear? Can desire, the moving spirit of the subject, ever evanesce?

In his more analytic mode, Fanon can impede the exploration of these ambivalent, uncertain questions of colonial desire. The state of emergency from which he writes demands more insurgent answers, more immediate identifications. At times Fanon attempts too close a correspondence between the *mise-en-scène* of unconscious fantasy and the phantoms of racist fear and hate that stalk the colonial scene; he turns too hastily from the ambivalences of identification to the antagonistic identities of political alienation and cultural discrimination; he is too quick to name the Other, to personalize its presence in the language of colonial racism—"the real Other for the white man is and will continue to be the black man. And conversely." These attempts, in Fanon's words, to restore the dream to its proper political time and cultural space can, at times, blunt the edge of Fanon's brilliant illustrations of the complexity of psychic projections in the pathological colonial relation. Jean Veneuse, the Antillean *évolué,* desires not merely to be in the place of the white man but compulsively seeks to look back and down on himself from that position. The white man does not merely deny what he fears and desires by projecting it on "them": Fanon sometimes forgets that paranoia never preserves its position of power, for the compulsive identification with a persecutory "They" is always an evacuation and emptying of the "I."

Fanon's sociodiagnostic psychiatry tends to explain away the ambivalent turns and returns of the subject of colonial desire, its masquerade of Western Man and the "long" historical perspective. It is as if Fanon is fearful of his most radical insights: that the space of the body and its identification is a representational reality; that the politics of race will not be entirely contained within the humanist myth of Man or economic necessity or historical progress, for its psychic effects question such forms of determinism; that social sovereignty and human subjectivity are only realizable in the order of Otherness. It is as if the question of desire that emerged from the traumatic tradition of the oppressed has to be denied, at the end of *Black Skin, White Masks,* to make way for an existentialist humanism that is as banal as it is beatific:

Why not the quite simple attempt to touch the other, to feel the other, to explain the other to myself? . . . At the conclusion of this study, I want the world to recognize, with me, the open door of every consciousness.

Such a deep hunger for humanism, despite Fanon's insight into the dark side of Man, must be an overcompensation for the closed consciousness or "dual narcissism" to which he attributes the depersonalization of colonial man: "There one lies body to body, with one's blackness or one's whiteness in full narcissistic cry, each sealed into his own particularity—with, it is true, now and then a flash or so." It is this flash of "recognition"—in its Hegelian sense with its transcendental, sublative spirit—that fails to ignite in the colonial relation where there is only narcissistic indifference: "And yet the Negro knows there is a difference. He wants it . . . The former slave needs a challenge to his humanity." In the absence of such a challenge, Fanon argues, the colonized can only imitate, never identify, a distinction nicely made by the psychoanalyst Annie Reich: "It is imitation . . . when the child holds the newspaper *like* his father. It is identification when the child learns to read." In disavowing the culturally differentiated condition of the colonial world—in demanding *"Turn white or disappear"*—the colonizer is himself caught in the ambivalence of paranoic identification, alternating between fantasies of megalomania and persecution.

However, Fanon's Hegelian dream for a human reality *in-*

itself-for-itself is ironized, even mocked, by his view of the Man-ichean structure of colonial consciousness and its nondialectical division. What he says in *The Wretched of the Earth* of the demog-raphy of the colonial city reflects his view of the psychic struc-ture of the colonial relation. The native and settler zones, like the juxtaposition of black and white bodies, are opposed, but not in the service of "a higher unity." No conciliation is possi-ble, he concludes, for of the two terms, one is superfluous.

No, there can be no reconciliation, no Hegelian "recogni-tion," no simple, sentimental promise of a humanistic "world of the You." Can there be life without transcendence? Politics without the dream of perfectibility? Unlike Fanon, I think the *nondialectical* moment of Manicheanism suggests an answer. By following the trajectory of colonial desire — in the company of that bizarre colonial figure, the tethered shadow — it becomes possible to cross, even to shift the Manichean boundaries. Where there is no human *nature,* hope can hardly spring eternal; but it emerges surely and surreptitiously in the strategic return of that difference that informs and deforms the image of identity, in the margin of Otherness that displays identification. There may be no Hegelian negation but Fanon must sometimes be re-minded that the disavowal of the Other always exacerbates the "edge" of identification, reveals that dangerous place where iden-tity and aggressivity are twinned. For denial is always a retroac-tive process; a *half*-acknowledgment of that Otherness that has left its traumatic mark. In that uncertainty lurks the white masked black man; and from such ambivalent identification — black skin, white masks — it is possible, I believe, to redeem the pathos of cultural confusion into a strategy of political subver-sion. We cannot agree with Fanon that "since the racial drama is played out in the open the black man has no time to make it un-conscious," but that is a provocative thought. In occupying two places at once — or three in Fanon's case — the depersonalized, dislocated colonial subject can become an incalculable object, quite literally, difficult to place. The demand of authority cannot unify its message nor simply identify its subjects. For the strategy of colonial desire is to stage the drama of identity at the point at which the black mask *slips* to reveal the white skin. At that edge, in between the black body and the white body, there is a tension of meaning and being—or some would say, demand and desire—that is the psychic counterpart to that "muscular tension" that inhabits the native body:

The symbols of social order—the police, the bugle calls in the barracks, military parades and the waving flags—are at one and the same time inhibitory and stimulating: for they do not convey the message "Don't dare to budge"; rather, they cry out "Get ready to attack."

It is from that tension—both psychic and political—that a strategy of subversion emerges. It is a mode of negation that seeks not to unveil the fullness of Man but to manipulate his representation. It is a form of power that is exercised at the very limits of identity and authority, in the mocking spirit of mask and image; it is the lesson taught by the veiled Algerian woman in the course of the Revolution as she crossed the Manichean lines to claim her liberty. In Fanon's essay, "Algeria Unveiled," the colonizer's attempt to unveil the Algerian woman does not simply turn the veil into a symbol of resistance; it becomes a technique of camouflage, a means of struggle—the veil conceals bombs. The veil that once secured the boundary of the home—the limits of woman—now masks the woman in her revolutionary activity, linking the Arab city and the French quarter, transgressing the familial and colonial boundary. As the "veil" is liberated in the public sphere, circulating between and beyond cultural and social norms and spaces, it becomes the object of paranoid surveillance and interrogation. Every veiled woman, writes Fanon, became suspect. And when the veil is shed in order to penetrate deeper into the European quarter, the colonial police see everything and nothing. An Algerian woman is only, after all, a woman. But the Algerian *fidai* is an arsenal and in her handbag she carries her hand-grenades.

Remembering Fanon is a process of intense discovery and disorientation. Remembering is never a quiet act of introspection or retrospection. It is a painful re-membering, a putting together of the dismembered past to make sense of the trauma of the present. It is such a memory of the history of race and racism, colonialism and the question of cultural identity, that Fanon reveals with greater profundity and poetry than any other writer. What he achieves, I believe, is something far greater: for in seeing the phobic image of the Negro, the native, the colonized, deeply woven into the psychic pattern of the West, he offers the master and slave a deeper reflection of their interpositions, as well as the hope of a difficult, even dangerous, freedom: "It is through the effort to recapture the self and to scrutinize the self, it is through the lasting tension of their freedom that men will be able to create the ideal conditions of existence for a human world." Nobody writes with more honesty and insight of this lasting tension of freedom in which the self—the peremptory self of the present—disavows an image of itself as an originary past or an ideal future and confronts the paradox of its own making.

For Fanon, in *Black Skin, White Masks,* there is the intricate irony of turning the European existentialist and psychoanalytic traditions to face the history of the Negro that they had never contemplated, to face the reality of Fanon himself. This leads to a meditation on the experience of dispossession and dislocation—psychic and social—that speaks to the condition of the marginalized, the alienated, those who have to live under the surveillance of a sign of identity and fantasy that denies their difference. In shifting the focus of cultural racism from the politics of nationalism to the politics of narcissism, Fanon opens up a margin of interrogation that causes a subversive slippage of identity and authority. Nowhere is this slippage more visible than in his work itself, where a range of texts and traditions—from the classical repertoire to the quotidien, conversational culture of racism—vie to utter that last word that remains unspoken. Nowhere is this slippage more significantly experienced than in the impossibility of inferring from the texts of Fanon a pacific image of "society" or the "state" as a homogeneous philosophical or representational unity. The "social" is always an unresolved ensemble of antagonistic interlocutions between positions of power and poverty, knowledge and oppression, history and fantasy, surveillance and subversion. It is for this reason—above all else— that we should turn to Fanon.

Today, as a range of culturally and racially marginalized groups readily assume the mask of the black, not to deny their diversity but to audaciously announce the important artifice of cultural identity and its difference, the need for Fanon becomes urgent. As political groups from different directions gather under the banner of the black, not to homogenize their oppression but to make of it a common cause, a public image of the identity of otherness, the need for Fanon becomes urgent. Urgent, in order to remind us of that crucial engagement between mask and identity, image and identification, from which comes the lasting tension of our freedom and the lasting impression of ourselves as others.

The time has come to return to Fanon, as always, I believe, with a question. How can the human world live its difference? How can a human being live Other-wise?

Notes

1. Fanon's use of the word "man" usually connotes a phenomenological quality of humanness, inclusive of man and woman and, for that very reason, ignores the question of gender difference. The problem stems from Fanon's desire to site the question of sexual difference within the problematic of cultural difference—to give them a shared origin—which is suggestive, but often sim-

plifies the question of sexuality. His portrayals of white women often collude with their cultural stereotypes and reduce the "desire" of sexuality to the desire for sex, leaving unexplored the elusive function of the "object" of desire. In chapter 6 of *Black Skin, White Masks,* he attempts a somewhat more complex reading of masochism, but in making the Negro the "*predestined* depository of this aggression" (my emphasis) he again preempts a fuller psychoanalytic discussion of the production of psychic aggressivity in identification and its relation to cultural difference, by citing the cultural stereotype as the predestined aim of the sexual drive. Of the woman of color he has very little to say. "I know nothing about her," he writes in *Black Skin, White Masks.* This crucial issue requires an order of psychoanalytic argument that goes well beyond the scope of this article. I have therefore chosen to note the importance of the problem rather than to elide it in a facile charge of "sexism."

Above and page 159 from *Breakdowns,* by Art Spiegelman. Copyright © 1972 by Art Spiegelman; reproduced by permission of Roter Stern, Frankfurt.

Pages 155, 156, 170 and 172 from *Maus: A Survivor's Tale,* by Art Spiegelman. Copyright © 1986 by Art Spiegelman; reproduced by permission of Pantheon Books, a division of Random House, Inc., New York.

Alice Yaeger Kaplan

THEWELEIT AND SPIEGELMAN:

OF MEN AND MICE

Too young to have known World War II, but born of it, what are
we to make of our parents' history? What can we possibly add to
the great testimonies of survival in the death camps—to Wiesel,
Levi, Bettelheim? What psychoanalytic insight, one generation
removed, could possibly equal those gleaned from the actual
subjects of history, from the great diagnostic monuments—*The
Mass Psychology of Fascism, The Authoritarian Personality*—from
countless interviews, vivid confessions, from a Speer who was
Inside the Third Reich. The subjects of these books, this history,
are retired from active life, they've borne their children. Among
them, Klaus Barbie was perhaps our last on trial, our last chance
to catch the lie.

As memory retreats from its object, a new kind of work on
the war is born. It can't approach its subject directly. It worries
as much about what it doesn't as about what it does have to say.
It speaks sometimes not about the war but in spite of it. It wants
to know not what happened in that war, but how it was desired;
how it was prepared in language, what use it is to speak of it
now. Its critical idiom, its analytical tools were sharpened on the
mass culture forms of the fifties and sixties. It knows that World
War II itself is not just a memory, but a memory industry, with
enormous political value. Bitburg, Gaza, Faurisson, Le Pen: by
necessity it thinks of World War II not in terms of memory but
in terms of forgetting.

All this could be said to apply most acutely to two
seemingly disparate books that have appeared in an American

context in the past two years. Klaus Theweleit's *Male Fantasies* is about the Freikorps and the S.S., *Maus* by Art Spiegelman about the victims of Auschwitz. *Male Fantasies* is a psychoanalytic reading extended over hundreds of pages and illustrated with artwork, advertisements, and a hundred other visual documents. *Maus* is a cartoon where Jews are represented by mice, Germans by cats, Poles by pigs. In *Maus,* the animals' words come out in balloons. It's an animal fable, an allegory adapted to the American comic strip genre. In *Male Fantasies,* German Freikorps officers speak their most revolting fantasies about murder and rape, conquest and rock hard resistance to a slimy female and communist menace, a red flood. What, beyond their age, could Theweleit and Spiegelman have in common?

For one, both start their books under the sign of paternal violence, maternal pain. For Theweleit it's a bad fascist father:

He was a good man, too, and a pretty good fascist. The blows he brutally lavished as a matter of course, and for my own good, were the first lessons I would one day come to recognize as lessons in fascism. The instances of ambivalence in my mother — she considered the beatings necessary but tempered them — were the second. [1]

Theweleit announces himself in his preface as an abused child, setting out to write about the violent world of his father. He begins his book as an autobiography, taking us in the few pages of his preface from his defeating family romance to a kind of victory that comes with the completion of his thesis. But his project is not in any obvious sense an autobiography. What follows the preface is the thesis he has completed, a thesis based on a very specific topic: the group of post-World War I soldiers known as the Freikorps, warriors who fought to put down communist insurgents after World War I. Two of them (Höss, Goebbels) became top-ranking Nazis; one, Ernst Jünger, a respected modernist writer; one of them even became an anti-Nazi resister. So while their legacy is mixed, even inconsistent, their writings as a whole sent an enabling message and set an emotional tone for the rise of National Socialism. Theweleit works from a broad corpus of novels, biographies, and journals written by Freikorps veterans. The books he quotes have sensational titles like *The Red Flood* and *Blood-Brass-Coal,* and he organizes their themes into titles and subtitles: The White Nurse; Exploding Earth/Lava; Defense Against Slime, the Morass, Pulp. He does, furthermore, what we're usually taught in graduate school not to do in academic writing: mentions everything that comes into his head. Lets it flow. Theweleit's document is powerful in its length; there's a kind of willful "Nuremberg trials effect" where the banality of the examples and their constant repetition force the reader into acknowledging the ubiquity of psychic horror.

Spiegelman's animal tale is brief. The simplicity of the cartoon form and of the dialogue hits you over the head with the strength of allegory. Art Spiegelman is an American from Queens and the narrator of his cartoon. He tells the story of his father's life while telling and showing how he gets the story: *Maus* is both an autobiography, a biography, and a novel of testimony, for it is Spiegelman's father Vladek who supplies the narration, the survivor's tale, while Spiegelman himself elaborates the frame. Vladek Spiegelman is a survivor of Auschwitz. His wife also survived, but she has committed suicide before the story begins—or rather the memory of her suicide intrudes into Spiegelman's attempt to get his father to tell their story. *Maus* strips down the conversations between Art Spiegelman and his father to the minimum, and yet the small book speaks volumes about the death camps, the postwar struggle for Jewish redefinition and survival, about war, memory, and forgetting.

Maus is structured around a series of "simple conversations." Spiegelman's father doesn't want to talk; he is stingy to a fault, repressive, the kind of guy who grabs paper towels from restrooms so he won't have to buy napkins. He keeps interrupting the story he tells his son about the camps while he takes his pills, picks up old telephone wire, throws his son's coat in the garbage and gives him his old one. He doesn't trust anyone and he's inculcated the mistrust in his son from a very young age. But finally the story takes over. Art Spiegelman shows some of his first drawings for *Maus* to his father, who's really happy—thinks Art will be successful and famous like Walt Disney. But while the father may be enthusiastic about the creation of a comic, he is far more ambivalent when it comes to the memory of the war. The story of Vladek's life proceeds at regular intervals toward the gates of Auschwitz, but the narrative frame of *Maus* builds up to a single act of violence committed by the father against memory: he has destroyed his wife's diary from the camp.

Father: After Anja died I had to make an order with everything . . . These papers had too many memories. So I burned them.
Son: You burned them? Christ! you save tons of worthless shit, and you . . .
Father: Yes, it's a shame! For years they were laying there and nobody even looked in.
Son: Did you ever read any of them? . . . Can you remember what she wrote?
Father: No. I looked in, but I don't remember . . . only I know that she said, "I wish my son, when he grows up, he will be interested by this."
Son: God DAMN you! You—you MURDERER! How the hell could you do such a thing!!
Father: Ach.[2]

The *Maus* published by Pantheon in 1986 is the first part of an eventual two-part book. It ends on a double register: the present, our present, and the flashback to 1944. Spiegelman's father at the gates of Auschwitz saying he knew he would be gassed and then an abrupt flash forward to Queens and to his survival, his confession about the diaries. The last frame of *Maus* is a narrow little frame of Art Spiegelman, mouse-cartoonist, walking out of

his father's house with portfolio in hand and a single balloon
coming out of his head as he thinks about his father. The balloon
reads ". . . Murderer." The reader is left with the impossible
double register: the certainty of Vladek's extermination and the
misery his survival has inflicted upon his family.

One of many extraordinary features of *Maus* is that Spiegelman gets the voices right, he gets the order of the words right,
he manages to capture the intonations of Eastern Europe spoken
by Queens. He puts us in the cultural space of those impossible
father-son dialogues without ever being obvious about it. It's
very hard to describe why the anthropomorphic universe of
Maus works so well. It begins on a white page with a single
quotation from Adolf Hitler: "The Jews are undoubtedly a race,
but they are not human." From then on, we're in a nightmare.
As if presenting Jews as Hitler saw them — as animals — were
Spiegelman's way of forcing us to experience anew that Hitler's
word did become law — that "what he said, went." Spiegelman's
resistance to Hitler's law is then all in the anthropomorphism, in
having made the Jews — and the Germans and the Poles — human
animals, all too human, each of them dressed with minute attention to cultural detail, from the naugahyde windbreaker and ex-
ercycle in Rego Park to the suit jackets and spectacles and the
hats of Sosnowiec. The possibilities of black ink on white,
scratched shading, solids, dots to convey documentary memory,
everydayness, and danger are a stunning surprise: there is much
of the beauty of nineteenth-century children's engravings here.

Spiegelman and Theweleit are genealogical opposites. One

is the child of Nazi ideology, one the child of an Auschwitz survivor. The parents of one attended the rallies at Nuremberg, the other's parents escaped the ovens at Auschwitz. They ought to be as distant as oppressor and oppressed. Why, then, do I have the overwhelming sense, reading one book after the other, that Klaus Theweleit and Art Spiegelman are brothers? There is, of course, the shared anger at their fathers. Theweleit at his for doling out the politics of the fascist state to his children in the form of domestic violence. Spiegelman at his for internalizing the hell of the camps and projecting it onto his wife and his son. There is the loss of history, and the loss of parents: Spiegelman's mother, who survived Auschwitz but committed suicide in 1968; Theweleit's father, who "succumbed to alcohol and German history" and died "a disappointed public servant."

Klaus Theweleit tells us, in passing, once again in the preface to his study of the Freikorps, how the act of naming children was, in the Theweleit family, politically overdetermined. The older siblings were named with operatic pride, Reinhold, Siegfried, Brunhilde, Günter: "for the coming Reich that somehow never came."[3] The author and his sister were the "latecomers" inasmuch as they came after the defeat at Sta-

lingrad. They were given names that lacked specific historic or
cultural associations, names that, by their very ordinariness,
hence their blamelessness, came into vogue for postwar children:
Klaus and Helga. This preface, of course, is only a small autobiographical aside in comparison with the rest of *Male Fantasies,*
but it enables what is to come. It makes a connection between
Theweleit's life and his work; it takes as its first step an autobiographical risk.

The parents of both Theweleit and Spiegelman bring their
children to life, name them, after their own survival, after their
defeat. All children must live with the historical signs imposed
on them by their parents: a first name, a place name, a series of
anecdotes. What happens when history cuts people off from
their name and place? I am reminded of that haunting exchange
at the end of Duras and Resnais's *Hiroshima mon amour.*[4] The two
main characters, lovers, have respectively lost and broken with
their families through separate tragedies of Second World War
history. They give themselves place names after those tragedies.
"Your name is Hiroshima." "Your name is Nevers. Nevers in
France."

Hiroshima mon amour is in fact the film that I think of when
I try to make the connection between *Maus* and *Male Fantasies.* It
is a story about memory and about a French woman who, as a
girl in the German-occupied town of Nevers, loved a German
soldier. He dies from a sniper's bullet at the end of the war. She
is shaved for her sins, *tondue* in her town square as part of the
Liberation festivities. When her hair is decently long, she is sent
off by her family to forget and be forgotten in Paris. Years later,
now an actress, she goes to Hiroshima to make a film about
peace. She meets a man, a "Hiroshiman" with whom she is able
to remember, and to whom she tells her war story. As she tells
of her love for the German soldier for the very first time, the
man from Hiroshima becomes, in her mind and in his, the German soldier. The two events—love in France, love in

Hiroshima—collapse, and with a remorse that drives her nearly to the point of madness, the woman realizes that the condition for telling her story is that she's become able to forget. *Hiroshima mon amour* is one of the most famous enactments of an impossible truth that *Male Fantasies* and *Maus* renew: the necessity of repressing in order to survive, the necessity of remembering as a condition of the survivor's dignity, the inevitability that if history is forgotten, or perhaps even if it is remembered, it will repeat. And the sense that when it does, it does so in the least expected ways.

But there is an important difference in the texts of Theweleit and Spiegelman, who are not the historic agents, but rather the sons of Hiroshima and Nevers. This generation was named by World War II survivors, learned to read and write in postwar schools. It's old enough now to have its own family history, its own signs: television, commodity and drug cultures, sixties militancy and rejection of middle-class parents, therapy, and more. There is a whole new generational perspective available to bring to bear on the world events portrayed in *Hiroshima mon amour,* a new perspective and radically new descriptive forms.

Theweleit's project is essentially archival, a Ph.D. dissertation: he's read all the diaries, the papers of the Freikorps, all the secondary psychoanalytic and theoretical materials on fascism. But he gives himself permission to take on the project by writing in the autobiographical genre. He begins by saying, the story of Nazism is also a story of families, of marriages, of German selfhood, of what we have inherited from our parents. The memory of Nazism is within. Spiegelman's project is construed in the style of his own generation, in comix. A generation ready at last to listen to the story of its parents but who insists on telling that story in its own language. Young Theweleit and young Spiegelman, characters at a generation's remove from war trauma, are marked by trauma in a different way than the lovers in Hiroshima. But even in their generational remove from the

events, there is still no emotional safety. Hitler has carried his effects one generation beyond. Your name is Stalingrad, Hindenburg, Kiel, your name is Czestochowa, Sosnowiec, Auschwitz, Queens. A new generation is marked, it is making its mark. What happens to the memory of history when it ceases to be testimony?

One generation removed, Nazi Germany is no longer an experience that can be narrated directly; it has been absorbed by the children who heard about it and grew up with it; it is worn. Hence the prominence in both Spiegelman and Theweleit's project of the narrative frame.

Theweleit's intuition of "Nazism within" gives to his writing an anger, and an impatience with academic method, theoretical language, with all the intellectual tools for understanding Nazism that he has also inherited along with the Nazi past. He tries to come at history already absorbed by the body, expressive only in lived experience. The authority he substitutes for the fascist one is female: "I am not about to use literature to make this point. Anyone who is interested can discuss it at length with actual women."[5]

Once again we can look to the preface for an autobiographical clue. Theweleit is indebted to his wife, the analyst, to her clinical experience with schizophrenics, so-called deviants, whom Theweleit calls "the true non-fascists." Unlike the women with whom Theweleit would have us discuss whether fascism is indeed the norm for males who live under capitalist patriarchy, schizophrenics can't be effective sources of information about fascism—they lack conceptual authority. Yet Theweleit claims a lot for them, in passing. He claims for them a freedom from categories and a language that is neither distant nor repressed. He wants something of the same freedom in his own writing process, though he acknowledges that the risk of identification is boundaryless disfunctionality. And his readers know that the radical forms of therapy proposed for schizophrenics by Laing and others twenty years ago have given way to drug therapies: Theweleit's empathy is a nostalgic one, his claim but a fragile claim for position. In order to make the connections between body, writing, and thought a part of the anti-fascist struggle, Theweleit posits schizophrenia as fascism's polar opposite.

His personal and bodily engagement with his archival material, his self-knowledge, allow Klaus Theweleit to do what I am tempted to call (still in the parlance of therapy) "emotional work" with his material that traditional historians are not likely to do. He gets close to the material, he establishes an emotional intimacy with his readers in a style I've rarely seen outside feminist criticism. His closeness can produce elation or discomfort in a reader. Sometimes you feel as though he—and you, too—are in an impossible therapy group. Theweleit is group leader, and he has gathered together from outside time a few fascist terrorists, uptight left-wing intellectuals, and boundaryless psychotics:

> Gisela Pankow has outlined one possible avenue of treatment for "psychotic" patients who, unlike the men under scrutiny here, are not equipped with any totality ego and have no awareness whatever of their body boundaries. . . .
>
> For her, the goal of therapy is that the patient, who often experiences a single part of the body only as the whole—and perceives the whole body as dismembered—develops a recognition of her or his body boundaries. "Every new area of the body perceived is a firm piece of ground extracted from the process of psychosis."
>
> For the soldier male, by contrast, locked as he is in his totality-armor, analysis might perhaps involve guiding him towards an acknowledgement of his bodily openings and of the interior of his body, in order to protect him from immediate inundation by the fear of dissolution if his bodily periphery becomes pleasurably invested.[6]

When I first read volume one of *Male Fantasies* in manuscript, I was writing a book of my own on French fascism, and I came to think of Klaus Theweleit as a friend who allowed me to write—I got incredible writing energy from the book, analytic energy, permission to use my intuitions.[7] I was swimming and writing and reading Theweleit; the book was having both an invigorating and a hypnotic effect. Effects such as these take *Male Fantasies* way outside the boundaries of conventional social theory, in terms of reception and in terms of consequences. How, and why?

Theweleit is not afraid of being "vulgar." Nor is he afraid of the ordinariness of the language he is quoting. His book is not about literature but about language that is repetitive, "obvious," "bad." There is no temptation, as there would be in reading a canonized novel, to lose one's grip on sadistic dynamics because the form itself is such a bribe . . . except perhaps with Ernst Jünger, the "real writer" among the warriors, but his words and his commonplaces are mixed in by Theweleit with those of all the rest of the warriors.

Some of the American critics have complained in reviewing Theweleit's book that he wasn't much good as an historian. The work of the historian, they argue, would be to show why some men became Freikorps sadists, others left-wing intellectuals. What in their background, their socialization, what in their specific historic moment made them so? Is this preoccupation with specificity important, I wonder? Or rather, which is the true historical project: the pinpointing of an empirical cause, or the trickier, less disciplined attempt to make links between past and present? I don't think that Theweleit is totally uninterested in why Höss became a fascist and Sartre didn't, but the question is, in an important way, beside the point of the book; it is not the move Theweleit himself is interested in making. He wants rather to insist on shared terrain. Not why Sartre and Brecht didn't become fascists, but how it is that they share so many misogynist themes, how it is that they occupy much the same psychosexual universe. Sartreian language makes for an especially tempting comparison: enough female murk inhabits his writings to com-

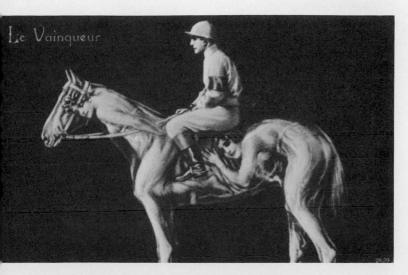

French postcard, from Klaus Theweleit, *Male Fantasies,* 1987. Reproduced by permission of the University of Minnesota Press.

"... Progress," from Klaus Theweleit, *Male Fantasies,* 1987. Reproduced by permission of the University of Minnesota Press.

pete with the slimiest texts in Theweleit's corpus of slime.[8]
Theweleit would celebrate such a comparison, for he is always
attempting to slide from the fascist to nonfascist, arguing especially about what the respectable, left-wing intellectual—his
reader—shares with the fascists he's examining in the way of
rhetorical rigidity, primitive fear, and hatred of the female body.
His most characteristic moves are juxtaposition and boundary
crashing. In image alone, we see Lenin and Brecht, a Frenchman
on a horse, an English comic strip, a panel of nine male psychoanalysts in 1977, mingling with fascist propaganda posters. Look
for fascist structures in your daily life, Theweleit says, in your
intellectual heroes, in your schoolbooks. And this is precisely
how Theweleit's book worked, how it inflamed in Germany, especially among young people who had been told by their parents
and teachers to remember the Holocaust *but* . . . to forget about
fascism. Theweleit is looking not for the truth about the fascists,
not for the specificity of their socialization, he is not even trying
to uncover new, unknown fascists. He is interested in their emotional legacy.

Male Fantasies is constantly metamorphosing. On one page
it's about the 1920s; then it becomes a book about intellectual
style, about now:

*To this day, it is required that the level of reflection be a high one, the
level of theory higher still; the drop to lower levels of feeling and con-
cretizations is considered precipitous. But is there any such thing as the
"height of theory," except as an element in masculine mystique?*[9]

You can't help thinking that something has been lost of the energy of the sixties when what used to be called "getting down"
gets articulated as "concretization" ("concretization" was, in
fact, a key word in leftist student circles—it doesn't translate
well). But Theweleit isn't nostalgic for the student left; he spares
neither left activists nor male feminists on the style question. A
recurring theme of his analyses is the attack on a national style

mmy's dream," British World War I poster, from Klaus Theweleit, *Male Fantasies,* 1987. Reproduced permission of the University of Minnesota Press.

common to both right and left that betrays its flight from the body in a penchant for abstraction:

If a male author chooses to write eulogies to the feminist movement, then he should at least accept that the language of penetration which he has, perhaps, used in the past to seduce long-suffering virgins, can no longer be used to take possession of virgin-white paper.

The language of the Left excludes the mysteries of the body . . . Over and over again, the Left blunders into engagements with the language of dominant groups without realizing it has mistaken its terrain. Such language cannot be "refuted" on the level of "political meaning": its primary territory of effectivity is elsewhere.[10]

"Primary territory of effectivity" is a difficult way of saying that language dominates not because it means X, Y, or Z, but because it gets to us, because it feels good, body and soul. And the "us" includes intellectuals, not some abstractly nondiscriminating "people" susceptible to manipulation. The mind/body problem isn't new, but Theweleit brings the body to his intellectual material in an acutely political manner that may be new. What's missing for Theweleit in the Theory he looks to in understanding fascist violence is any sustained sensitivity to the power and mystery of our body's relationship to our minds. The theorists Theweleit is finally most interested in are the ones who try to start "at home," with the body, rather than with the idea. He's especially indebted to Wilhelm Reich, to Deleuze and Guattari, and most of all to the entire field of radical psychotherapists, beginning in the preface with Monika Kubale and Margret Berger, for whom bodily functions are the starting point of all psychoanalytic work. Theweleit is promoting neither a "distant" (phallic) nor simply identificatory type of criticism. His method is perhaps best described as a new way of "knowing" politics through the body.

How can we hope to understand fascist defenses, he implores, if our intellectual methods for understanding are rigid and defensive, too? Here's the crux of Theweleit's argument and here is where I begin to lose him, or, perhaps, where he makes me defensive: I don't want to believe that the analogy he's making between his original object of study — the Freikorps officers — and the various political and psychoanalytic theories he dismisses is so complete, nor even so useful. I want some hierarchies, or maybe just more boundaries. Between fascist terrorists, phallic psychoanalysts, between 1870 and 1977. I want context.

So let me attribute the author's own rejection of boundaries to his context. This slipping and sliding from rigid fascists to rigid intellectual methods has several important functions in the postwar German context. Theweleit believes that the Holocaust was not an accident. It was a working out of desires for fusion, for mastery, for control that all people experience on a daily basis. The project of analyzing the Nazi past is itself imbued with, informed by the same psychic needs for mastery, distance, control. What is the message then? It's about guilt, and responsibility. Not that "they" were perverts, and we are innocent, but look at what "they" and "we" share. The length of the book is not just, as I surmised earlier, an insistence on the psychic horrors of the Nazi past, but a smashing of boundaries between real time and reading time that Theweleit wants to visit upon his reader as a part of the anti-fascist cure.

It's important in understanding Theweleit's work in the German context to remember the message of Fassbinder's films: that postwar German society was caught up in a massive social project where reconstruction and forgetting were intertwined. Theweleit's context is, as he states it, "the injunction prevailing in Germany against learning about fascism and its antecedents."[11] My friend Margret, a member of Theweleit's generation, learned about the camps not from her parents but from her grandmother, on the sly. When she became a teacher in a German secondary school, she devoted much of her energy to that near impossible task: fostering an atmosphere where students could learn about recent German history in a critical but not self-hating way. Her story, she tells me, is not unusual.

I learn as I finish writing this article that it was Roter Stern, the same publisher who published *Male Fantasies,* who published segments of *Maus* in a German version, even before it was published by Pantheon in the United States.[12] And I learn that it was Klaus Theweleit who introduced Spiegelman's work to the German public, in a brochure packaged with the volume that contains an interview with Spiegelman and a history of the American comic strip. Roter Stern is a left-wing publisher, progressive, anti-fascist. The segments from *Maus* raise questions in the German context of 1980. Is demystifying the camp survivors a luxury? In an intellectual climate where so-called revisionists write literal-minded texts to persuade people that much of what we've learned about the camps *is* a Disney tale, what does it mean for people to read *Maus,* whose allegorical characters look like cousins of Mickey and Minnie? Is this aesthetic insensitivity or is Spiegelman's brilliant formal invention—the rendering of a high tragic story in comic strip form—incomprehensible in a society so troubled by its racist past?

Related, perhaps, is the trouble at the University of Minnesota Press over the advertisements used to publicize the American translation of *Male Fantasies.* The editor received a number of complaints that the illustrations from *Male Fantasies* published in the Minnesota Press catalogue were violently anti-feminist: a woman bound and gagged with a gun aimed at her face, an ink drawing of multiple female nudes. The complaints came from that unholy alliance: the conservative right and the anti-pornography feminists. A cover, a catalogue, is meant for people who *don't* read a book, not for those who do. It occurs to me that Theweleit, reader of symptoms and distant effects, would probably be pleased and amused by these critics who saw something of what he did without the benefit of his words.

For us in the U.S., the necessity of learning about Nazism does not exist in the same form as it does in Germany. The equations that Theweleit insists upon between intellectual methods and political crime do seem excessive; the connections are too numerous, too messy. Not that we don't have our own national repressive structures. What can the American reader take away from Theweleit? What is our equivalent of the Freikorps officer, the seminal fascist male with male fantasies? If we were to read the book in an American context the way he might hope we would, we'd have to start asking a lot of questions about an American fascism.

How easy it is to forget our own nationalist genocides, our manifest destiny that wiped out those others—Indians, Filipinos. Vietnam seemed almost to have ruptured the pattern, until revisionism came its way. We now need a Theweleit, a Spiegelman, to write about My Lai and Rambo without disdain. In Germany the memory of the Holocaust is an issue inseparable from national identity. The suggestion that the Holocaust should be relativized in the name of national pride is met with outcries and serious debate. We do not bear a personal burden of guilt or shame for our own war crimes, and scarcely the memory. We don't want to let our history bleed. But Spiegelman insists: "My father bleeds history," though his father tells him to separate the events from their effect on his person: "I can tell you *other* stories, but such *private* things, I don't want you should mention."[13]

"Okay, okay, I promise," Art Spiegelman answers, raising his mouse hand in a defensive gesture that looks oddly like a "sieg heil."

Someone who picks up this essay when it appears in a year or two will not automatically know that it was written the month the American literary world learned that Paul de Man, a man it knew as a teacher and literary theorist until his death in 1984, wrote articles for a collaborationist Belgian newspaper at the age of twenty-one and twenty-two. It's the year, too, of the

Heidegger revelations in France. We are busy with surprise. I hope that revelations like these will fill us with energy for research, with desire for a new look. The initial reactions, however, have shown not so much a curiosity as a defense against intellectual debt, an estrangement, a cutting of ties.

We live in an era of denouncement. We denounce, clean and simple, the past of one or two individuals *instead* of thinking about history, instead of thinking about how we, too, bleed history. Theweleit is angry and polemical on the subject of those who thought they knew what fascism was:

The "symbol seekers" are fundamentally misguided in assuming fascist language to be easily open to interpretation — as misguided as are the "anti-fascists" who characterize fascist language as "stupid" or "politically senseless." Since neither group takes account of the structure from which fascist language emanates, they inevitably underestimate its explosive political power, ignore its dynamic force; they are interested only in what it says, not in how it functions. And once they have framed their questions in terms of "what it says," they are able to pose fascist language in opposition to signifiers of their own preferred meanings, which they immediately claim to be "superior." "Fascism can never tri-

umph since we are more clever" — *this was the dictum on which almost all "assessments" by the 1920's Left were founded.*[14]

To find an analogy with the kind of error Theweleit warns against in our own context, I would need to produce in myself and my readers that uncomfortable, compromised feeling of recognition: "my God, we haven't learned a thing." I don't want to believe Theweleit on this score. The belief seems, like so much in Theweleit, wandering, tedious, irresponsible. Which brings me again to Spiegelman and to *Maus.* The fascism within, the way Spiegelman shows it to us, is the fascism visited upon his father in the camps, a fascism his father has come to embody and project even as he has triumphed in his survival. "My father bleeds history," Art Spiegelman tells us. "My father is a murderer." We don't like to think about it this way: we like our victims pure, and our intellectual heroes untouched by history.

In *Male Fantasies* and *Maus,* there's a horrible echo, a haunting of personal history by the political. Theweleit seems to me to greet the echoes with anger and resignation, despite his alliance with the therapeutic option; Spiegelman greets it with an overwhelming sadness, a determination that just as his father survived, he must survive his father. If I were tempted to put their books together before knowing why, it was undoubtedly out of the sense of generation that I share with them. Therapy becomes a dominant method and metaphor for Theweleit because therapy is the way our generation has learned to understand history. And to resist it, at the bodily level. Fascism, for Theweleit, is still around to be resisted. In Spiegelman, the form — the radical comic strip — brings into the cultural mainstream of the eighties a sixties militancy, with its hallucinogenic imperative to transform our parents' dusty reality. By using that radical form to tell his father's story, Spiegelman consecrates it with his own vision and voice. Both men have claimed their parentage in the fullest sense in order to free themselves from its bonds.

Notes

1. Klaus Theweleit, *Male Fantasies,* Vol. 1: *Women, Floods, Bodies, History*, trans. Stephen Conway (Minneapolis: University of Minnesota Press, 1987), p. xx.

2. Art Spiegelman, *Maus: A Survivor's Tale* (New York: Pantheon Books, 1986), p. 159.

3. Theweleit, *Male Fantasies,* vol. 1, p. xx.

4. See Marguerite Duras, *Hiroshima mon amour,* scenario for a film by Alain Resnais (New York: Grove Press, 1987).

5. Theweleit, *Male Fantasies,* vol. 1, p. 444, note 1.

6. Klaus Theweleit, manuscript of volume 2 of *Male Fantasies* (forthcoming); manuscript pp. 328-329.

7. Alice Yaeger Kaplan, *Reproductions of Banality: Fascism, Literature, and French Intellectual Life* (Minneapolis: University of Minnesota Press, 1986).

8. Margery L. Collins and Christine Pierce, "Holes and Slime: Sexism in Sartre's Psychoanalysis," *Philosophical Forum* 5, no. 1-2 (Fall-Winter 1973-1974); reprinted in *Women and Philosophy: Toward a Theory of Liberation,* ed. Carol C. Gould and Marx W. Wartofsky (New York: G. P. Putnam's Sons, 1976), pp. 112-127.

9. Theweleit, *Male Fantasies,* vol. 2, manuscript p. 67.

10. Ibid., manuscript p. 132.

11. Theweleit, *Male Fantasies,* vol. 1, p. 57.

12. Art Spiegelman, *Breakdowns. Gesammelte Comic Strips,* with an interview by Martin Langbrin and Klaus Theweleit; adapted by Dieter Karl; trans. Emigholz Heinz (Frankfurt: Roter Stern Verlag, 1980). This is a collection of Spiegelman's work, much of which was to be incorporated into *Maus.* The book is not available in any American library or inter-library system that I know of. I am grateful to Miriam Hansen for the reference.

13. Spiegelman, *Maus,* p. 23.

14. Theweleit, *Male Fantasies,* vol. 2, manuscript p. 328.

John Wayne in *The Green Berets*, 1968. Courtesy Photofest.

VIETNAM: THE REMAKE

While movie-going has long since ceased to be a national habit
for just about everyone but teenagers, the movies themselves remain a privileged instrument in the symphony orchestra of
American—indeed, international—mass culture. Entertainment
aside, they function as social metaphor, showcase utopian possibilities, present new personality types, provide socially cohe-
sive cocktail party conversation. While television is a
continuum, a transmission, a guilty pleasure, a consumer ap-
pliance; and pop music a way of life that generally exhausts itself
by the age of thirty-five, each new movie is an aspiring Event—a
conflagration, a potlatch, a public burning of celluloid and
money, whose success is dependent on inspiring the public's fascination, instigating a kind of mass need-to-know, the secret fantasy that this might change your life.

The Vietnam War—to take the central event of many people's lives—was something else. It was, to paraphrase historian
Gabriel Kolko, an epic event. It was both the longest single war
and the most sustained revolutionary effort of the twentieth century, as well as the most challenging military experience in U.S.
history—"a synthesis of politics, technology, the residues of past
wars, convoluted logic, and symbolism,"[1] delivered with the
greatest volume of firepower the world has ever seen. The cost
in human suffering was monumental and difficult to calculate. In
South Vietnam, the war produced seven million displaced
persons—one-third of the population, over half the peasantry; it
precipitated a forced urbanization, the most "brutal and disori-
enting that a large Third World nation has ever experienced."[2]
Here in the United States, we experienced another sort of
disorientation.

In a brilliant essay occasioned by the American Bicentennial, Hannah Arendt wrote that the Vietnam War "was exclusively guided by the needs of a superpower to create for itself an image which would convince the world that it was, indeed, the mightiest power on earth." Such "image-making as global policy," Arendt observed, was "something new in the huge arsenal of human follies recorded in history . . . [Image-making] was permitted to proliferate throughout the ranks of all governmental services, military and civilian—the phony body-counts of the search and destroy missions, the doctored after-damage reports of the air force, the constant progress reports to Washington."[3]

So the Vietnam War was spectacular—in the literal sense. Waged in the name of "credibility," it was intended to project a superpower's image as the mightiest on earth. But image-making has its own logic and imperatives. The war was also something less rational and more delirious, harder to control and easier to get high on, than just a ten-year public relations campaign. Vietnam was also a movie. Our movie. Our greatest hit. Our biggest bomb.

As orchestrated by two administrations, this movie became the greatest episode in American show business—the longest, costliest, most ambitious, best-attended catastrophe ever staged. Or rather filmed, videotaped, and televised. *Cleopatra* and *Heaven's Gate* have nothing on this debacle—a cost of billions, a cast of millions, some sixty thousand American casualties (plus the death of forty times as many foreign "extras," eighty or ninety times as many if you include the Cambodian sideshow). I don't have to tell you what the ratings were like—or the word of mouth. Indeed, we've never stopped talking about it.

It's not simply that Vietnam was perceived as a living-room war by those of us who used to watch the instant replay on television. The experience of those who participated was intimately bound up with our national fantasy life. Out in the field, dangerous areas were called "Indian country," Vietnamese scouts were known as "Kit Carsons," the infamous one-liner "The only good Indian is a dead Indian" was updated as the slogan "The only good gook is a dead one." It's not a coincidence that the base to which John Wayne was assigned in *The Green Berets* is named Dodge City.

When an American captain invites war correspondant Michael Herr on a search-and-destroy mission, he says, "Come on, I'll take you out to play Cowboys and Indians." (This is in *Dispatches*.) Later, Herr muses over the combat performance given by nineteen-year-old kids when they realized a television crew was in the vicinity: "They were actually making war movies in their heads, doing little guts-and-glory Leatherneck tap dances under fire, getting their pimples shot off for the networks. They were insane, but the war hadn't done that to them."[4] Like the election of Ronald Reagan, the war was the fulfillment of something.

In his analysis of the role American cultural attitudes played in our Vietnamese involvement, Loren Baritz observes that "It is astonishing how often American GIs in Vietnam approvingly referred to John Wayne, not as a movie star, but as a model and a standard . . . Nineteen-year-old Americans, brought up on World War II movies and westerns, walking through the jungle, armed to the teeth, searching for an invisible enemy who knew the wilderness better than they did, could hardly miss these connections. One after another said, at some point, something like 'Hey, this is just like a movie.'" You probably remember the famous scene in *Dispatches* where a wounded marine turns to Herr and says, "I *hate* this movie!"[5]

The men that served in Vietnam used to call America "the World"—short for the Real World. Vietnam by inference, was somewhere else—somewhere imaginary. But this isn't exactly what I'm going to talk about—I was never in Vietnam, I only know it second-hand, so for me it's doubly imaginary. The rubric under which these talks are being given is "Remaking History," and—as literal-minded as I am—this is "Vietnam: The Remake."

Now, for Hollywood as elsewhere, the 1960s was a period of much fertile confusion. Among other things, the previous decade had been characterized by a cycle of Biblical or Roman spectaculars that not only demonstrated Hollywood's wealth and power but were also suggestive of an imperial Pax Americana. With the twin disasters of *Cleopatra* (1963) and Vietnam (1964-75), this cycle came to an end—or rather, it reached its apotheosis.

The movie industry was in the midst of an identity crisis— it groped in the dark for the huge youth market, attempting to develop new formulae. By 1969, around the time that the war was wisely conceived to be unwinnable, five major studios were in the red. At its best, this disorganized state encouraged considerable genre criticism and directorial nonconformity. The old verités had crumbled, anything was possible. The quintessential sixties mode is the apocalyptic genre film—*The Wild Bunch, Bonnie and Clyde, Easy Rider, Wild in the Streets, 2001, Myra Breckinridge, Night of the Living Dead.* (The latter is a film of particular significance, having been made outside Hollywood, using the techniques of underground movies to offer the most literal possible image of America devouring itself.) The war film alone remained quite traditional.

Of course, the whole idea of a war film is bizarre— particularly if you suspect, as I do, that entertainment is by its nature somewhat utopian and compensatory, concerned with pleasure and wish fulfillment. Samuel Fuller, who was wounded twice in World War II and made a number of powerful combat movies, maintained that it was impossible to "show war as it really is on the screen," adding that it might be preferable to "fire real shots over the audience's head" and "have actual casualties in the theater." The analogy between dreams and movies has been endlessly rehearsed and so it's suggestive that, after studying the dreams of traumatized World War I veterans, Freud considered their nocturnal flashbacks as a distinct category of dream that arose less from wish fulfillment or anxiety than a compulsion to repeat the traumatic experience.

The megabuck World War II epic was still a viable form of entertainment during the period of U.S. escalation. Each year, from 1965 through 1970, brought at least one large-scale replay of Big Two: *Battle of the Bulge* (1965), *Is Paris Burning?* (1966), *Beach Red* (1967), *Anzio* (1968), *The Battle of Britain* (1969), *Tora! Tora! Tora!* (1970). Yet, with the exception of *The Green Berets* (which, although produced in 1968, took its cues from World War II combat films), the current war was entirely absent from American movie screens. This was virtually true of popular music as well. There were a few songs dealing with unhappy soldiers, but the Vietnam War produced no "Over There" or "Don't Sit Under the Apple Tree."

Now, John Wayne and *The Green Berets* notwithstanding, the Vietnam War has always had an odd history in American films. Indeed, once the Vietnam War became widely perceived as unwinnable—that is, once Nixon and Kissinger began to withdraw American ground forces—all war vanished from the movie screen. Although Hollywood released nine war films in 1970 (the most since the big-budget World War II epic was launched in 1958), the genre was abruptly terminated once Richard Nixon set about withdrawing American combat troops. Only two war films were released in 1971, and none at all for the next four years (which, significantly, coincides with the heyday of disaster films). Not until the war was over did *Midway* (1976), *A Bridge Too Far* (1977), and *MacArthur* (1977) appear—along with the first wave of Vietnam combat films.

So, right from the start, Hollywood seemed to want the war in Vietnam over and done with—thus operating within the regime of wish fulfillment. The initial cycle of Vietnam movies were set mainly on the home front, where the battle was being fought for the hearts and minds of the American viewing public. These movies were considerably less interested in combat heroics than in the often nightmarish situation of the returning vets—alternately shown as a guilty society's violent redeemers or its victimized scapegoats and often an ambiguous combination of the two.

The 1967 *Born Losers* not only introduced the messianic half-Indian, ex-Green Beret, Billy Jack (a now-forgotten left-wing precursor to Rambo in his agonized vigilantism), but spawned an entire subgenre in which alienated Viet vets either joined up with or battled marauding motorcycle gangs (the most malevolent manifestation of the youth culture). With the rise of blaxploitation, the turf shifted so that ex-Green Berets played by Jim Brown or Paul Winfield came back to war against ghetto dope dealers and exploitive gangsters. While only a few horror flicks—the 1971 *Fiend with the Electronic Brain,* Bob Clark's 1972 *Deathdream*—were crude enough to use returning Viet vets as literal monsters, movies like *Welcome Home Soldier Boys* (1972), *Tracks* (1976), *Taxi Driver* (1976), and *Rolling Thunder* (1977), not to mention scores of TV shows, made the psychotic, violence-prone Viet vet a mass culture cliché.

But the purpose of war, as Elaine Scarry reminds us, is to injure—"to alter (to burn, to blast, to shell, to cut) human tissue, as well as to alter the surface, shape, and deep entirety of the objects that human beings recognize as extensions of them-selves."[6] And so, more disturbing perhaps than those vets who returned to the World to run amok were those who came back visibly or invisibly scarred—the wounded vets of *Coming Home* (1978), *Who'll Stop the Rain?* (1978), *Cutter's Way* (1981), and *Some Kind of Hero* (1982)—who appeared to suffer some partic-ular sexual malaise, if not an out-and-out mutilation. Something of theirs is missing. Vietnam, it would seem, hit America below the belt.

The first recuperation of the sixties can be found in the cycle of disaster films inaugurated in 1970 by *Airport*—and peaking four years later with *Earthquake, The Towering Inferno, The Hindenburg,*

Juggernaut, The Taking of Pelham One Two Three, the resignation of Richard Nixon, and *Airport 1975.* These featured all-star casts in the guise of ordinary, middle-class people who have to cope with the total breakdown of institutions thought to be safe. Such institutions are clearly microcosms of America but, although the disaster is worsened by mendacious, greedy, corrupt, and incompetent leaders, it does not reflect a fundamental flaw in the system. Actually, the system works. Disaster films demonstrate the fundamental decency of ordinary people, their allegiance to traditional moral virtues. All the middle-class values reign victorious at the end.

By asserting that America's enemies remained nature and/or technology, disaster films denied that Americans had become decadent or that consensus had shattered. Indeed, they suggested that the sixties never happened—traditional virtues are intact and, unlike in *Night of the Living Dead,* enable people to help each other survive the crisis. So disaster films were fundamentally reassuring and they also reassured the alienated audience with the old-time entertainment religion of conspicuous consumption, happy endings, and all-star casts. They were typically filled with familiar faces from the forties and fifties—had he not decided on another career, Ronald Reagan would have fit right in as a secondary character in *The Towering Inferno.*

In recuperating the apocalyptic breakdowns of the sixties, disaster films were the first wave of reillusionment. There would be others. With the fall of Saigon in June 1975, the American public was left to contemplate the futility of its great disaster film—the wasted lives and squandered wealth. This was depressing. Small wonder that, from 1976 on, Americans indulged in an orgy of born-again genres and exercises in feel-good regression, a prolonged fascination with the fabulous fifties that functioned like Freud's notion of the fetish—that is, a defense against castration anxiety fixating on a substitute phallus, often the last thing experienced before a traumatic discovery or loss. For the past fifteen years, the era we call the fifties (really the 1955-62 period between the Korean and Vietnam wars) has been a kind of lost paradise within American popular culture. George Lucas's 1973 *American Graffiti* was the harbinger of this trend—not just because it was the first film to periodicize the 1955-62 period, but because it deliberately used the disaster of Vietnam as a structuring absence.

Since then and up until very recently, American movies, TV, and politics have continued to privilege the fifties, even to the point of superimposing that happy era over the eighties. Only in *Blue Velvet* (1986) does this contradiction begin to manifest itself; in the more seamless *Back to the Future* (1985), "1955" is a place for the hero to play—a theme park or Disneyland (which, perhaps not coincidentally, opened that very year). *Back to the Future* is a kind of historical Moebius strip that negates the idea of history, by suggesting that the troublesome past can be rescripted to improve the present.

In terms of war movies, this usually occurs several years after the war is over. Hollywood began to ponder World War I in the mid-twenties and World War II after 1949, while Korean War movies were a staple of the late fifties. Not until several years after the fall of Saigon did Hollywood attempt to reenact the war as a period spectacle. A cluster of films released in 1978 and 1979 established and/or epitomized the basic thematics that, in various combinations, have gone in and out of favor through to the present day: the returning vet melodrama (Hal Ashby's *Coming Home*, 1978), the grunt ensemble film (Sidney Furie's *The Boys in Company C,* 1978), and the macho back-to-Nam fantasy (Michael Cimino's *The Deer Hunter,* 1978).

These were preceded by the publication of Michael Herr's *Dispatches,* a vivid work of gonzo journalism that established certain basic koans about Vietnam and the American relationship to its triply elusive antagonist, the Vietcong—"Under the ground was his, above it was ours . . . We had the days and [Charlie] had the nights."[7] *Dispatches* further paved the way for the psychedelic spectacle of Francis Coppola's *Apocalypse Now* (1979) that, in its brazen megalomania and dazzling concern for the power of special effects, may be truer to the sense of the original Vietnam War than any remake yet produced—up to its confused, anticlimactic ending, not to mention the destructive effect it had on Coppola's subsequent career (which most recently included a hack, maudlin tribute to Viet era heroism).

For all this, however, the war remained as dark and primal as a murder witnessed by a two-year-old. For Herr, "Night was the war's truest medium; night was when it got really interesting in the villages, the TV crews couldn't film at night."[8] Our popular culture hadn't evolved language to describe it, beyond the grandiose failure of *Apocalypse Now*'s final movement. As mad Dennis Hopper said of crazy Marlon Brando when he met a dogged Martin Sheen at the heart of darkness: "I wish I had words." Despite the success of *The Deer Hunter* and *Apocalypse Now,* their unresolved ambiguities proved far less attractive than the clearcut fantasies generated by something like *Good Guys Wear Black* (1979), an early Chuck Norris vehicle in which the ex-karate champ searches for the Washington politicos who betrayed him and his commando unit, or *First Blood* and *Uncommon Valor,* two early eighties sleepers both directed by Ted Kotcheff.

Released almost simultaneously with the dedication of the Vietnam Veteran's Monument in Washington, *First Blood* proved the surprise hit of late 1982—as well as Sylvester Stallone's first commercial hit outside the Rocky cycle. A property that spent a decade on Warner's shelf, *First Blood* turned the assumptions of the returning vet films inside out. This incendiary plea for tolerance, designed to appeal to both hawks and doves, introduced John Rambo—a taciturn, hippified ex-Green Beret driven to acts of insane violence by the relentless persecution of a redneck sheriff.

In effect, Rambo brought the war home and cast himself as

Sylvester Stallone as Rambo in *First Blood, Part II,* 1985. Courtesy Photofest.

a victimized, victorious guerrilla fighter. In the novel from which the film is adapted, Rambo is clearly a Frankenstein monster. He kills the entire posse that chases him up into the hills, returns to burn down Main Street, and is finally terminated by the very Green Beret officer who trained him. The movie Rambo, who anticipates Bruce Springsteen in his ambiguous mixture of left- and right-wing symbols, is more like a reverse neutron bomb—destroying property rather than lives. Although Rambo never succeeds in wrestling the Phallus from the possession of the sheriff, when he's hauled off to prison, it's clearly for our sins.

Rambo's equally haunted if less neurotic and more securely masculine equivalent was Tom Magnum, the hero of CBS's long-running *Magnum, P.I.* The show is set in Hawaii but Vietnam is continually manifest in its characters and situations, not to mention the hero's frequent flashbacks to his commando experiences — often accompanied by soulful sixties pop songs or moody riffs for electric guitar. (Clearly, Magnum was a man who had once smoked pot and brooded over Eric Clapton.) An eruption of orange and green, the war is represented as a mad succession of meaningless missions or chaotic combat. But for all its incomprehensibility, it is clearly a male testing ground. Son and grandson of American war heroes (his father was killed at Inchon), the Magnum Man exudes a tough melancholy that substituted Vietnam for some prehistoric unhappy love affair in his private-eye mystique. (*Simon and Simon* is another hit detective show, born during the 1982-83 season, that proposed to bind America's wounds by splitting Rambo in two. The protagonists are a brother team, one a Viet vet, the other a college-educated peacenik.)

By the early eighties, the idea that Rambo — if not all those who fought in Vietnam — had been betrayed at home, then "spat upon" when they returned, became an article of faith. This ingratitude lent piquance to the fantasy of an American victory in Vietnam and an aspect of implied revenge to the imaginative appropriation of the Vietcong's guerrilla tactics. In 1983, this scenario was canonized with the unexpected success of *Uncommon Valor,* co-produced by John Milius, in which a retired officer trains guerrillas to spring his son and other MIAs held captive in a Laotian prison camp.

Uncommon Valor basically appropriated the premise of *The Losers* (1970), in which a group of bikers returned to Nam on their motorcycles to rescue a captured presidential adviser from a Chinese prison camp. (Anticipating the self-pity endemic to early eighties Nam films, the surviving gang members have to hear themselves denounced as "trash" for their troubles.) But, with its emphasis on patriarchal authority, mutilated genealogy, and male rites of passage, *Uncommon Valor* took the lead in visualizing Indochina as the site of America's symbolic castration. Unlike *Apocalypse Now* or even *The Deer Hunter* (in which De Niro's possession of the Phallus seems tentative and depressed), it offered itself as a clear-cut exorcism of the shame and dishonor of American defeat.

Milius's 1984 *Red Dawn* provided a guilt-free version of *First Blood* that managed to refight the war in Colorado—identifying his youthful protagonists with the VC while projecting America's wartime activities onto the Soviet and Cuban invaders. In the wake of *Uncommon Valor* (and the euphoria produced by Grenada, surely the most successful American war movie since *Bridge on the River Kwai*), subsequent Vietnam exorcisms grew increasingly fantastic and compensatory. Films like *Missing in Action* (1984), *Rambo* (1985), and the futuristic *Top Gun* (1986) changed the emphasis from teamwork to the glorification of a supermasculine principle.

In recuperating the war, these movies finally (after twenty years) recapitulated something of its initial appeal. The American policy makers of the early sixties were obsessed with the issue of American military potency. The nuclear stalemate between the United States and the Soviet Union only intensified their frustration—you can see this again in *Top Gun,* which is like a celebration of *ejaculatio retardata.* Once upon a time, back in the bold, Kennedy-inflected sixties, war was an invitation to manliness . . .

Now, given the shame inherent in missing a war and thus foregoing the opportunity to demonstrate one's manhood, it seems appropriate that the movies most expressive of America's humiliation would have been produced by John Milius and Sylvester Stallone, both of whom avoided service during the Vietnam War. (*Top Gun's* co-producer, Don Simpson, actually bragged to one interviewer that he deliberately wrecked his motorcycle to beat the draft.) No less than the war itself, the fantasies of *Red Dawn* and *Rambo* reflected a nostalgia for what Philip Caputo, in *A Rumor of War,* yearns for as "that savage, heroic time . . . before America became a land of salesmen and shopping centers."[9]

As Elaine Scarry has noted in her essay, "Injury and the Structure of War," it's scarcely uncommon for an army to be envisioned as a single gigantic individual, often named for the commanding officer, with an Achilles heel or an underbelly or a rear that may be penetrated. For the American ground forces in Vietnam, that individual only appeared some years after the war was over. This colossus is Rambo—a thing built to absorb punishment, whose illusion of mastery complements Ronald Reagan's mastery of illusion.

Rambo is a superb icon: a hippie he-man (he manages to keep his talismanic long hair even in prison), a patriotic loner. Once in the Nam, he strips down to his trademark tank top and sweatband—he's a high-tech primitive incinerating battalions of gooks with his special TNT-tipped arrows. You might reasonably assume that Rambo is the American descendant of a nineteenth-century French poet, back for another Season in Hell. As it turns out, he's of "Indian-German" descent, a sort of Apache *Übermensch* or a Prussian noble savage, the ultimate Karl May fantasy. But mainly, Rambo is a torso: absurdly muscular, perpetually taut, a sort of Nautilus-built hard-on. One critic wrote that "Stallone is so pumped up his veins have erections." Rambo is so phallic, he really should be called Dildo.

If you've seen the movie, you know that the love object is killed in Rambo's arms seconds after he clasps her to his pecs, thus the VC saves him from even a moment's relaxation. Rambo, as Klaus Theweleit wrote of the Freikorps, is one of those "men [who] look for ecstasy not in embraces, but in explosions,"[10] the great balls of fire that the guys in *Top Gun* are always singing about. Rambo can never be satisfied, he can never detumesce, he presents himself as the embodiment of unrequited patriotic love:

with him, that unwinnable war had at last (and at least) been successfully repackaged.

Magnum and Rambo (we might call him Cro Magnum) redeemed the American fighting man, thus making the world safe for their lesser buddies. With *Platoon* (1986), *Gardens of Stone* (1987), *Full Metal Jacket* (1987), *Hamburger Hill* (1987), *Good Morning Vietnam* (1987), the documentary *Dear America* (1987), and the television series *Tour of Duty* (shot, like *Magnum, P.I.,* in Hawaii), the Vietnam exorcism has taken a turn for the "naturalistic," focusing on the actual experience of ordinary combatants. Not surprisingly, a number of these movies are statements by Viet vets who have been trying, in some cases for years, to get their experience of the war on the screen.

The emphasis having shifted from the humiliation of the elite POWs, mainly air force bomber pilots, and the fantasy exploits of their supermasculine rescuers, to the less glamorous suffering of the teenage recruits who were most often sent into combat, the new Vietnam films are less virulently right-wing than their immediate predecessors and more attuned to the specific nature of the war. (As Herr observed, "Flying over the jungle was almost pure pleasure, doing it on foot was nearly all pain.")[11]

Now on the American side, Vietnam was a war fought mainly by working-class teenagers—half of them black or Hispanic. Their average age was nineteen (as opposed to twenty-six in World War II). These kids knew that most of their peers were beating the draft, that the better educated enlistees were enjoying American-style amenities. In short, they understood that they were suckers, and they were resentful. Consequently, they developed their own anti-authoritarian subculture: more than any previous American army, they were prone to go native, take scalps, wear earrings, shoot drugs, scrawl weird slogans on their helmets.

The grunt ensemble films acknowledge that the war's human cost was born largely by the disadvantaged. Still, they do so only obliquely: poor blacks are prominent, but the protagonists of these movies are middle-class whites. There has been as yet no Vietnam film made from a black point of view although, overrepresented as they were in the worst assignments, black grunts were far more politically radical and disaffected than were whites. *Hamburger Hill* allows a taste of black rage, albeit focusing on micro-incidents of racial tension rather than addressing the essential racist component of the war.

Instead, war is shown as terrifyingly existential: a sense of abandonment amid meaningless conflict is as central to the grunt ensemble films as it is to the MIA rescue films, but here it is less tragic than pathetic or, in the case of *Full Metal Jacket,* ironic. *Gardens of Stone* is the lone current example to even bother with traditional forms of patriotic sentiment. Like, it wasn't them who started "that crazy Asian war." Bereft of even the most minimal ideological support, the teenage warriors nevertheless perform their "patriotic chore." As befits a TV show, *Tour of Duty* is the most didactic when it comes to this: the last episode I saw had a peacenik learn to kill, a Puerto Rican win the respect of his black comrades, a middle-class lieutenant come to appreciate his tough sergeant. But the acme of excruciatingly pointless heroism is *Hamburger Hill,* where the central battle for control of a slope in the Ashau valley has no intrinsic meaning, strategic or otherwise. With the collapse of the greater values, the minor ones are drafted into service. The film escapes the bleakest sort of absurdism only by making it seem a virtue to be cannon fodder—a tragic and noble fate.

Given the close identification between Rambo and Ronbo, one suspected that when *Platoon* swept the 1987 Oscars, six months after the Iran-contragate revelations, the Reagan revolution was receding from its high water mark. But even as *Platoon* provided a gutsy correlative to the fantasies of bellicose noncombatants

Milius and Stallone, it initiated another round of mythologizing. Drenched in sixties rock and a perverse Viet nostalgia (one's youth is still one's youth, whether spent in Kansas or Khe Sanh), grunt ensemble films shy away from any sense of the war's moral basis or its political significance. In this, they may reflect the conflict of Vietnam veterans who want to forget the horrors of war but recognize that the experience was the high point of their lives.

Historical context is secondary to the re-creation of the period—and, by extension, American innocence. Hence the stunning popularity of *Good Morning, Vietnam* in which Robin Williams appears as an irreverent Saigon-based disc jockey. Aside from playing the man who brought rock 'n' roll to Vietnam—thus making possible Vietnam movies—Williams's major accomplishment is his attitude. He reads classified news items or rags on LBJ's family on the air, insults uptight officers and teaches Vietnamese students to talk street jive. Williams's hipness distances him from the war. Like the protagonists of *Platoon* and *Full Metal Jacket,* his cynicism is a form of militant naiveté, if not denial. Moreover, despite his insolence, he's protected by a friendly general who recognizes his value for morale. Thus, *Good Morning, Vietnam* doesn't satirize the war so much as celebrate the illusion—and the impotence—of "telling it like it is."

The first Vietnam films had two themes: the vet's return home and the vet's return to Vietnam, embodying a restless movement back and forth in some fruitless search for closure. The more naturalistic grunt ensembles plunge headlong into the war's center, an attempt to ward off inevitable defeat. The machine is still engorged: it's Good Morning, Vietnam rather than Good Night World.

This is why virtually all Vietnam combat films are set during the present tense of Johnson's war—that is, at the peak of American involvement, before Nixon's troop withdrawals de-

Poster for *Full Metal Jacket*, 1987. Courtesy Photofest.

stroyed what was left of army morale, the exposure of the My Lai massacre eroded America's moral position, before the invasion of Cambodia made a mockery of Nixon's promise not to widen the war, before new recruits had experienced the antiwar movement and the counterculture, black power, and urban riots. The post-1969 recruits were less docile and, as the troop withdrawals signaled the retreat from military victory, the army was plagued by escalating disorders that raised questions as to the ability of the U.S. armed forces to continue to function at all.

The grunt ensemble films strongly suggest the dreams that Freud attributed to traumatic neuroses, "repeatedly bringing the patient back into the situation of his accident." (In fact, there was an article in *Newsday* about the value of *Platoon* as therapy.)[12] This repetition, according to Freud, is an attempt at mastery: overpowered by the initial experience, the subject actively repeats it, as children might as play. But, a neurotic in the grip of a repetition compulsion is "obliged to repeat the repressed material as a contemporary experience instead of . . . remembering it as something belonging to the past."[13]

Defusing blame is a key aspect of the new Vietnam film. Although the war is named for a foreign country, it must always be shown as an American struggle. It can never be acknowledged that in waging this war, the U.S. orchestrated the most massive display of firepower in human history. As in the original movie, the stars of every Vietnam film are entirely American. *Hamburger Hill* and *Good Morning, Vietnam* might be considered mildly revisionist for the cameos they award the locals but, a bit of hand-to-hand combat and a few flashes of North Vietnamese artillery aside, the indigenous population is almost entirely female and thus designed for subjugation. The enemy is only perfunctorily the VC: *Platoon* refights the American Civil War with blacks and northern white dopers pitted against Southern juiceheads; in *Full Metal Jacket,* women are the enemy; in *Hamburger Hill,* it's the media.

Bill Coutrie's *Dear America,* produced for Home Box Office, is the documentary corollary to *Platoon* and *Hamburger Hill.* Sentimental and horrific, it juxtaposes actual GI letters to parents, wives, and girlfriends read by a small galaxy of Hollywood stars with candid footage, as well as the obligatory sixties rock track, to create a sort of transpersonal home movie. These letters are often expressions of pure terror and disorientation. But this powerful raw material makes the result doubly disturbing. The paradox is that Coutrie's documentary is the most heavily mythologizing grunt ensemble film yet. Not only are the musical juxtapositions stupefyingly literal-minded ("I'm 18" for boot camp, "Gimme Shelter" during an air assault, "A Hard Rain's A Gonna Fall" used to accompany a monsoon), but the filmmakers conveniently forget that war is war and one doesn't necessarily tell Mom all.

Although insistent on its authenticity, *Dear America* is Vietnam without racism, drugs, fraggings, atrocities, sex weirdness, or any of the perks of an occupying army. Historical context dissolves in subjectivity, the war emerging as a no-fault collision whose victims are entirely American. *The Deer Hunter* has been replaced by Dear Hunter.

In their retreat from the realm of the sociohistorical, recent Vietnam films stress the subjective experience of the individual combatant—thus, the importance of voice-over letters in *Platoon, Gardens of Stone,* and *Dear America,* the frenzied flashbacks of *Magnum, P.I.,* the immersion in sixties pop music. The war becomes a personal affair or a generational coming of age. Grunt ensemble films honor the Viet vet by extolling his situational loyalty to his buddies. Although in this, they are true to the experience of a war where the continual rotation of ground troops discouraged cohesion and a soldier's overriding concern was to survive his twelve-month tour of duty and get out, these movies can never address the ideological conditioning that suckered

Americans into Vietnam to begin with.

Imperial America is now in syndication: it's a perpetual re-run. As the TV ads for the video release of *Platoon* told us: "It's not too late to do something about Vietnam. See *Platoon* and understand." The World War II combat film had addressed the question *Why We Fight?* It explained who our adversaries were, located the war in our national history, and directed us towards our individual responsibilities. It provided instruction in what it meant to be an American while reassuring us that, whatever the provocations of the enemy and horrors of war, we were still nice guys and square-shooters who played by the rules.[14] Vietnam films could do none of this. Nor can they. *The Green Berets* aside, there were no such movies produced during the course of the Vietnam War. Instead, *The Dirty Dozen* (from the right) and *How I Won the War* (from the left), both 1967, initiated a cycle of cynical war stories that had nothing to do with patriotism, democracy, or fair play. If anything, these issues were displaced onto the dying form of the western. *The Wild Bunch* (1969), *Soldier Blue* (1970), *Little Big Man* (1970), and *High Plains Drifter* (1973) had more to do with Vietnam than any war film.

This quintessential American genre was typically the way that, however honestly or meretriciously, America used to explain itself to itself. Who makes the law? What is the order? As American soldiers played "cowboys" in Vietnam, it is significant that the antiwar counterculture identified itself with the Indians, adopting beads and headbands, tribal lifestyles, peyote, eco-politics, a return to the land. This split in historical consensus made the western obsolete. The genre, which enjoyed its Golden Age during the quarter-century Pax Americana that followed World War II, grew increasingly apocalyptic throughout the Vietnam War, with the ultimate desecration of *Blazing Saddles* (1974) capping the assorted anti-, post, spaghetti, revisionist, psychedelic, and burlesque westerns of the early seventies.

The decline and eclipse of the western effectively redefined the screen image of the masculine hero. When Dustin Hoffman finally made a western, he played an Indian; the seventies saw a whole generation of stars who never donned stetsons (Robert De Niro, Sylvester Stallone, Al Pacino, Richard Dreyfuss). The mythology had been discredited. No wonder *Top Gun's* press book was emblazoned with a quote to the effect that "there are only four occupations worthy of a man: actor, rock star, jet fighter pilot or President of the United States." The difficulty inherent in constructing a winner out of a loser is at least a partial factor in the abject failure of Senator Albert Gore, the first Vietnam veteran to run for president. He really should have spent less time listening to Martin Peretz and more time watching *Magnum, P.I.*

Vietnam offered no great battles and no clearly defined enemy. Its casualties included our longstanding sense of national innocence and masculine identity, not to mention the broad national consensus that had defined American foreign policy since World War II. This has made the war particularly difficult to represent: inherently polarizing and depressing, with a built-in unhappy ending, it both broke the conventions of civilized warfare and the basic rules of Hollywood entertainment. It was the last picture show.

The impossible longing for a satisfactory conclusion tempts each Viet film to sell itself as definitive. It is precisely that bummer of a finale—more the film just running out of the projector, than the roof caving in—that has left us with a compulsion to remake, if not history, then at least the movie.

Notes

1. Gabriel Kolko, *Anatomy of a War: Vietnam, the United States, and the Modern Historical Experience* (New York: Pantheon Books, 1985), p. 176.
2. Ibid., p. 201.
3. Hannah Arendt, "Home to Roost: A Bicentennial Address," *New York Review of Books,* June 26, 1975, p. 4.

4. Michael Herr, *Dispatches* (New York: Avon Books, 1978), pp. 61 and 209.

5. Ibid., pp. 188-189.

6. Elaine Scarry, "Injury and the Structure of War," *Representations,* no. 10 (Spring 1985): 1-51.

7. Herr, *Dispatches,* p. 14.

8. Ibid., p. 41.

9. Philip Caputo, *A Rumor of War* (New York: Holt, Rinehart and Winston, 1977), p. 5.

10. Klaus Theweleit, *Male Fantasies,* Vol. 1: *Women, Floods, Bodies, History,* trans. Stephen Conway (Minneapolis: University of Minnesota Press, 1987), p. 41.

11. Herr, *Dispatches,* p. 10.

12. *New York Newsday,* May 10, 1988.

13. Sigmund Freud, *Beyond the Pleasure Principle* (New York: W. W. Norton, 1961), p. 12.

14. See Jeanine Basinger's comprehensive *The World War II Combat Film: Anatomy of a Genre* (New York: Columbia University Press, 1986), p. 79.

Carol Squiers

AT THEIR MERCY:

A READING OF PICTURES

FROM 1988

An instantly consumable and hyperbolically inflated type of history is produced each and every day by the American news media. Writ in mass-culture platitudes, shorthand redundancies, and bureaucratic jargon, journalists strive to make simple that which is complex and to provide a behind-the-scenes look at power without ever revealing the true underpinnings, suppositions, and beneficiaries of the system that they labor to explain and maintain: who wins and who loses and why the losers are never going to win; who controls what; who the owners of the system are and what that means; how money can indeed buy you a kind of love; and how honest labor and the sweat of your brow will in many cases earn you a progressively lower standard of living and an uncertain future for whatever children you are optimistic enough to bring into a democracy in which most people are created unequal.

An important part of the newsmaking process is the visual image. It takes a variety of ever-more pervasive forms, from the video footage of the world's killing fields unreeled nightly on the national news to the still images reproduced in newspapers and magazines to Hollywood's factoid-based dramas, which are predicated on "real life" events. Each visual mode has its own rules and uses in the greater scheme of the maintenance of American democratic capitalism and the concurrent achievement of maximum corporate profit, with a middling consideration given to actually providing information or insight to the general public.

Within this system, the news photograph has an almost wholly symbolic function. Most often a single picture will be used to "tell" an entire story, both illustrating and supplementing a journalist's words. Take a situation in which the Israeli military blows up a Palestinian's house on the West Bank in revenge for an alleged act of violence. It is a picture of the moment the house explodes that is printed in the newspaper—not the moment the soldiers arrive at the house and begin laying the explosives, or the look on a woman's face when she is given twenty minutes or one hour to clear out of her home before it is totally destroyed. Such a profound injustice will almost always be inadequately portrayed in a single photograph. What is recorded instead is the instant of greatest action and high drama. And that instant collapses any notion of injustice, brute force, and human violation into an image that replays repeatedly the idea that the Middle East is somehow mysteriously and willfully violent, that nothing can be done about the violence, that the Palestinians bring it on themselves. In addition to the political complexities and human tragedy that are effaced is the fact that violence is constituted as so essentially exciting: the violence *makes a better picture* than any other visual aspect of the situation.

Whether they are shooting politicians in Washington or poverty in Bangladesh, all good news photographers know what their wire service or news magazine or newspaper wants. Their job is to deliver "fresh" images of subjects within a range of acceptable stereotypes. Anything less than this is to risk seeming uninformed and even unintelligent. Anything more is to be labeled too "political" and therefore unobjective. The following commentaries strive to untangle the ideology of news and its representations, showing how news imagery illustrates the cultural suppositions that construct the news.

I

During the second half of 1988, the American public was subjected to a thoroughly dreadful and some might even say *heinous*
presidential campaign. Rather than trying to forget that it ever
happened, however, we should take time to meditate on the system of party politics—and political representation—that
brought us this miserable travesty.

One of the most obvious points that springs to mind about
said party system is how the spectrum of the politically permis-
sible in this country runs the gamut only from A to B. Despite
this disheartening fact, there is indeed a difference between the
Democratic and Republican parties, as evidenced by pictorial
analysis of large groups of people from both parties attending
their respective national conventions. Thus, even acknowledging
all the prevarication, hypocrisy, evasiveness, quibbling, fibbing,
faking, dissembling, and perversion we have been subjected to,
we might still be able to discern why we should continue to involve ourselves in a process presided over by a bunch of humor-
less, immoral numbskulls. Consider the following photographs,
taken while the author was documenting the way the news media covered the presidential campaign. Although they are simulations of political photography (the author is not a photo-
journalist), they do cover the general range of typical sights photographed at conventions—and in the process, point up visible
philosophical differences between Democrats and Republicans.

People in Funny Hats. A staple of political conventions and the
photographer's best friend, few people in funny hats can escape
looking like born fools. Some, however, such as this Jesse Jackson delegate, can convey a message of progress and optimism
with their decorative headgear. Having experienced a lifetime of
our government at work, however, this delegate also wears an
expression indicating an underlying skepticism that this political

process is ever going to do jack zip for her.

Other hats, such as the one worn by this Pat Robertson supporter, remind you that Diane Arbus didn't invent the people she photographed. She simply waited for them to tear the rims off their Styrofoam campaign hats, smash an old army helmet over them, grab an American flag, and goosestep in her direction.

Young People. What does it take to get a young Republican to turn himself into a one-person billboard for death and destruction? Not much, judging from the spooky self-desecration happily exhibited by this youthful enthusiast. Notice too the conflict

he shows about his appearance. Is it modesty and the desire *not* to be recognized that inspires him to wear his Ray Bans, along with his "SDI" stickers, at eleven o'clock at night?

In contrast, witness the young man wearing the Dukakis feed-'n'-seed cap and festooned with traditional political buttons—none of them on his face. Clean-cut, well-behaved, psychologically stable, and probably working for nothing at the Democratic convention, he's the type of youngster the Republicans pretend is *just like one of their children.*

Politicians Who Are Not Running for the Presidency. New York's Democratic governor Mario Cuomo has lots of negatives, including not being the kind of leader that the people who voted for him wanted, and not running for the presidency in 1988. Nevertheless, he still has plenty of admirable attributes. The most obvious—a cuddly, pliable face capable of squeezing itself into some of the most ironic expressions ever sported by a politician. Here he is doing his turn on the perennial disbelief all elected officials seem to feel about the things people say to them.

On the Republican side, however, we have the likes of Utah senator Orrin Hatch, the man who went high profile during the Iran-contra hearings by congratulating Oliver North for his criminal behavior, and who has called the Democrats "the party of homosexuals." The strange deathmask-like illusionism in this picture, which makes it look as if the senator's face is detached from his body, is actually a quite realistic depiction of a man whose usual demeanor suggests that he probably gets his skin screwed on.

Signs Bearing Political Sentiments. CBS's Lesley Stahl looked none too happy about being photographed holding the *No Contra Aid* sign that her cameraman used for some kind of test, the myth of objectivity still being the general masquerade amongst many journalists. Stahl's predicament aside, it shows the kind of stuff you could readily lay your hands on at the Democratic convention: signs that spelled out concern for issues such as AIDS (*Silence = Death* buttons were highly visible), the environment, and equal rights, many of them problems that a majority of Americans in both parties are vitally concerned about, even though their government has ignored or otherwise purposefully defeated them for many long years.

At the Republican convention, signs were either of the happy-faced Hallmark variety—*Welcome Dan!* and *Ohio Loves Bush!*—or the deeply disturbed. At the river's edge rally where George Bush sprang Dan Quayle on an expectant world, nutso conservatism manifested itself in anticommie sentiments and the

pummeling of AIDS protestors. Of course, the signs were home-spun. Utilizing squadrons of young Republicans armed with magic markers and a decided lack of design ability, thousands of hand-lettered signs were turned out for use at the convention, giving the entire corporate fiesta that homey, hand-made look.

Prayer. There was entirely too much praying at both conventions. Invocations, benedictions, Billy Graham—heads bent in prayer during events that are essentially television commercials are a revolting sight to witness. Once again, though, there was an essential difference between the two parties. Democrats assumed a variety of pious attitudes, from unctuous devotion to barely faking it. Republicans, however (although they probably span the same spectrum in terms of real attitude), treated prayer as a form of revenge. Our father—*we'll get every last one*—who art in heaven—*of you dirty, card-carrying*—hallowed be thy name—*liberals.* Luckily, despite the impediment of prayer, ABC's Sam Donaldson always stayed on top of his job, although when the Republican supplication was over he inadvertently brushed past the devout young blonde woman at right. When she saw who it was, she bared her teeth, glared, and heatedly wiped off her arm, belying the dog-eared platitude about prayer being a balm to the spirit.

Balloons. Like funny hats, balloons are a beloved and indispensable part of our political process. The release of red, white, and blue inflated orbs over a crowd during emotional convention finales is deemed the festive way to celebrate the candidate, the acceptance speech, and the end of four days of living hell. On the night Dukakis delivered his acceptance speech in Atlanta, the

tricolors were a nice finishing touch to an emotional evening that had been capped by the spectacle of every Democrat of any stature taking to the podium along with the beaming candidate. The balloons wafted down gently over the excited crowd, a bonus to a heartwarming event.

In contrast, by the final night of the Republican convention, the crowd worked itself into a frenzy of hysterical self-interest masquerading as morality. Prayer in the schools! The pledge to the flag! Eight more years of escalating profits! Suddenly huge cachés of killer balloons were released from the heights of the Superdome and somewhere in the range of two hundred thousand of them dumped on the crowd. These orbs didn't waft: they came down with a vengeance, pelting and bashing. Giddy, the Republicans cast off their Sunday school demeanor and jumped and stomped on their attackers. Lest any escape unbroken, they turned their little American flags upside down and, using the gold points at the ends, stabbed until all the balloons were destroyed. Haiti, one veteran campaign photographer said, standing back in disbelief. It's like Haiti during the elections.

II

These are the outlines and accessories of transgression: an empty chair, a paper cup, and a used condom discarded surreptitiously in shame and disgust on the carpet next to the chair. A hanky furtively swiped across the shriveled member. A jogging suit with easy frontal access. And a woman who was badly paid to perform a series of naughty poses and meager costumings. A woman with a memory that had recorded, in seemingly exacting detail, the verbal commands given and obediently obeyed, perhaps because they were so simple and pathetic. Down goes another televangelist, Jimmy Swaggart this time, a multimillion-dollar gilded goose slaughtered on the altar of voyeurism, masturbation, dirty words, and short-term motel rentals.

Oh sure, it's easy to say in hindsight that it all makes sense. These taunting, prancing preachers, these wailing maws of money lust—it stands to reason that they are hypocrites, scam-

mongers, and opportunists through and through. And so the longings of Swaggart, however sad and puny, were bound to make the news. The news in this case takes a particularly interesting route through varied venues. From the local media outlet that first "breaks" the story, it then progresses through the national network newscasts, daily newspapers, and national news magazines, and into the secondary purveyors such as news-oriented talk shows, late-night talk shows, lifestyle magazines, and sex rags. Round and round the news of Swaggart's misdemeanors goes, swelling with conjecture and ridicule and embellishment. Once hidden from all but a single observer's eyes, the small and shameful ejaculations in hastily arranged encounters are magnified into major events that audiences across the land could almost see. Events that they would lust to see, would pay to see. Events that they, predictably, can see, for the cost of the July 1988 issue of *Penthouse: The International Magazine for Men.*

In more ways than one, *Penthouse* is a public-service publication. Suspecting that its readers' minds might be less than razor sharp, *Penthouse* (like *Playboy*) helpfully characterizes each listing on its contents page. Some pieces are called "Comment," while others are "Article" or "Service." Most popular, probably, are those sections called "Pictorial." A pictorial is what "Debbie Does Swaggart" is, but what it was called by *Penthouse* was "Reportage," a term that usually means "the act or process of reporting the news."

Jimmy Swaggart getting "done" was certainly news. A rival televangelist's son snapped pictures of Swaggart outside a motel with a prostitute, evidence that placed him in a compromising position. Unfortunately, no original photographs that we know of were taken of the encounters between Swaggart and Debra Murphree, a self-admitted worker in the sex industry—not a church secretary claiming wanton violation or an aspiring model/actress who likes to party with the powerful and randy, but a woman who makes her living servicing the unmet needs of men you wouldn't usually hear about.

But in this richly fictionalized era, just as documentary proof of presidential lies is totally ignored, so can documentary proof of just about anything be materialized from thin air. A reportage can be created in both words and pictures. So Debra Murphree re-posed and re-cited for two *Penthouse* writers and a photographer the things that Swaggart had her do that brought him down. Presented as a two-part package, an article included a detailed narrative of Swaggart's "secret sex life" as described by Debra Murphree, while a series of black and white photographs, isolated in a sealed section of the magazine that had to be cut open after purchase, provided the reenactment of the sordid scenes.

But what kind of pictures are these—as either "reportage" or pornography? Shot in square format, they are printed full-frame with black borders in the self-conscious art photo style that was popular in the 1970s. Oddly, there is no photographer's credit given, leading one to suspect that someone intimately familiar with both this artful style and this kind of cheeky trespass has taken these snaps.[1] Odder still, they are ironic and untitillating, like medical photos or pictures from a women's self-examination manual. Murphree faces the camera and pantomimes her dirty deeds with a knowing, bemused expression. Or she lies back and demonstrates, with clinical precision, the moves and positions that Swaggart wanted to see. Rather than being exploited by the anonymous shooter, Murphree is in cahoots with him, giving a deadpan, tongue-in-cheek performance that is cool and unseductive.

Penthouse's reasons for producing this parodic piece are perplexing but hardly indecipherable. The magazine's editors must have realized that Murphree doing *Penthouse* was not going to be convincing in the cheesecake marketplace. A plain woman, she lacked both the trashy stylization and pendulous physical endowments of a Jessica Hahn or Donna Rice and would thus have limited charm for a jack-off clientele. Still, because she was an upfront sex worker and not a supposed innocent trying to recover her self-respect through extortion, Murphree would feel freer to enact for the camera what had transpired in private. She didn't need to be portrayed, as Hahn was, musing soulfully—and toplessly—in healing waters and open fields. She issues no disclaimers, although she clearly judges most of Swaggart's desires as sick, thus separating his twisted needs from her own more pragmatic motives. Unlike the typical pictorials, where *Penthouse* supplies brief, suggestive captions, the editors here could flesh out the entire sordid scenario: Murphree's words printed beneath became the dirty images that defined the otherwise schematic visuals.

What could *Penthouse's* readers gain from seeing this "reportage"? We are positioned as viewers, as surrogates for Swaggart. We look across a car seat at this woman, with her blouse unbuttoned and her shorts pulled down in order to display and rub herself. We take his position on a bed as she stands over him and we peer up her skirt. We watch her pull her panties up her "crack" and kneel, "doggie-like," on a bed. The chill, anti-erotic staging of all these pictures, coupled with Murphree's almost condescending "memoirs," tells us that this is the performance of a woman who has contempt for her spectator's incapacity to join in the performance. And this message makes us question Swaggart's sexuality even more strongly than we mock his hypocrisy.

This might just be the rationale behind the pictures. For consider this man's television performance before his fall. Striding back and forth and back and forth across his stage, he was like an animal in heat. Strutting and shouting, he appeared in cheap-looking suits that weren't necessarily cheap (this man had money but he had to appeal to his mainly lower-middle-class constituents), with their fabric often drawn taut across his thighs and his crotch. A pimp for Jesus. A cock of the walk. A cock that walks and throbs and thrusts itself, again and again, across the stage. It shouts and moans and yells its incantations of sin and lust and god and hell, its moving, brutal mouth pulled wide open and snapping shut, again and again. But words are secondary here. What mesmerizes and what really counts is this motion, this ramming plunging power. More than the logic of the words, this motion is convincing—so powerful, so demanding, so essential.

A man of insatiable desires could have been imagined, a man of many lusts. Yet the "truth" as it's staged and framed in *Penthouse* presents us with a lust so diminished, so stunted, so repulsive. More than bringing Swaggart down as a holy roller of a preacher, these pictures bring him down as a sexual performer. "I don't think evangelists mean to be sex symbols," says University of Alabama historian David E. Harrell, Jr., in *Newsweek* magazine, "but they are frequently handsome and highly masculine in behavior. The audience response is not unlike bobby-soxers swooning." Among those who most demanded and elicited that sublimated swooning was the unfortunate Mr. Swaggart. But the boys at *Penthouse* figured how to stop the swoon and chasten that high-stepping cock. Mere scandal in the pulpit is now old hat. The stakes are higher, and the market demands a more profound, more permanent psychic disgrace.

III

From all of the newspaper images of the months-long Palestinian uprising in the Israeli-occupied Gaza Strip and West Bank, one stands out. This small photograph, printed on page 8 of the *New York Times* for April 9, is captioned "A house in the Palestinian village of Beita, in the occupied West Bank, being blown up by Israeli troops." It is a simple and somewhat abstract picture, because the photographer's view is so close to the exploding

Beita, West Bank, April 8, 1988. Photo: Reuters/Bettmann News.

house—either physically close or brought close by the use of a powerful lens—that little besides the explosion, the smoke, and the blasted clouds of debris is visible in the image. Underneath the picture and caption is a headline: "Army Says Israeli Girl Was Killed by Her Guard." And under that, in boldfaced type, a single sentence stands alone: "The guard had shot at Arabs before."

This refers, of course, to a much-publicized incident in which a teenage Israeli girl was reported, with great hysteria and horror, to have been "stoned to death" by Palestinian villagers. Immediately after the first reports of the rock-throwing melee that led to her death, Israel's justice minister called for the demolition of numerous Arab homes and the expulsion of hundreds of Palestinians.

Two days after the incident, and before some of the punishments could transpire, the Israeli army issued a statement that the girl had in fact been killed not by Palestinians but by her Israeli guard. Yet the army subsequently dynamited eight houses belonging to families of Palestinians accused of taking part in the rock-throwing, despite its own report that the rocks did not directly cause her death. What is so distressing about the picture, then, is its evidence of retribution against a family of a nameless accused at least partially vindicated by Israeli officials who nevertheless continued to carry out a punishment decreed in the heat of hatred and rage.

Yet it is just a small photograph that offers this evidence, in conjunction with the news story that accompanies it. In some ways the picture seems even insignificant—it is far less dramatic, for example, than the images of dead children, angry soldiers, or weeping women that have also been printed. But the situation of these people, with their grievous problems and appalling solutions, is essentially alien to us, even while we sympathize with them or damn them, and even while pictures of them evoke our emotions. What is not alien to us is the idea of due process—of arrest, charges brought, judgment passed, punishment decided. And what we see in the picture is the collapse of all those processes into one immediate, and apparently acceptable, spasm of revenge.

Under what circumstances would a similar punishment be acceptable on American soil? What black activist arrested during a violent street confrontation would expect the U.S. Army to arrive at his home, evacuate him and his family—parents, wife, children, whatever kin lived there—and blast the house to ruins? What antinuclear demonstrators, after crawling through a fence and damaging a nuclear warhead, would expect, in addition to arrest, the destruction of their homes? It seems unthinkable, yet in 1985 there was an officially sanctioned bombing of an American dwelling. The Philadelphia house of a group of black Americans who belonged to an organization called MOVE was bombed by the city police department, in a disastrous maneuver that resulted in the destruction of sixty other homes. MOVE, a radical fringe organization, was unacceptably troublesome to its neighbors and local authorities, and its intractability gave Philadelphia officials an excuse to use extraordinary force against it.

Usually, such force can only be gotten away with when it is applied to people considered too far outside the realm of human society to be rendered even the most basic of rights. What has happened with the Palestinians in the current insurgency is that their disruptive, violent, and essentially nonlethal behavior (at least in the events in question) has convinced the world community to allow them entree to the human society from which they had thus far been excluded because of their prior abstraction into "terrorists." The opposition of their teenagers' stones to Israeli guns and armored cars has proved much harder to label and categorize than the PLO's bombs and assassinations, and has provoked a kind of sympathetic identification. The images of their dead children, angry women, and ruined homes have conveyed a tragic message that had never before reached the majority of the American population with such force.

Out of all the terrible images pouring out of the occupied territories, that picture of the exploding house, and the news that the excuse for its destruction was no longer even valid, sums up the frightening force that has been mobilized against Palestinian demands. It also asks each viewer to consider where the use of unbridled force against an entire people will lead.

IV

As the 1980s draws to a close, the image of women in the mass media is still taking a beating. In part, this is the result of a well-orchestrated right-wing campaign against independent women. Spearheaded by the attack on abortion rights, most so-called feminist issues have been steadily torpedoed during the Reagan era. Overall, women made no economic gains, except for that minority of genteel women—mainly Anglo-Saxon Protestant— who were enlisted by Wall Street during its "bull" market,

Jean Harris at Westchester County Jail, 1981. Photo: AP/Wide World.

Hedda Nussbaum testifying at Joel Steinberg trial, 1988. Photo: AP/Wide World.

which only widened economic disparities. But it will not be an image of the successful, economically upwardly mobile woman who will stand for the eighties. Rather, it will be the image of a beaten, genteel woman—Hedda Nussbaum—who apparently will represent the feminine status quo.

This is only fitting. The eighties began with the image of another abused (emotionally rather than physically) genteel woman—Jean Harris, who did away with randy diet doctor Herman Tarnower. In concert with the decade-long campaign against women, New York governor Mario Cuomo has decided that Harris, despite good arguments to the contrary, must continue her penal servitude.

Cuomo's denial of clemency for Harris occurred during the Christmas holiday season for 1988, a time that seemed to breed a great spasm of antiwoman activity. Releasing a sixty-six-year-old woman with advanced heart disease, who has already suffered two heart attacks in prison, would apparently send a dangerous signal. Any other homicidal female might take up arms and slaughter an unfaithful or abusive husband or lover.

This trend, it seems, would interfere with a system that is firmly entrenched. In it, husbands and lovers feel relatively free to maul or kill their wives and girlfriends. During that last extraordinary week of 1988, New Yorkers were also confronted with images of two women gunned down by their estranged husbands. At the time of their deaths, both women were under "court protection" orders because of threats and physical abuse by their husbands. Yet the men were still on the streets despite their violation of those orders. According to local police, "hundreds" of violations of court orders occur and each violation can't be considered a "top priority."

So the representation of bloodied women remains a tolerable cultural norm, even though the image of women bloodying men is utterly taboo. And even though proof exists that this situation can be altered: the murder rate in Bergen County, New Jersey, dropped 44 percent in 1987, "five years after a comprehensive state law took effect *requiring* the police to arrest violators of protective orders" (emphasis added). Reluctantly, men round up their fellow men, and in so doing give up some measure of power over their own domestic situations.

In line with the presumption that the bloodlust of men is socially tolerable, the supposed bloodlust of women is played out nowhere more ferociously than in the abortion rights struggle. And the *New York Times* gave abortion foes a juicy present in a front-page, Christmas Day story on the sex testing of fetuses. "In a major change in medical attitudes and practice, many doctors are providing prenatal diagnoses to pregnant women who want to abort a fetus on the basis of sex alone," wrote Gina Kolata. "Even doctors who will not provide this service themselves will often tell women where to go to get it."

Telling women where to go seemed to be the point of the story, as it laid out a sordid tale purporting to expose the growing trend of *women* who decide to abort fetuses based on sexual preference. Patiently, Kolata built up evidence against the lying, calculating females who tricked doctors into giving them abortions for this reason. "We've been burned," one doctor bitterly intoned.

Unspoken in the *Times* piece, except where it related to "women from India and Asia," is that sexual preference usually means a preference for the male sex and a devaluation of the female. But neither the cultural forces that compel a woman to worry over the sex of her child or the father's role in sexual preference were even mentioned. Clearly, the American family is being destroyed by the country's women, painted as demented manipulators who con innocent doctors into performing medical procedures for their own diabolical end. Women, if the *Times* is to be believed, will stop at nothing in order to control the human race.

Control, submission, credibility, and victimization are issues played out repeatedly in the media, mainly to the detriment of women. Among the most recent have been the "preppy" murder victim Jennifer Levin and the brutalized Tawana Brawley, along with Hedda Nussbaum. And the reportage, day in and day out, poses a certain repetitious and insidious set of questions about each of them: whether she was asking for it, whether she allowed it, whether she is telling the truth, whether her death or violation or beating was in some sense deserved. By the way the questions are framed, the frequency with which they are asked, and the sheer reiteration of words and images, the answer seems to be affirmative: women are getting what they deserve.

In 1980, Jean Harris was represented as an outcast and an anomaly. It seemed certain that no woman could make common cause with her, driven as she was by frightening self-delusion and reprehensible class philosophy. But Hedda Nussbaum, conversely, is being touted as everywoman, as the victim potentially lurking within each woman alive, waiting to be abused. As we enter the Bush years and look toward the 1990s, the antiwoman rhetoric—and the ghastly actions and images that result—is being played out with macabre new twists and unabated ferocity. With every new day, that violation comes to seem more familiar, more common, more expected, more normal. Conditioned by the steady stream of sordid images, the injured and deformed face of a Hedda Nussbaum begins to look more essentially sympathetic than any smiling, self-confident woman could ever be.

Notes

1. In his "Real Life Rock Top 10" column of June 21, 1988, in the *Village Voice,* Greil Marcus mentioned that David Kennedy was the photographer.

Victoria de Grazia

THE ARTS OF PURCHASE:

HOW AMERICAN PUBLICITY SUBVERTED

THE EUROPEAN POSTER, 1920-1940

On a summer Sunday in 1931, a Fiat Spider 509 scrambled up a donkey path one thousand meters to a village in the Apennine Alps of Emilia. It was the first car ever seen there. Just arrived, the drivers, two debonair youths, hopped out and to the perplexity of the villagers pasted up a symbolist poster advertising Midas Motor Oil. This event equally perplexed the Italian advertising expert who reported on it. In a town so poor and out-of-the-way, there was simply no market for engine oil. The only machines in need of lubrication thereabouts were sewing machines; and gasoline and olive oil aplenty were available for that. If nothing else, our sophisticated urbaner concluded, this episode documented once more the futility of postering.[1]

For students of mass culture, the advertiser's dilemma—namely, whether or not the campaign paid off by boosting markets for car oil—is of slight interest. The episode is telling for other reasons. Not least of all, it presents in neat paradox how capitalist market relations separate exchange from use values. Here, no less, the machine had come to announce its own needs! The story acquires yet more significance when it is put in historical context. Students of market cultures have emphasized that exchange and consumption are embedded in complex cultural and social meanings; commodities come loaded with ways of thinking about human relations; and acts of purchase foster new individual and collective identities.[2] Accordingly, we might ask whether profit alone motivated this enterprise and whether the young men were not conscious of their own role as interpreters of culture; we might query how the villagers regarded it and what significance should be given to the motor oil's American origin. Indeed, the young men's bravado did not go unremarked at the time, as if, from the centers of consumer culture in the plains, they came as civilizing knights, bringing urbanity and modern ways to a rough rural backwater. Aside from causing a commotion that disrupted Sunday mass, their deed impressed the local priest and community leader that the donkey path could be made transitable. The roadbed was upgraded soon thereafter, and before long, this little Italian village, like many others, emptied out as emigrants made their way down to urban centers to find work and partake in the amenities of modern consumer mores.

This micro-event, interpreted both as a market ploy and for its social-cultural implications, is a fragment of an even more complex story. The variations thereon are practically innumerable and can be conjured up with any of the myriad images in which American cultural and consumer artifacts set jarringly amidst the semi-rural environs of other societies, sometimes to be interpreted as representing modernity, sometimes as degeneracy and corruption. The Coke bottle that plummets from a passing airplane onto the Khoisan, Xi, in *The Gods Must Be Crazy;* the comic-pathetic scene of bleach-blond Hamoua shimmying with a Coke bottle in Youssef Chahine's 1957 film *Central Station;* the Coca-Cola-induced high of desperate 1950s teenagers in the Hungarian Peter Gothar's *Time Stands Still* — these images are all emblematic of a world-changing set of events in this century: namely, the transposition of American models of marketing and consumer culture beyond U.S. borders in the last seventy or eighty years as the United States acquired world economic preeminence.

In this essay, I want to explore some aspects of this global

process of "Americanization" by focusing on how in a particular
region of the world, continental Europe, and in a particular
period—namely, the interwar years—conceptions of market,
merchandising techniques, and advertising design of American
provenance forced the development of new patterns of consumer
culture and thus came to define what it meant to be modern.[3]
By consumer culture, I mean broadly a society-wide structure of
meaning and feeling organized primarily around acts of purchase. In the forms we know today, it originated in the United
States. Since the turn of the century, as the main circuitry of
mass commerce was established, techniques devised to promote
national markets for the branded, standardized products of large-
scale manufacturers were honed in a huge industry specialized in
preparing, placing, and disseminating advertising messages. Increasingly, the contractual relations of market shaped notions of
community, pressures for entitlement, and the modalities of political consensus. This change was accompanied by the construction of new social subjects, such as the consumer, and of new
social mediators including the salesman, the advertising expert,
and the press agent. It also gave rise to new organizations such
as the Rotary businessmen's clubs. Not least of all, it gave rise to
a new language of goods. Both in the U.S. and abroad, this complex system of representation cast capitalist relations in a new
light: the dynamic principal was not so much production as distribution and consumption; the consumer was, if not sovereign,
a subject empowered by his or her spending capacity; social col-
lectivities increasingly appeared to be based on choice in the
marketplace rather than the vagaries of geography or the bonds
of craft or class; finally, social conflicts seemed subject to resolution by widening access to commodities rather than by revolu-
tionizing capitalist society root and branch.[4]

The responses of European societies were in some sense
special inasmuch as American consumer culture appeared less
abruptly and in less brutal forms than in Third World areas:

there was no colonial heritage and no physical conquest was involved. From the start, American models competed with well-defined market cultures, which themselves had contributed much over the previous century to developments in the U.S., and that continued to produce the finely wrought craft goods held up as models of taste and quality by American elites. Nonetheless, American consumer culture presented a real challenge to local notions of market, craft, and modernity. Reconstructing the process by which certain American values and techniques were assimilated into European commercial culture demonstrates not just the power exercised by the U.S. economy, but also the process by which certain local economic patterns and cultural alternatives were altered, abandoned, or suppressed.

American business methods, with their powerful emphasis on creating productive capacity, took hold after World War I in societies in which markets were still regarded as finite. Most European business firms continued to be guided by a residual economic Malthusianism: markets, like resources, being naturally limited, the best policy was to cleave to traditions and stick to one's tried and true clientele. Commercial culture was organized around old city centers and catered to bourgeois rather than mass tastes.[5] Generally, politicians could not conceive of changes in consumption or cultural habits such as would have caused them to alter their appeals. Indeed, consumer identities being so bound up with class cleavages, it was hard, even for social reformers, to imagine that workers would develop "needs" that were not strictly economic necessities or consonant with their class position. Any ulterior desires reflected "false consciousness" or "embourgeoisement."[6]

In the 1920s, American consumer culture started to challenge these assumptions. This was especially manifest in what is the specific focus of my essay, namely the *grande querelle* among European advertisers and commercial artists over how to represent goods in the marketplace. In its most elementary form, this debate centered on whether to pursue the editorializing copy style used in the American mass-circulation press or to prefer the design aesthetic associated with European postermaking traditions. Should European promoters stake their future on a textual style that promised profits and new professional dignity? Or should they stay loyal to pictorial representation in the hope of preserving artistic autonomy and defending local traditions? Underlying these positions, broader issues were in dispute. Thus the debate reflected conflicting assumptions about the operations of the market, the extent of "communities of consumption," the logics motivating consumer behaviors, and even the means of constructing human desire. The contending positions also reflected diverse notions within the advertising sector and, more generally, within bourgeois culture about the relationship between art and commerce. In particular, they differed about the aesthetics of representation itself; should goods be represented realistically to highlight what they did for the consumer, as the American practice indicated? Or should they be animated by strong symbolic and pictorial design traditions in order to activate latent desire, as European practitioners held out?

Both the allure and fear of American commercialism fueling this contest reflected a more pervasive ambivalence among the elites in post-World War I Europe about a model of development that, while promising prodigious growth, also threatened uncontrollable cultural and social changes. There was a kind of unanimity in favor of economic modernity: from conservatives and liberals to the far left, the response to Taylorism and Fordism was generally positive.[7] But the implications of Americanizing trends for culture and values were judged unpredictable if not outright pernicious. American society might well have tolerated the continuous turnover in custom generated by mass consumption. After all, its constitutional structures were regarded as being sufficiently sturdy to withstand the fads and wild fluctuations of opinion that European observers had associated with the "civilization" of the New World ever since Tocqueville's travels to America. Moreover, American capital appeared powerful enough to satisfy the desires unleashed by consumer culture. In any event, American society, it was argued, was already so homogenized or so hybrid—views differed as to which—that the risk that novel mores would disrupt status hierarchies, declassing the bourgeoisie and disquieting the lower orders, seemed minor. In Europe, by contrast, cultural traditionalism and highly stratified consumer habits appeared to stand as a bulwark against social upheaval. Thus, for the cultural conservatives who most anguished about the conquest of European culture by American material civilization, the "democratization of consumption," as conservative commentator André Siegfried wrote, could "only be obtained at a tragic price . . .": namely, workmen becoming automatons, leisure ruled by standardized products, and spiritual values forsaken for mechanistic conduct.[8]

At the same time, American commercial culture seemed to offer much to professionals in quest of social and cultural legitimacy: this was true not just for advertising experts, but also for engineers, architects, journalists, and movie producers, indeed for all of the professions associated with constructing and communicating in mass society. For advertising agents, in particular, American technologies of distribution and publicity offered three opportunities: first, to make big profits, much as they saw were being made in America in the 1920s; second, to bolster their own professional status at a time when interest-group organization was firming up everywhere; and third, to manage what might be described as a crisis of representation of the bourgeois order, consequent on the social upheavals following the Great War and compounded by the double challenge of Americanism and Bolshevism in their wake.[9] Thus modern publicity might help overcome the zero-sum logic of economic nationalism by deepening and broadening markets across national boundaries. It would eliminate irrational consumer choices by applying behavioral studies and psychological testing to human motivation. Above all, advertising's stripped-down language, its mass appeal, and its display of business tempos bespoke the vigor of new elites and their endeavor to publicize the virtues of technological civilization. These virtues, they argued, were being contested, not least of all because modern industrial society's accomplishments had been furtively concealed by retrograde businessmen. Flashing the name of the French Henry Ford, Citroën, from the Eiffel Tower with two hundred thousand bulbs, or illuminating the Milan Duomo Square with thousands of megawatts of publicity, or faking advertising copy to suggest industrial patronage for innovating architecture—as Le Corbusier did in his journal *L'Esprit* in the mid-1920s—these feats signaled the compatibility of cultural iconoclasm, technology, and a reformed community of workers and capitalists. In advertising, modernists saw a new language, the idiom of youth embattled against the rhetorical conventions of the old, the sacrosanct, and the academic. Advertising promised to become the Esperanto of a dynamic capitalism, "the key to world welfare," to use the slogan of the 1929 Berlin World Advertising Conference, and, as such, the guarantor of a new international order.[10]

Their zeal was all the stronger because the structure of European economies and the nature of consumer habits seemed so unpropitious to promoting American-style techniques. U.S. advertisers had the advantage of serving oligopolistic firms and working with brand-products devised for broad, homogeneous, and affluent markets. However, in the 1920s, most European business firms served local markets, at best regional ones. Marketing consumer commodities across national boundaries was practically unheard of. Domestic markets were generally shallow, even in the most affluent nation, namely late Weimar Germany; the European working classes were still not regarded as potential consumers in these pre-Keynesian economies.[11] Even among those producers of consumer durables who had gone over to American production systems, there seemed to be a real gap between innovations in production techniques and distribution methods. Meanwhile, the most visible advertisers were not the producers of consumer durables, but an ill-reputed lot of vendors of patent medicines and entertainment.

Above all, the organization of space and publics seemed little suited to the marketing practices developed to sell standardized brands in a relatively homogeneous and incomparably more wealthy market, using the press and other media to reach out to increasingly suburbanized publics. Traditionally, European markets were dominated by major capitals of consumption; the *goût parisien,* we know, set the dress style of all Western society. The department store *étalage,* the open-air market, the exposition pavilion, and the grand boulevard were the typical institutions of a market culture organized around city centers. Retailers publicized their merchandise by elaborate displays and customers were primarily bourgeois. Local markets might appear luxury at the core. But outside of the great metropolitan centers and a few wealthy provincial towns, they were still straitened by poverty, status differences, and regional fragmentation. Under the circumstances, the poster, along with window and shopfloor displays, still offered the major mediums of communication: placarded kiosks, handbills, postcards all signaled, with no special need for detail and little class specificity, the physical proximity of centers of consumption. The mass press absorbed increasing amounts of advertising revenues by the early 1920s. Even so, the political character and class specificity of most leading national news organs, the regional dispersion, and the great jumble of rates and formats made the print medium still an ungainly and costly undertaking for advertisers.[12]

Although beleaguered advertisers banked on U.S. precedents, they were not indifferent to the dangers of American-

style modernity. Some features of U.S. marketing technologies
were not readily digestible. One was the exploitativeness of U.S.
advertising: it was with awe and trepidation that advertisers remarked on American ruthlessness. Everything could be publicized: from deodorants to furs, babies to burials, the intimate
to the afterlife. Not even religion was sacred, as the marketing
director of a French pharmaceutical concern observed in *Vendre,*
a leading French trade journal. He illustrated his point with ad
copy showing a soldier offering to quaff Christ on the Cross'
thirst with gall and apologizing that it wasn't Vinegar X.[13] The
intense competitiveness caused uneasiness as well. It was one
thing to urge Taylorized work rules for sales personnel or to up-
grade the profession by purging the unfit; it was quite another to
introduce humbling competition into the ranks of the profession
itself.

Above all, there was the giant problem of "taste." U.S. advertisers abroad contended that there was "one best way" in advertising. Carefully studied in terms of markets and product
qualities, their advertising pitches were deemed universally appealing. Hence they would need only minor tuning to adjust to
local conditions. However, in Europe, bourgeois status was identified with conserving cultural traditions, and advertising was
still close enough to being considered art to want to uphold aesthetic standards alongside commercial ones. Each nation—and
in the case of Germany, each major region as well—had its own
identifiable style of publicity. Should these customs be jettisoned
in the interest of building up sales? Were advertisers and their
clients really ready to foresake the old cultural alliances underlying their class position to pander to the tastes of volatile mass
publics? It might be possible to argue that publicity was at bottom just business, opening the way to all stylistic conventions,
regardless of national provenance. Yet questions remained. Did
American advertising styles promote alien values? Did they sub-
vert national traditions? Was there indeed a national "taste,"

not just among advertisers but among consumers as well, that should be protected and perhaps even promoted against U.S. commercialism?

These issues were most sharply formulated in discussing what in trade journals was commonly referred to as the "crisis of the poster." In its heyday in the Belle Epoque urban centers of prewar Europe, the poster was lamented to have "decayed" and "declined" in the years thereafter. This complaint was especially strong in Italy and in France. In Germany, with its exceptionally strong commercial design traditions, well-organized advertising and commercial art corporations, and much stronger domestic and international markets, the poster held its own, at least until the early 1930s.[14] But there, too, commercial artists fretted about their future and advertisers weighed the merits of new American systems against the familiar German styles of representation.

Was the poster really "in crisis"? Crisis is a strong word: that it was used suggested that the poster had become the focus of a whole set of anxieties. These were perhaps spurred by fears of American competition. But they also reflected little understood and ill-tolerated changes going on in European societies of the period. For sure, the poster had occupied pride of place in prewar advertising. The great expansion of merchandising after the turn of the century had put a premium on inventiveness. To market the special article for the bourgeois trade, the stock posters that lithographic companies kept in hand for all-purpose advertising and that could be adopted indiscriminately for promoting soap, chocolate, sewing machines, or whatever were judged ineffective. Enterprising merchants in search of specialized designs were thus hospitable to the aesthetics of Art Nouveau or Jugendstil, as well as to Arts and Crafts movement styles. Intensely local schools evolved within national boundaries or in reference to regional markets: the leading artists were renowned locally, like the British Hardy, Pryde and Nicolson, or

the French postermasters André Cheret, Raffet, and Gavarni, or
the Germans Hohlwein and Lucian Bernhard; a few, like Cappiello, who moved between France and Italy, acquired broader
recognition.[15]

For urban residents who idealized the halcyon days of pre-Great War Europe, the poster was a soothing reminder of the
past: amidst social turmoil, it recalled the comfortable human
dimensions of the Belle Epoque. "The cry of the posters from
the concrete walls/ Proclaims a fairyland that we have lost,"
wrote the Dadaist poet Richard Huelsenbeck. In the bleak, chaotic cities of Weimar, "Man might stand naked among tramway-cars/ And not know a word of human speech/ The colored
poster-world would break down the bars/ And his own heart the
secret meaning teach."[16]

The tendency to identify the poster with a more humane
order heightened perceptions of how uneasily it fit with the
tempo of postwar commercial life. The poster's crisis was thus
perceived as having a threefold dimension. First, the poster had
become politicized, having become identified with left-wing
street politics and mass mobilizations after the war. Second,
businessmen were increasingly uncertain about what aesthetic or
style was more suited to selling goods. Third, the commercial
artist was in increasingly precarious circumstances, beset by
competition and unemployment. All of these combined to
jeopardize the poster's value as *commercial art*. Thus, since the
war, and especially in the wake of the "red years," the poster
had become a much-debated form of mass culture (hence
Huelsenbeck's evocation of the poster's symbolic and social
value). In Germany, the revolution of 1918 and the subsequent
polarization of national political life had produced an outpouring
of wall manifestos. Experimental in form, often inspired by Expressionist motifs, they were designed as propaganda, that is, to
rally public opinion rather than to market goods. Second, older
conventions very successful in the prewar years, such as Lucian

Bernhard's emphasis on the "thing-ness" of objects *(Sachplakat),* were worn to death by imitators. Although the exhaustion of old formulae led to a greater variety of figurative and pictorial motifs, the conventions about what best sold goods broke down. Commercial culture in the big cities was conducted on too large a scale to permit regular contact between businessmen and the arts. Forced to take up their portfolios to make the rounds in search of clients, artists tended to pitch their sketches more loudly and cast their personal idiosyncrasies in crasser form; and when executed, the designs presented stronger traits of conventionalization than the goal of advertising usually warranted. Finally, young artists everywhere were discouraged by the ease of plagiarism, not to mention the difficulty of plying their trade as commercial artists as commissions declined. This insecurity fed the fear, polemically evoked by Grosz and Herzefelde in *Die Kunst in Gefahr* (1925), of the "dismantling of the artist in his present form." In their radical vision, the artist now had but two choices, namely, "he could merge in industry as a designer or advertising man, or else he might become a propagandist for the revolution."[17]

At the same time, there were growing doubts about whether postering itself was an effective medium of advertising. Marketing was becoming a more complicated process, with new products, new publics, and new uses of urban space. Firms advertising consumer durables, including automobiles and household appliances, as well as personal products such as soap, cosmetics, and cleansers, realized that these new products called for explanation. They also sought new consumers outside of the city centers. At bottom their concerns about the effectiveness of postering reflected its high costs. Paper and color printing were expensive, and postering was encumbered by heavy taxation. More and more, local governments treated street advertising as a luxury or a nuisance: strapped for revenues in the 1920s, town councils assessed taxes of all kinds, and practically no revenues went to maintain the emplacements. In Italy, local taxes on size, product, and the kind of posting (whether it was on board, metal, or concrete) added 50 percent to the price of production. Even then, it was not uncommon for new rulings to cause entire print runs to be warehoused. Moreover, regulations were so diverse that they discouraged any but the most local marketing endeavors.[18]

But the real issue was cost-effectiveness. In most big urban centers, city life was changing: in the 1920s, renewal projects designed to ease the flow of motor traffic and clean out the sign-cluttered confusion of the old central districts cleared away poster emplacements and speeded up the pace of urban life. Among the major cities, except perhaps for Paris, residential districts were more and more separate from the commercial center. New systems of public transportation speeded up daily life. In any case, the poster was simply too generic in its appeal. It was unable to target specific publics for particular products. Nor did it readily lend itself to provincial distribution networks where prosperous small-town or rural customers might be found. The bourgeois clientele formerly concentrated in city centers had moved to the suburbs. True, advertisers might study the subway routes, as they were invited to do in Berlin, so as to determine which led to proletarian quarters and which led to bourgeois suburbs. They might then specify the goods to be advertised on each route. However, the costs of this more extensive coverage were high. There was also a problem of turnover: it was alleged that the quicker pace of urban life, shorter attention spans, and more rapid turnover of products called for a more frequent postering. As a mid-1920s Berlin advertisers' adage, loosely translated, put it in Warholian terms: "Every effective poster is a celebrity — for twenty-four hours" ("Ein effektvolles Plakat an der Saule macht unsterblich — für 24 Stunden").[19]

Finally, the use of public space was becoming more competitive and conflictual. The garish outsize cinema posters, distributed by the promoters of American films and often produced on giant presses in the U.S., crowded out smaller placards of local production. In Italy, there were complaints that vandals ripped up the hoardings for fuel. New products and leisure pastimes vied for position. During the great German inflation of 1923, the commercial poster was literally buried on the hoardings. The situation was bleak. According to the account of Professor H. E. Frenzel, director of Berlin's refined commercial art magazine *Gebrauchsgraphik*, "The principal space [had been] occupied by the movie poster with its pernicious excrescences and high-sounding titles, calculated to appeal to cooks and kitchen-maids. Next in importance came the numerous announcements of offices for the buying and selling of gold and jewels, advertisements of pleasure resorts, 'beauty dances,' go-go girls, etc." These were interspersed with "red placards topped with fabulous sums in millions of marks for this or that criminal." Between these, "small and modest like the agonized sighs of a man being suffocated, [were] official state announcements for the benefit of people who, in reality were no longer to be regarded as part of the economic life of the nation."[20] In sum, consumption was no longer comfortably contained within the commercial spaces of town centers. Those spaces were increasingly being subverted by urban renewal and shifting networks of distribution, by the poor from below, and by Americanism from abroad.

Ultimately the poster's apparent inability to represent the new world of consumer goods was brought home by the growing use of a potentially more commercially effective alternative. This was the newspaper or periodical insert. Throughout Europe, it is true, the print medium was already increasingly widely used for publicity purposes by the early 1920s. But press advertising was still generally treated as a shabby enterprise: crowded, competing for space, smudgily copied, with heavy black lined designs, they were often but mere announcements. Insofar as long copy was used, it was devoted to the most heavily advertised goods and services, namely patent medicines, quack remedies, fortune telling, and nostrums of various sorts. For their sale stood or fell on the results of advertising. Nationwide campaigns for new products treated the newspaper as if it were a poster: using heavy black on white, emphatic with a single word, displaying the name of the article advertised in as large a typeface as possible, without any decoration or illustration, publicity inserts seemed intended, according to the characterization of a contemporary observer, to give "a blow between the eyes, as hard as it is possible to deliver it, through the medium of printer's ink."[21]

The real alternative then was an entirely new style of print advertising, identified with the American consumer industry. This was the carefully argued, meticulously designed, sometimes multicolor insert in especially conspicuous display in the mass-circulation magazines of the interwar years, in particular, the *Ladies Home Journal, Saturday Evening Post,* and *Good Housekeeping.* Employed by American companies such as Erwin Wasey and J. Walter Thompson in their European advertising campaigns in the late 1920s, it was also much-cited in European sources as the American national style of advertising. In design, print ads were densely packed, sometimes three columns of several paragraphs, illustrated with titles and decoration. Yet, at its best, as in the so-called "reason why" studies of Helen Resor, it was uncluttered to look at and readable; it combined much information and persuasive reasoning, and it was backed up with ostensibly scientific data or testimonials by social leaders. "Salesmanship in print," as it was sometimes called, the text insert emphasized the attributes of goods and how the consumer could use them. Thus, it "sold the benefit instead of the product: illumination instead of lighting fixtures, prestige instead of automobiles, sex appeal instead of mere soap."[22] Often the advertisement imitated the look and layout of the medium in which it was printed, as if to play on the indistinctiveness in a highly commodified culture between "real" reading matter and editorializing for consumer products.

This style, sometimes called "stupid realism," or perhaps with more analytical rigor, "capitalist realism,"[23] worked through different psychological mechanisms from those at play in the poster and print copy derived from it. So European contemporaries frequently pointed out when they contrasted the publicity that worked through seduction with that which worked by evocation, or when they contrasted American puritanism, with its purported emphasis on interpreting the text, with European paganism, with its worship of the idol.[24] Indeed, unlike European poster advertising, in which symbolic goods were represented with symbolic forms, as was increasingly common in the 1920s, the American style relied, in Michael Schudson's words, on the "common understanding of its audience."[25] One American advertising layout played on emotions and insecurities; it reassured the consumer that the sponsor was likewise a patron of shared ideals, and the product being endorsed concretely and actively contributed to their perpetuation. Democratic by its claim to represent common social values, this style manipulated their social meanings by implying that they were individual acquisitions, available solely through the marketplace. American advertising may not have depended on the scientific market surveys that firms like J. Walter Thompson swore by, much less on any real respect for public opinion. But it did command a strong if temporary dose of empathy for popular susceptibilities and enough familiarity with the qualities of the product to be able to write persuasive copy.

Just as the poster represented turn-of-the-century European urban commercial culture, this advertising form reflected the state of development of early twentieth-century American marketing. Text advertisements carried, as it were, heavy freight over long distances, reaching out to diverse, nonhomogeneous publics at a time when markets were increasingly distant and impersonal. They had a strong power of projection when the medium, to recall McLuhan's familiar phrase, was not yet the message and the presentation of new brands still called for considerable explanation. More generally, the adoption of capitalist realism seems to have responded to what Pierre Bourdieu described as the "popular aesthetic," that of people who, dominated by ordinary interests and urgencies, expect the conventions of representation "to allow them to believe 'naively' in the things represented." They reluctantly accept abstraction, "not just from lack of familiarity but from a deep-rooted demand for participation, which formal experiment systematically disappoints . . ." In this sense, they behave differently from "aesthetic elites" who "believe in the representation . . . more than in the things represented" because they experience the world "freed from urgency and through the practice of activities which are an end in themselves."[26]

By the 1920s, U.S. advertisers had come around, not without conflict, to sharing the aesthetic of capitalist realism with their audience; indeed they promoted it to legitimate their social leadership. For no aesthetic seemed to represent so well the complex modernity of market relations. This was twofold. On the one hand, advertising promoted an impersonal marketplace of vast scale, stimulating the conviction that "what was new was desirable," indispensable to a modern world outlook. On the other hand, advertising denied its essentially economic nature as the mass communications system of the marketplace by striving after a subjective, personal appeal. Thus, at the same time as publicity promoted economic modernity, it protected against the uncontrollability of market operations. It accommodated the public to new conveniences while it comforted them against the stressful competitiveness and the cultural strictures that went along with them.[27]

Naturally, this conception of how modern goods should be

sold was not uncontested in the European advertising milieu. One typical response, shared not just among the more tradition-bound, but even by individuals working in Americanizing firms and trade journals was that American copy style was simply in bad taste. The grossly literal sensibility, the pretentious didacticism, the mix of stylistic conventions were perhaps suited for a "young people"; that mix would not appeal to the complex sensibility of the old world. Europeans would not tolerate such long texts; and for technical reasons, such as the low quality of reproduction and the high costs of premium space, emulation of such methods was inadvisable. Not least of all, there was the fear that the American style, produced by giant bureaucratic juggernauts, would snuff out the expressivity of the advertising staff itself; in the name of efficiency, profits, mass markets, it denied "fantasy, initiative, personality—in sum all that gives pleasure to the existence of our publicity experts *[téchniciens]*."[28]

Indeed, one reaction to this formidable rival was to defend European poster traditions. This defense used two quite different strategies. One might be described as resistance; this was associated with the weaker commercial markets of Southern Europe. The other strategy might be called reformist: this was associated with the powerful position of Germany in European markets, and it sought to commercialize the poster by developing a more varied idiom and wider marketing appeal. Both strategies presumed that commodities needed only relatively simple visual signing and that their uses were familiar enough not to require any complex system of textual signification.

The strategy of resistance was most militantly put forward by the Italian Giuseppe Magagnoli, founder and director of the poster workshop Maga. A former salesman with the leading French poster concern, Vercasson, Magagnoli had established his own atelier just after the Great War. This firm was exclusively devoted to commercial postermaking. With showrooms centrally located in Milan and Paris and business connections as far away

l bearings and such are the "material ∘structure of our civilization." Print advertising m *Fortune,* late 1920s.

Poster advertising ball bearings produced by Fiat's subsidiary Riv, Maga workshop, mid-1920s.

as Rio de Janeiro and Buenos Aires, it was largely responsible for the reputation of Italian poster art for individuality and bold expression. Magagnoli's contemporaries, bothered by his factiousness as they sought to professionalize their métier, charged the firm with being "old school" and overly specialized. The latter charge was true in a way, and perhaps contributed to the firm's bankruptcy in 1932. Magagnoli himself died the next year of heart failure.[29]

In its prime, however, Maga employed the talents of leading French and Italian artists, including Cappiello, the Italians Nizzoli, Sinopico, and Pozzati (Sepo), the French-born, Italianized Lucien-Achille Mauzan, and other lesser known and often unnamed figures working in the house style. In his house organ published through the 1920s under the title *Pugno nell'Occhio,* or *Pans dans l'Oeil* (Punch in the eye), Magagnoli ranted against "all the old, rancid and idiotic systems used up to now," and especially against the purported scientificity and academicism of U.S. advertising.[30] Typically, Maga's posters were "materialized ideas": they performed as large trademarks for goods, though they were always unmistakably Maga products. The color effect was forced by giving them a colored, black, or blue background, and the lettering, brief and legible, did not form part of the design. Indeed, the text, far from being integrated into the design, was generally added on afterwards, once the customer had selected the sketch for his product from a roster of proposals.

The work of Lucien-Achille Mauzan was crucial to Maga's reputation. He was not only a virtuoso designer, but also an inventive lithographer. Drawing posters according to a technique of his own, directly upon the stone or zinc, he had so mastered the method that he could turn out daily two press-ready posters 140 by 140 centimeters worked in four colors. Indeed, his output was prodigious. From 1906 when he started through 1929, Mauzan was estimated to have produced 3,200 items. Like other Maga artists, Mauzan played on quick visual wit, the cunning of "la trovata" (the gimmick), the odd juxtaposition, and the ostensibly animate qualities of the object. The poster was a barker; it had to grab your attention; it was the voice of the object calling out, clamoring for attention (and Clamor, fittingly, was the name of the first Italian roadsign company). In Italy, as a British publicity expert commented, "you have to increase the sound of your voice—to be heard."[31] In common, Maga and its entourage eschewed any reference to the social attributes of objects or the potential needs they might serve. It was through their rendering of the object that they preserved a strong sense of human agency; the machine, domesticated and individualized, was vivified through representation.

The entry into a society of new distinctions, it has been argued, is fraught with the "anxiety of exposure" and aestheticizing becomes a distancing mechanism to preserve social position.[32] In Magagnoli's case, but not only his, aestheticizing offered a means to establish control over the modernizing process. This claim to leadership rested on his capacity to caricature goods rather than to communicate to new consumers about their utility. His Americanizing compatriots contested his position as factious, backward, and inefficient. Yet Magagnoli was only being true to what he was—a skilled craftsman plying a trade geared to older market circuits: to have done otherwise would have called for a different professional identity, a different relationship with commodities, and a different rapport with the mass consumer.

By contrast, the leading German commercial art schools, being better connected both to national marketing networks and to international markets, embarked on what might be called a program of reform. This was sparked by the recognition that as American commercial competition overran specialized markets, it threatened to destroy the specialized design traditions associated with them. The endeavor to keep German commercial art abreast of rapidly changing commercial and aesthetic conventions was led primarily by Professor Frenzel, who founded *Gebrauchsgraphik* in 1924. The Berlin-based monthly, starting out as a journal "to promote artistic publicity" ("zum förderung kunstlerische reklame"), in 1928 changed its subheading to journal of "international advertising art." Covering design innovations from all over the world, but especially focusing on the U.S., it was an awesomely cosmopolitan affair, its mission being to modernize German commercial art by measuring it against the international competition.

The task of relating local styles to Americanizing trends is especially interesting in Germany, because two very different options were available. One was the "object-ness" of the Berlin school of Lucian Bernhard, which, in the postwar years, easily fed into the modernist experimentation of the International school. Basically, Bernhard, and like him, Fritz Rosen and Wal-

What electric lighting can do for the consumer: U.S. print advertising, *Fortune,* late 1920s.

Updated German poster advertising for Osram. Walther Nehmer, 1927.

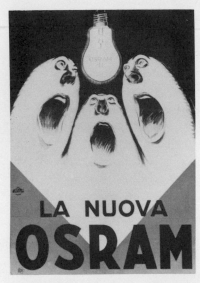

Updated poster advertising for Osram. Lucien-Achille Mauzan, circa 1928.

Face to face: the bourgeois family reacts to Lucien-Achille Mauzan's poster for Osram in a caricature by Mauzan, displayed at a show of his work, late 1920s.

"Sachplakat," for Osram. Lucian Bernhard, c. 1908.

ther Nehmer, to name but two of the figures more in evidence after Bernhard moved to New York in 1925, held to the notion that there was rationality in the functional form; good advertising, by mustering symbolic representations — early morning, the crowing cock; speed, an arrow; flight, a bird — might construct, with astonishing economy of form, an international language. Progressive, internationalist, experimental, artistically rigorous, it seemed in every way an alternative to America's capitalist realism.[33]

The other style was identified first and foremost with the Bavarian artist Ludwig Hohlwein. Influenced by local traditions of genre painting and growing out of a vigorous local art industry, his "amiable and soliciting" pictorial style found favor elsewhere in Germany; its expressive sentimentality was remarkably close in spirit to American commercial realism. Indeed, prior to and much more than Bernhard, Hohlwein found favor in U.S. advertising circles, though it was argued that his character types were too local and his artistic personality perhaps too strong to work on competitive accounts—at least not without firm guidance from an agency art director.[34]

What more concretely did *Gebrauchsgraphik*'s promoters urge be done? First, they advocated a willingness to experiment; then, a turnover in styles; finally, a greater responsiveness to commercial pressures. To these ends, the German commercial artists mounted extraordinary regional and national shows, the culminating event being held at Leipzig in 1927, on the occasion of the huge annual commercial fair.[35] Over the long run, these endeavors did not save the German commercial poster. By promoting a critical awareness of the aesthetic conventions underlying local schools, they may even have helped call these conventions into question. Nevertheless, they did draw attention from abroad, and they related local traditions to the syncretic commercial mill of American publicity. One outcome was that German artists were welcomed in the U.S.; though they did not fundamentally alter the nature of the appeal of American publicity in the 1930s, they significantly embellished American design traditions with modernist motifs.

Even while the canons of commercial art were under review, the American-style advertising campaign was going native. At first much discussed, by the mid-1930s, its American origins were no longer always labeled as such. Apparently some elements had become so familiar as to be taken for granted; they had become the "natural" way of promoting goods. However, American business was also becoming less visible. As American firms pulled out of Europe altogether in the wake of the Great Depression or cut back on their European staffs, former employees sought positions elsewhere, sometimes in firms of their own, sometimes in branch subsidiaries of U.S. firms. As less now was to be gained from identifying techniques as American—the Depression having destroyed the myth of America's infallible economic might—the citing of U.S. models diminished. Local advertising might henceforth be in the American style. But it

Examples of "cluttered," "uninformative" German press advertising and more simplified direct style, both from *Die Woche,* early 1920s.

now passed as local production. Finally, the Great Depression, by aggravating worry over sales, counseled paying close attention to any technique or ploy that promised to build up markets. Not everywhere, not usually systematically, the American model was most closely followed for the promotion of goods such as automobiles, foodstuffs, and cosmetics that potentially had a mass market, might benefit by national advertising, and were similar to commodities already marketed successfully by American firms. Just as in the U.S., and as a result of American competitors like General Motors and Ford on European markets, the European automobile industry, together with car products, such as motor oil and tires, were the biggest and most innovative advertisers. If for many other goods, full-fledged campaigns were not the rule, still Americanisms had begun to crop up everywhere: in the heavier reliance on text, the structure of argumentation, the use of photography, the look of capitalist realism, and the styles of typography.

Unquestionably, trends outside of the advertising world reinforced stylistic changes. American movies, so widely distributed all over the continent through the mid-1930s, and so very influential in the popular imagination, established new con-

ventions for female beauty; the Hollywood set, with its rendering of the "thing-ness" of American everyday life, made objects
such as the telephone, boudoir sets, automobiles, and home appliances appear quintessentially modern. Meanwhile, the major
aesthetic alternative, German modernist experimentation, was
destroyed by the triumph of Nazism. It is sufficient here to recall
that the ban on non-Gothic typefaces destroyed the international
leadership of German typographic arts, to the benefit of the
more romanticized and eclectic American styles.[36]

This is not to argue that the poster disappeared from the
European scene in the 1930s. Far from it: commercial "high
art," as it might then have come to be called, was beautifully
represented in the modernist verve of 1930s postermaking. Yet
its meaning had changed significantly: sometimes it had become
a mere ploy in the gamut of means available to commerce; it justified itself on aesthetic grounds, concealing the hurly-burly of
commerce; it was used as a propaganda device, legitimating state
intervention in the market. Its major sponsor was no longer private commerce, but the interventionist state of the Great Depression and interest groups sponsoring collective advertising
campaigns. In this capacity, the poster advertised social messages; rather than selling, strictly speaking, the poster appealed
for sacrifice and social involvement in an effort to transcend
market relations. Thus, national governments stepped up their
promotional and welfare activities to compensate for the mal-
functioning of the marketplace. Thus, by appealing to citizens as
consumers of national goods and services, they in effect rejected
the claim of American market society that individual desires and
collective well-being could be satisfied through mass consumption. Like Magagnoli in the 1920s, theorists of the poster continued to emphasize the importance of focusing on the object
rather than the consumer, aestheticizing it with a still powerful
design tradition rather than socializing it by publicizing its "us-
able" qualities. So the new commodities of a society of abun-

"Mommy, Aunt Ilse's hands are as rough as sandpaper . . ." Americanized press advertising from *Die Woche*, late 1930s.

"Tartar, the greatest danger." American-style therapeutic advertising from *Die Woche*, late 1930s.

Pierre Fix-Masseau, *Exactitude-État,* 1932. Poster commissioned by the French State Railways.

dance were recast as the icons of scarcity. In the words of a well-known French advertising entrepreneur, R.-L. Dupuy: "No need to construct a scenario: the object, the object alone, the object-king, just solicit it, it will tell its own story . . ."[37]

The triumph of American methods was not, however, simply a function of changing strategies of merchandising. It was in no small extent propelled by broader changes, some of which were related to American influence elsewhere in the economy, others to deeper processes of capitalist transformation sometimes identified with the United States by virtue of it being the leading capitalist economy. Much more study has to be done to determine whether there was any significant increase in disposable income, such as to create the kind of broad middle-market associated with the growth of the advertising industry in the U.S.; this appears not to have been the case, though allocations within the lower-middle and working-class family budgets may have shifted to accommodate more expenditure on consumer items.[38]

Certainly, an important determinant of change was the appearance in Europe of the conditions that had made print advertising so profitable in the United States. The first of these was the restructuring of the mass press itself. If one recalls, unreliable circulation figures, provincial dispersion, difficulties of placement, poor layout and reproduction, the multiplicity of print formats, uncooperative editors, and partisan audiences had prevented the press from being used effectively as an advertising medium in the early 1920s. However, by the middle of the next decade, there had been remarkable changes: everywhere bureaus of audit had been established to check on circulation figures; rotogravure techniques transformed layout and quality, standardizing formats; the successful penetration of local markets by American distribution and advertising networks prompted more interest in wealthy regional markets and the provincial newspapers that served them. In turn, the press itself was more hospitable to advertising: not just the politically neutral, the tabloid or centrist mass press, appealed for advertising, but also party organs such as Mussolini's *Popolo d'Italia* and the Nazi *Volkische Beobachter*. By the mid-1930s, too, there was a spate of new illustrated periodicals, the European counterparts of *True Story Magazine, Cosmopolitan,* and *Life,* along with a whole run of fan magazines, all advertising in the American style.[39]

The second condition was the growth of advertising agencies. In the early 1920s, most advertising was placed in the press by jobbers, who made the rounds, picked up copy, and on a commission basis, bought space. By the 1930s, specialized agencies had begun to take care of these tasks, as well as all others involved in promotion. In theory, they were free agents, owing no allegiance to any one form of medium; they had no space in publications to sell, no favorite means of expression, and no interest beyond profits. However, the better to enlist and keep clients, they were inclined to experiment with campaigns with ostensibly proven worth. American business offered myriad examples. The well-studied agency was also better able to manage complex sets of information than the publicity department of any single firm; and they were freer to experiment with a variety of styles. Self-promoting through the trade journals, they set the styles for others. Most of the founders of advertising agencies in the interwar years referred to U.S. models. Locally, they acted as the catalysts of an "international demonstration effect."[40]

A third condition was of course the greater willingness on the part of manufacturers to advertise. It is difficult to speak yet of a marketing revolution such as there would be in Europe in the 1950s, when changes in marketing would go hand in hand with a huge increase in consumer spending. Nevertheless, during the 1930s especially, sales distribution networks became more centralized and retailing systems more standardized. By the mid-1930s, in Germany as well as in France (if to a lesser degree), national advertising, combined with chain stores and new wholesale distribution networks extending out into the provinces, had established more centralized control over consumer tastes and retailer's supplies.[41]

In the last analysis, merchandisers responded more positively to American styles of representing goods because they had trouble fathoming the changing nature of the market in the wake of the Depression. Advertisers could no longer rely on conventional notions of class and taste to intuit what customers wanted. They needed to find new methods of studying consumer habits, especially the habits of the urban lower classes and of provincial customers with whose tastes they were wholly unfamiliar. They needed to find a new language to communicate with mass publics. American advertising offered such a method: Marcel Bleustein-Blanchet, the French advertising pioneer whose "rage to persuade" was periodically renewed by trips to the United States from the 1920s, once wrote that the major discovery of prewar advertising was that "to sell well, you must reverse the communication process. The route is no longer from product to consumer but from consumer to product."[42] The founder of French radio advertising, he had begun to introduce the market study as well by the 1930s. Even so, as he recalled, "advertising was like aviation in those days: we could fly farther than before, and with greater safety, but flying still relied on sight— we did not have radar, automatic pilots, or all-weather landings. Those would come later." Bleustein-Blanchet, the founder of Le Drugstore and Prénatal, both inspired by American models, would have had no difficulty acknowledging that in the wake of World War II, the U.S. offered not just a blueprint, but a detailed map; in the 1940s, American sociologists and marketing experts joined with their European counterparts to construct modern European consumers in the image of their American forebears.

The fact that the remapping of the marketplace was thus so closely identified with American commodities, techniques, and images was certainly a source of power for the United States. This was perhaps less true in the 1930s, when American-style modernity was still strongly contested and, in any case, divorced from the exercise of political influence in Europe. However, after 1945, as European national sovereignties were overrun by free-trade doctrines, conservative cultural legacies were discredited, and the economic miracles of the 1950s opened the way to mass consumption, American models were rarely contested. Since then, European consumer culture has been tied ever more firmly to American models. With the mass market a fixture for a second, then a third generation of European consumers, the need to translate the American idiom into local vernaculars lessened; a universal language of commodities now connected America's vast empire of goods.

Notes

I wish to thank the Shelby Cullom Davis Center of Princeton University for its generous hospitality while I was drafting an earlier version of this essay in spring, 1987.

1. P. Brunazzi, "Del cartello pubblicitario," *L'Ufficio Moderno,* July 1932, pp. 433-434.
2. More generally on the social and cultural meanings of market culture, see the semiotic and structural approach of the "French School": Jean Baudrillard, *For a Critique of the Political Economy of the Sign,* trans. Charles Levin (St. Louis: Telos Press, 1981); also Henri Lefebvre, *Everyday Life in the Modern World,* trans. Sacha Rabinovitch (New York: Harper & Row, 1971). Mary Douglas and Baron Isherwood, *The World of Goods* (New York: Basic Books, 1979), seek to reconcile the approaches of neoclassical economics and cultural anthropology. Arjun Appadurai, ed., *The Social Life of Things* (New York: Cambridge University Press, 1986), offers insightful historical and conceptual examples. See also Jean-Christophe Agnew, "The Consuming Vision of Henry James," in *The Culture of Consumption: Critical Essays in American History, 1880-1980,* ed. T. J. Jackson Lears and Richard W. Fox (New York: Pantheon Books, 1983), pp. 65-100, and his

Worlds Apart: The Market and the Theater in Anglo-American Thought, 1550-1750 (New York: Cambridge University Press, 1986).

3. This essay develops themes in a book-length study of European responses to American models of mass and consumer culture called *Americanizing Europe, 1920-1945,* themes that have been developed in "Americanism for Export," *wedge,* no. 7-8 (Spring-Winter 1985): 74-81, and "Mass Culture and Sovereignty: The American Challenge to European Cinemas," *Journal of Modern History* 61, no. 2 (March 1989).

4. The peculiar fusion between market and civil cultures in American society has been remarked upon in various ways. See in particular: David M. Potter, *People of Plenty* (Chicago: University of Chicago Press, 1954); Daniel Boorstin's *The Americans: The Democratic Experience* (New York: Random House, 1973), especially his discussion of "communities of consumption," pp. 89-90; and Lears and Fox, eds., *The Culture of Consumption.* On the development of U.S. commercial culture, especially advertising, see Michael Schudson, *Advertising: The Uneasy Persuasian* (New York: Basic Books, 1984), and Daniel Pope's business history, *The Making of Modern Advertising* (New York: Basic Books, 1983). Roland Marchand studies advertisements as "social tableaux" in *Advertising the American Dream* (Berkeley: University of California Press, 1985). The emancipatory aspects of U.S. consumer culture in the early twentieth century are discussed in William R. Leach, "Transformation in a Culture of Consumption: Women and Department Stores, 1890-1925," *Journal of American History* 71, no. 2 (September 1984): 319-342. Its implications abroad are traced in Emily S. Rosenberg, *Spreading the American Dream* (New York: Hill and Wang, 1982).

5. On French consumer culture before the war, see Rosalind H. Williams, *Dream Worlds: Mass Consumption in Late Nineteenth-Century France* (Berkeley: University of California Press, 1982), Michael B. Miller, *The Bon Marché* (Princeton: Princeton University Press, 1981), and Rachel Bowlby, *Just Looking: Consumer Culture in Dreiser, Gissing, and Zola* (New York: Methuen, 1985).

6. An important statement of this position is contained in Maurice Hawlbachs, *L'Evolution des besoins dans les classes ouvrières* (Paris: Alcan, 1933).

7. For an excellent overview of the response to U.S. production models, see Judith A. Merkle, *Management and Ideology: The Legacy of the International Scientific Management Movement* (Berkeley: University of California Press, 1980), in addition to C. S. Maier, "From Taylorism to Technocracy," *Journal of Contemporary History* 5, no. 2 (1970): 27-61.

8. André Siegfried, *America Comes of Age* (New York: Harcourt, Brace and Company, 1927), p. 348; other examples of this cultural pessimism are documented in David Strauss, *Menace in the West: The Rise of French Anti-Americanism in Modern Times* (Westport, Conn.: Greenwood Press, 1978); the role of culture in bourgeois class formation is analyzed in Edmond Goblot, *La Barrière et le niveau* (Paris: Presses universitaires de France, 1927), p. 192, and in reflections by Jürgen

Kocka, "La bourgeoisie dans l'histoire moderne et contemporaine de l'Allemagne: Recherches et débats récents," *Le Mouvement social,* no. 136 (July-September 1986): 5-27. On upper-class hostility to broadening consumer markets, see Albert O. Hirschman, *Shifting Involvements* (Princeton: Princeton University Press, 1982), esp. pp. 46-61.

9. Except for a sketchy work by a former adman, Edward A. McCreary, *The Americanization of Europe* (Garden City, N.Y.: Doubleday, 1964), there has been no general study of the influence of the U.S. advertising industry on European firms or styles. For an analysis of the pre-World War I situation, see Daniel Pope, "French Advertising Men and the American 'Promised Land.'" *Historical Reflections* 5, no. 1 (Summer 1978): 117-139; national histories such as Gian Paolo Cesarani, *Vetrina del Ventennio* (Rome and Bari: Laterza, 1981) and Antonio Valeri, *Pubblicità italiana* (Milan: Edizioni del Sole 24 Ore, 1986). For France, see Pierre Bruneau, *Magiciens de la publicité,* 2d ed. (Paris: Gallimard, 1956); also Philippe Schuwer, *Histoire de la publicité,* 2d ed. (Geneva: Edito-Service, 1966), suggests the influence of American methods in the formation of national industries, without giving them systematic study.

10. The expectations for advertising are eloquently stated in the various trade journals as well as in numerous pamphlets and manuals published for the advertising trade. Key examples include for France: *La Publicité, Vendre, Presse-Publicité;* for Italy: *La Pubblicità, L'Ufficio Moderno, La Pubblicità d'Italia, La Campana d'Italia, Pugno nell'Occhio;* for Germany: *Die Reklame, Gebrauchsgraphik.*

11. The major comparative source on market structure is L. Urwick and F. P. Valentine, *Europe—United States of America: Some Trends in the Organization and Methods of Distribution in the Two Areas* (Geneva: International Chamber of Commerce, 1931). Some comparisons are useful here: in the 1920s, the French working-class family spent 60 percent of income on food, and after household expenditures, estimated at 32 percent, disposed of 8 percent for sundries; cf. the U.S. working-class household, spending only 35 percent on food and 45 percent on household items, with 20 percent classified as disposable. Overall, the average per capita income in the U.S. was 3.5 times as great as the European, and from 1913 to 1929 grew an estimated 33 percent compared to 5.5 percent in Europe (pp. 50ff.).

12. J. Murray Allison, "Continental Advertising," *Advertising World,* April 1927, pp. 728-732; May 1927, pp. 16-18; and June 1927, pp. 130-132. In 1927, according to J. Walter Thompson's man in Berlin, Ned Crane, the 135 newspapers in which Thompson placed ads used 127 different column sizes, ranging from six to twelve centimeters wide (J. Walter Thompson Archive *Newsletter,* November 15, 1927). According to Italian sources, coverage for a national campaign involved inserts in 40 newspapers; see *L'Ufficio Moderno,* April 1930, p. 308. (Information on the activities of J. Walter Thompson comes from the firm's ar-

chives, formerly in New York City and now located at Duke University. I wish to thank the former director, Cynthia Swank, for her assistance.)

13. A. Le Flobic, "Comment un directeur commerçent a vu l'Amérique," *Vendre,* March 1931, p. 218.

14. For examples, see J. Neuilly, "L'affiche vend-elle?" *Vendre,* February 1928, pp. 153-157; anon., "L'affiche decade," *La Publicité* 1, no. 1 (April 1925); L. P. B. (L. Balzaretti), "La decadenza del manifesto," *Campana d'Italia,* December 1932; L. Cusmano, "Il cartello in crisi?" *L'Ufficio Moderno,* December 1928, pp. 679-680. See also D. Gualtieri, "Street Advertising in General," *International Advertising Conference, 1933* (Milan: A. Lucin, 1933), pp. 163-167.

15. H. K. Frenzel, "25 jahre Deutsches Plakat," *Gebrauchsgraphik* 4 (1925): 4-21; W. S. Crawford, "Das Plakat—The Poster," *Gebrauchsgraphik* 5 (1925): 3-9; Valeri, *Pubblicità italiana,* pp. 1-50.

16. "Das Lied der Plakate," *Gebrauchsgraphik* 1 (1927): 4.

17. Cited in John Willett, *Culture and Society in Weimar Germany* (New York: Pantheon Books, 1974), p. 114.

18. For an example, C. W. Frerk, "The Publicity Poster in Italy," *Advertising World,* June 1928, pp. 224-225, 230; and complaints as referred to in the accounts above, footnote 14.

19. Julius Steiner, ed., "Einfulle: Gebrauchs-Graphorismen," *Gebrauchsgraphik* 3, no. 5 (May 1927): 15.

20. Frenzel, "25 Jahre Deutsches Plakat," p. 13.

21. Allison, "Continental Advertising," p. 18.

22. Marchand, *Advertising the American Dream,* p. 10 and passim; see also, Stephen Fox, *The Mirror Makers* (New York: Morrow, 1984), chapters 2 and 3.

23. Schudson, *Advertising,* pp. 214ff.; The term "stupid realism" is used by T. J. Jackson Lears in "The Artist and the Adman," *Boston Review* (April 1986).

24. See in particular: L. Jones, "Pourquoi l'annonce française est differente de l'annonce américaine," *Vendre,* September 1929, pp. 201-204; also R.-L. Dupuy, "Panorama de la publicité française," *Vendre,* March 1930, p. 191; and various articles in *Die Reklame:* H. W. Brose, "Goût Americain," August 1927, pp. 519-523; G. Haug, "Wirksame verkaufstexte und wie man sie gestaltet," June 1928, pp. 393-395; H. Sakowski, "Amerikanisches-Allzuamerikanisches," October 1930.

25. Schudson, *Advertising,* pp. 218ff.

26. Pierre Bourdieu, *Distinctions* (1979), trans. Richard Nice (Cambridge, Mass.: Harvard University Press, 1984), pp. 4-5, 32, 54ff.; William Leiss, "The Icons of the Marketplace," *Theory, Culture, and Society* 1, no. 3 (1983): 10-22, makes the point that for a first generation of consumers, advertising appeals literally had to be spelled out. This was the first step in creating an advertising culture. The problem was not merely to familiarize consumers with brand names, but also to

confer "natural" attributes to goods that until only recently had been produced locally or in the home.

27. Marchand, *Advertising the American Dream*, pp. 9, 13-14.

28. Paule de Gironde, "Si nous faisions une annonce américaine," *Vendre* 10, no. 64 (March 1929): 175-181.

29. On Magagnoli and Maga, see G. Passavento and A. Palieri, *Chi è in pubblicità* (Milan: L'Ufficio Moderno, 1953), p. 202; Frerk, "The Publicity Poster in Italy," pp. 224-225, 230; Valeri, *Pubblicità italiana,* pp. 51, 55; Hermann Behrmann, "Maga," *Gebrauchsgraphik* 3, no. 7 (July 1927): 41-47.

30. *Pugno nell'Occhio* 1, no. 1 (January 1922): 1.

31. Frerk, "The Publicity Poster in Italy," p. 230; on Mauzan, H. K. Frenzel, "L. A. Mauzan, Ein Erfolgreicher italienischer Plakat-Kunstler—A Successful Italian Poster-Artist," *Gebrauchsgraphik* 6, no. 3 (March 1929): 53-61.

32. Bourdieu, *Distinctions*, p. 57.

33. "Lucian Bernhard a New York, ein Interview von Oskar M. Hahn," *Gebrauchsgraphik* 3, no. 2 (February 1926): 8-12; Fritz Hellwag, "Die Berliner Gebrauchsgraphik," *Gebrauchsgraphik* 3, no. 5 (March 1926); H. K. Frenzel and Frederick Suhr, "Was Weiter? And What Now?" *Gebrauchsgraphik* 5, no. 10 (October 1928): 33-38; also W. S. Crawford, "Das Plakat—The Poster," *Gebrauchsgraphik* 5 (1925): 3-9. The modernist ethos underlying the European representation of commodities is discussed in Reyner Banham, *Theory and Design in the First Machine Age,* 2d ed. (New York: Praeger Publishers, 1960); Roberto Tessari, *Il mito della macchina* (Milan: Mursia, 1973); and Sigfried Giedion, *Mechanization Takes Command* (New York: Oxford University Press, 1948). A comparable idolization of the machine may have occurred in late nineteenth-century America according to Leo Marx's *The Machine in the Garden* (New York: Oxford University Press, 1964).

34. "Einfuhrung zum Sonderheft münchenen Gebrauchsgraphik," *Gebrauchsgraphik* 3, no. 1 (January 1926): 3-8; Frenzel and Suhr, "Was Weiter? And What Now?," p. 36.

35. Ibid., pp. 33-38; Marchand, *Advertising the American Dream,* pp. 140-150.

36. *La Publicité* (1936), pp. 87-104.

37. Dupuy, "Panorama de la publicité française," p. 194. The shift toward collective advertising usually under state sponsorship was well illustrated in the reports at the 1933 conference of the Continental Advertising Association held in Milan-Rome. In Germany, state control had paradoxical effects: the Law of September 1933, reorganizing the advertising profession, literally closed the profession, increased fiscal charges on postering, and stipulated one posterer for each town, while other Nazi measures closed down hundreds of newspapers, eliminated "Jewish" advertising, and drove out modernist poster designers. Subsequent measures also banned radio publicity, standardized newspaper formats and rates, and forbade any invidious comparisons in advertising, emphasizing an

upbeat Teutonic social realism. The results were twofold: poster art eschewed the modernist style and, although heavily employed for propaganda, almost ceased being used for commercial purposes. In 1937, 87 percent of advertising budgets were spent for newspapers, a higher percentage than in the U.S. See H. Canzler, *Wirtschaftwerbung im neuen Reich* (Stuttgart: Muth, 1935), and Karl-Dietrich Abel, *Pressenlenkung im NS-Staat* (Berlin: Colloquium-Verlag, 1968), in addition to a fascinating report by L. D. H. Weld, director of services of McCann Erikson, in *Presse-Publicité,* June 21, 1938, pp. 20, 30, and August 15, 1938, pp. 20, 30, which argues that the Nazi state had finally achieved the order Americanizing reformers had advocated.

38. See Urwick and Valentine, *Europe–United States of America,* p. 52-55.

39. On changes in the press during the interwar decades, see Claude Bellanger et al., eds., *Histoire générale de la presse française* (Paris: PUP, 1969), vol. 3, passim; Nicola Tranfaglia, *La stampa italiana nell'età fascista* (Rome: Laterza, 1980). On France, see especially *Presse-Publicité,* founded in 1937 and specifically devoted to problems of newspaper advertising.

40. In addition to the histories cited above in note 9, see "De la naissance et de la vie des grandes agencies françaises de publicité," *Presse-Publicité* 23 (May 1937): 3-4, 25-26; on the Italian profession, see Passavento and Palieri, *Chi è in pubblicità.*

41. Gaston Defosse, *Le Commerce intérieur* (Paris: PUP, 1944), pp. 63, 90-103; F. Simmet, *Le Petit commerce de détail* (Paris, 1937), pp. 150-251. On Germany, see H. Laufemburger, "La consommation dirigée en Allemagne," *X Crise* (1937), Wolfgang Greve, *Die Rationalisierung der Werbung und ihre Bedeutung fuer die deutsche und englische Wirtschaft* (Munich: Neumann, 1933), and especially L. R. Coleman, "How to Make the Consumer into a Customer," and other contributions to the *International Chamber of Commerce: Berlin Conference 1937 #5* (Berlin, 1937).

42. *The Rage to Persuade* (New York and London: Chelsea, 1982), p. 53.

DE-, DIS-, EX-

The following is a largely verbatim transcription of a lecture given in February 1988. Its purpose — to question the focus on meaning that in whatever guise, invariably pertains to the dominant account of architectural history — was then illustrated by a project now under construction in Paris, the Parc de la Villette, in which the fixed meaning of architectural structures is eroded in a travesty of functionalist ideology.
— Bernard Tschumi, January 1989

Despite the nostalgic wishes of some conservative architectural ideologists, cities have no visible limits. In America, they never had. In Europe, however, the concept of "city" certainly once implied a closed, finite entity. The old city had walls and gates. But these have long ceased to function. Are there other types of gates, new gates to replace the gates of the past? Are the new gates those electronic warning systems installed in airports, screening passengers for gun control? Have electronics and, more generally, technology replaced the boundaries, the guarded borders of the past?

In fact, rather than speaking about the *technology of construction,* architects today should start worrying about the *construction of technology.* As Paul Virilio says, built space is not only built through material and concrete structures, through the perfection of visible architectonic signs, but also (and above all) "through the proliferation of *special effects,* that affect time and distance consciousness — and the perception of the environment."

The walls surrounding the city have disappeared; most

cities ceased to be finite over a century ago. The rules that carefully made the distinction between inside and outside have gone, despite politicians' and planners' guidelines, despite geographical and administrative boundaries. Cities have become *deregulated*.

Much of the city does not belong to the realm of the visible anymore. What was once called "Urban Design" has been replaced by a composite of invisible systems. Why should architects still talk about monuments? They are invisible now. They are *disproportionate* — so large (at the scale of the world) that they cannot be seen. Or so small (at the scale of computer chips) that they cannot be seen either.

Remember: architecture was first the art of measure, of proportions. It once allowed whole civilizations to measure time and space. But speed and the telecommunications of images have altered that old role of architecture. *Speed* expands time by contracting space; it negates the notion of physical dimension. A dimension depends on the relationship between the object and the observer, that is, on "the *nature* of the distance between the observer and the observed," as Benoit Mandelbrot has noted.

Of course, physical environment still exists. But the appearance of permanence (buildings are solid; they are made of steel, concrete, glass) is constantly challenged by the immaterial representation of abstract systems, from television and electronic images to electronic surveillance, and so on. Architecture is constantly subject to reinterpretation. In no way can architecture today claim permanence of meaning. Churches are turned into movie houses, banks into yuppie restaurants, hat factories into artists' studios, subway tunnels into nightclubs, and sometimes nightclubs into churches. There the supposed cause-and-effect relationship between function and form ("form follows function") is forever condemned the day function becomes almost as transient as those magazines and mass media images in which architecture now appears such a fashionable object.

History, memory, and tradition, called to the rescue by architectural postmodernists, become nothing but modes of disguise, fake regulations, so as to avoid the question of transience and temporality. The resulting architectural vignettes—collages of Lutyens with Ledoux—far from suggesting some sophisticated "double-coding," are nothing but the terminal crisis of the referent, "the incapacity to take the measure of events in an environment where appearances are against us" (Virilio). Media reality—we have known this for a while—is more real than immediate reality.

When the philosopher Jean-François Lyotard speaks about the crisis of the grand narratives of modernity ("progress," the "liberation of humanity," etc.), it only prefigures the crisis of *any* narrative, *any* discourse, *any* mode of representation. The crisis of these grand narratives, their coherent totality, is also the crisis of limits. As with the contemporary city, there are no more boundaries delineating a coherent and homogeneous whole. On the contrary, we inhabit a fractured space, made of accidents, where figures are disintegrated, *dis*-integrated. From a sensibility developed during centuries around the "appearance of a stable image" ("balance," "equilibrium," "harmony") today we favor a sensibility of the disappearance of unstable images: first movies (twenty-four images per second), then television, then computer-generated images, and recently (among a few architects) disjunctions, dislocations, deconstructions. The abolition of permanence—through the collapse of the notion of distance as a time factor—of course confuses reality. First deregulation of airlines, then deregulation of Wall Street, finally deregulation of appearances: it all belongs to the same inexorable logic. Some unexpected consequences, some interesting distortions of long-celebrated icons are to be foreseen. The city and its architecture lose their symbols—no more monuments, no more axes, no more anthropomorphic symmetries, but rather fragmentation, parcellization, atomization as well as the random superimposition of images that bear no relationship to one another, except through their collision. No wonder that so many architectural projects sublimate the idea of *explosion*. A few "deconstructivist" architects do it in the form of drawings in which floor plans, beams, and walls seem to disintegrate in the darkness of outer space. Some even succeed in building those explosions and other accidents (by giving them the appearance of control—clients want control—but it's only a "simulation").

It is as if the theoretical foundations of the newest architectural work were to be found in the combustion chambers of guns and cannons. This is not surprising. After all, the most important developments in science—chemistry, physics, astrophysics (the A-bomb, the Big Bang Theory) take as their model the deflagration of gunpowder. Architecture, after all, is a form of knowledge and, obviously, it imports and exports from all kinds of disciplines.

Hence the fascination for cinematic analogies: on the one hand, moving cranes and expressways and, on the other, montage techniques borrowed from film and video—frames and sequences, lap dissolves, fade-ins and fade-outs, jump cuts, etc.

One must remember that, initially, the sciences were about substance, foundation: geology, physiology, physics and gravity. And architecture was very much part of that concern: solidity, firmness, structure, hierarchy. Those foundations began to crumble in the twentieth century. Relativity, quantum theory, the uncertainty principle: this shakeup occurred not only in physics, as we know, but also in philosophy, in the social sciences, in economics.

Today's contemporary science resembles a science of *accidents:* sudden electromagnetic shifts, instant transfers of energy or light, "violent cosmic accidents," a constant detachment from solids and permanence toward immateriality and transience.

How can architecture maintain some solidity, some degree of certainty? It seems impossible today—unless one decides that the accident or the *explosion* is to be called the rule, the new reg-

ulation, through a sort of philosophical inversion that considers
the accident the norm and continuity the exception.

No more certainties, no more continuities. We hear that
energy, as well as matter, is a discontinuous structure of points:
punctum, quantum. Question: could the only certainty be the
point?

The crises of determinism, or cause-and-effect relationships, and of continuity completely challenge recent architectural thought. Here, bear with me if I go through a rather
tedious but quick recapitulation of "meaning" in architecture—
without entering into a detailed discussion of Ferdinand de Saussure or Émile Benveniste. Ethnologists tell us that, in traditional
symbolic relations, things have meanings. Quite often the symbolic value is separated from the utilitarian one. The Bauhaus
tried to reconcile the two into a new functional duo of signifier
and signified—a great synthesis. Moreover, the Bauhaus attempted to institute a "universal semanticization of the environment in which everything became the object of function and of
signification" (Jean Baudrillard). This functionality, this synthesis
of form and function, tried to turn the whole world into a homogeneous signifier, objectified as an element of signification: for
every form, every signifier, there is an objective signified, a function. By focusing on denotation, it eliminated connotation.

Of course, this dominant discourse of rationality was bound
to be attacked. At that time, it was by the Surrealists, whose
transgressions often relied on the ethics of functionalism, *a con-
trario*. In fact, some fixed, almost functionalist expectations were
necessary to the Surrealists, for they could only be unsettled
through confrontation: the surreal set combining "the sewing
machine and the umbrella on the dissecting table" only works
because each of these objects represents a precise and unequivo-
cal function.

The transgressed order of functionality that resulted re-
introduced the order of the symbolic, now distorted and turned

into some poetic phantasm. It liberated the object from its function, denounced the gap between subject and object, and encouraged free association. But such transgressions generally acted upon singular objects, while the world was becoming an environment of ever-increasing complex and abstract systems. The abstraction of the following years — whether expressionist or geometric — had its architectural equivalent. The endlessly repeated grids of skyscrapers were associated with a new zero-degree of meaning: perfect functionalism.

Fashion upset all that. It had always addressed issues of connotation: against fashion's unstable and ever-disappearing image, the stable and universal denotations of functionalism appeared particular and restrictive.

Partly fascinated by such connotations, partly longing for some long-lost traditional forms, architectural postmodernism in the seventies attempted to combine — to quote Charles Jencks — "modern techniques with traditional building, in order to communicate both with the public *and* with an elite" (hence "double-coding"). It was above all concerned with *codes*, with communicating some *message*, some *signified* (perhaps characterized by irony, parody, eclecticism). Architectural postmodernism was totally in line with the mission of architecture according to dominant history, which has been to invest shelter with a given meaning.

Ten years later, the illusion is vanishing. The Doric orders made of painted plywood have finally begun to wane and peel. The instability, the ephemerality of both signifier and signified, form and function, form and meaning could only stress the obvious, what Jacques Lacan had pointed to years before: there is no cause-and-effect relationship between signifier and signified, between word and intended concept. One should not "cling to the illusion that the signifier answers to the function of representing the signified, or better, that the signifier has to answer for its existence in the name of any signification whatsoever"

(Vincent Leitch). As in literature, as in psychoanalysis, the architectural signifier does not represent the signified. Doric columns and neon pediments suggest too many interpretations to justify any single one. Again, there is no cause-and-effect relationship between an architectural sign and its possible interpretation. Between signifier and signified stands a barrier: the barrier of actual use. Never mind if this very room was once a fire station, then a furniture storage room, then a ritualistic dance hall, and now a lecture hall (it has been all of these). Each time, these uses distorted both signifier and signified. Not only are linguistic signs arbitrary (as de Saussure showed us long ago), but interpretation is itself open to constant questioning. Every interpretation can be the object of interpretation, and that new interpretation can in turn be interpreted, until every interpretation erases the previous one. The dominant history of architecture, which is a history of the signified, has to be revised, at a time when there is no longer a normative rule, a cause-and-effect relationship between a form and a function, between a signifier and its signified: only a *deregulation* of meaning.

The deregulation of architecture began long ago, at the end of the nineteenth century, with the world fairs of London and Paris, where light metallic structures radically changed the appearance of architectural solids. Suddenly, architecture was merely scaffolding supporting glass, and it was discrediting the "solid," symbolic character of masonry and stone. Human scale ceased to be an issue, as the logic of industrial construction took over. Human proportions of the ages of classicism and humanism were rapidly replaced by grids and modular systems, a superimposition of light and materials that were becoming increasingly immaterial—another form of deconstruction.

In the mid-seventies, nostalgic postmodernist architects, longing for meaning and tradition, applied sheetrock and plywood cutouts to those scaffoldings, but the images they were trying to provide were weak in comparison to the new scaffoldings of our time: the mediatized images of ephemeral representations.

"To represent construction or to construct representation" (Virilio): this is the new question of our time. As Einstein said, "There is no scientific truth, only temporary representations, ever-accelerating sequences of representation." In fact, we are forced to go through a complete reconsideration of all concepts of figuration and representation: the constant storm of images (whether drawings, graphs, photographs, films, television, or computer-generated images) increasingly negates any attempt to restore the Renaissance ideal of the unity of reality and its representation. The concept of double-coding was the last and futile attempt to keep some of that ideal intact by establishing a new relation between communication and tradition. It is the word "tradition" that misled much of the architectural scene in the late seventies, and made some aspects of architectural postmodernism what I think will soon appear as a short-lived avatar of history: a form of contextual eclecticism that has been recurrent throughout architectural history, with and without irony, allegory, and other parodies.

In any case, the problem is not a problem of images: gables and classical orders, however silly, are free to be consumed by whoever wishes to do so. But to pretend that these images could suggest new rules and regulations in architecture and urbanism by transcending modernism is simply misplaced.

There are no more rules and regulations. The current metropolitan deregulation caused by the dis-industrialization of European and American cities, by the collapse of zoning strategies, contradicts any attempt to develop new sets of regulating forces, however desirable it may be for some. The 1987 Wall Street "crash" and its relation to the economic deregulation that immediately preceded it is another illustration that an important change has taken place. Let me go back a little again. In the Middle Ages, society was self-regulated, auto-regulated. Regulation took place at its center. The prince of the city was the ruler; there was a direct cause-and-effect relationship between rules and everyday life, between the weight of masonry and the way that buildings were built.

In the industrial era, societies became artificially regulated. The power of economic and industrial forces took over by establishing a coherent structure throughout the whole territory: control was defined at the limits, at the edges of society. The relation between rules and everyday life ceased to be clear, and so large bureaucracies and administrators took over. Regulation was not at the center anymore, but at the periphery. Abstract architecture used grids on its sheds International-style, before it discovered that one could decorate the same shed Multinational-style—regardless of what happened in them. Function, form, and meaning ceased to have any relationship to one another.

Today we have entered the age of deregulation, where control takes place *outside* of society, as in those computer programs that feed on one another endlessly in a form of autonomy, recalling the autonomy of language described by Foucault. We witness the separation of people and language, the decentering of the subject. Or, we might say, the complete *decentering of society*.

Ex-centric, dis-integrated, dis-located, disjuncted, deconstructed, dismantled, disassociated, discontinuous, deregulated . . . DIS-, DE-, EX-. These are the prefixes of today. Not post-, neo-, or pre-.

Gayatri Chakravorty Spivak

WHO CLAIMS ALTERITY?

As a postcolonial, I am concerned with the appropriation of "alternative history" or "histories." I am not a historian by training. I cannot claim disciplinary expertise in remaking history in the sense of rewriting it. But I can be used as an example of how historical narratives are negotiated.[1] The parents of my parents' grandparents' grandparents were made over, not always without their consent, by the political, fiscal, and educational intervention of British imperialism, and now I am independent. Thus I am, in the strictest sense, a postcolonial. As a caste Hindu, I had access to the culture of imperialism, although not the best or most privileged access. Let me, then, speak to you as a citizen of independent India, and raise the necessary critical and cautionary voice about false claims to alternate histories. False claims and false promises are not euphoric topics. I am also a feminist who is an old-fashioned Marxist and some of that will enter into this discussion of the cultural politics of alternative historiographies.

How are historical narratives put together? In order to get to something like an answer to that question, I will make use of the notions of writing and reading in the most general sense. We produce historical narratives and historical explanations by transforming the socius, upon which our production is *written* into more or less continuous and controllable bits that are *readable*.[2] How these readings emerge and which ones get sanctioned have political implications on every possible level.

The masterwords implicated in Indian decolonization offered four great legitimizing codes consolidated by the national bourgeoisie by way of the culture of imperialism: nationalism, internationalism, secularism, culturalism. If the privileged subject operated by these codes masquerades as the subject of an alternative history, we must meditate upon how they (we) are written, rather than simply read their masque as historical exposition.

Writing and reading in such general senses mark two different positions in relation to the uneven many-strandedness of "being." Writing is a position where the *absence* of the weaver from the web is structurally necessary. Reading is a position where I (or a group of us with whom I share an identificatory label) make this anonymous web my own, even as I find in it a guarantee of my existence as me, one of us. Between the two positions, there are displacements and consolidations, a disjunction in order to conjugate a representative self. (Even solitude is framed in a representation of absent others.) In the arena of cultural politics, whose disciplinary condition and effect are History, Anthropology, and Culture Studies, this disjunction/ conjunction is often ignored. The socius, it is claimed, is not woven in the predication of writing, not text-ile. It is further claimed that, when we push ourselves, or the objects of our study, forward as agents of an alternative history, our own emergence into the court of claims is not dependent upon the transformation and displacement of a writing into something readable. By that reasoning, we simply discover or uncover the socius and secure the basis of cultural or ethnic power through the claim to knowledge. By that reasoning, power is collective, institutional, political validation. I do not advise giving up this practical notion of power. If, however, we "remake history" only through this limited notion of power as collective validation, we might allow ourselves to become instruments of the crisis-management of the old institutions, the old politics. We forget at our peril that we get out of joint with the pre-text, the writing of our desire for validation, which one can only grasp by being "nominalistic, no doubt: power is not an institution, and not a structure; neither is it a certain strength some are endowed with; it is the *name that one lends* to a complex strategical situation in a particular society," so that one can read that writing.[3]

I will soon go on to discuss Indian postcoloniality from this perspective. But first I will make a brief detour via Marx.

Of all the tools for developing alternative histories—gender, race, ethnicity, class—class is surely the most abstract. It is only when we forget this that we can set aside class-analysis as essentialist. In the volumes of *Capital,* Marx asks the German worker to grasp, as a preliminary to the planned change involved in remaking history, the abstract determinations of what is otherwise merely suffered as concrete misery. In the language that I have been using, one might summarize Marx as saying that the logic of capitalism weaves the socius like the textile of a particular set of relationships. Power and validation within it are secured by denying that web and transforming/displacing it into "natural" readability. I think it is not excessive to see these general senses of reading and writing at work, for example, when Marx asks the worker to understand (read?) the coat s/he produces as having more signification than it does as itself.[4] Capital is a writing, which we must not read merely in terms of producing objects for use, a few for ourselves and many more for others, and not being given enough money to get more for ourselves. Reading the *archives* of capitalism, Marx produces a critique, not of cultural, but of economic politics—hence a critique of *political* economy, political economism.[5] In the current global postcolonial context, our model must be a critique of political culture, political culturalism, whose vehicle is the writing of readable histories, mainstream or alternative. I think it might be useful to write power in Marx this way: "Power is the name that one attributes to a complex strategical situation—the social relations of production—forming a particular society, where 'society' is shorthand for the dominance of (a) particular mode(s) of production of value."

The most useful way to think value is as something "contentless and simple" that must be presupposed as the name of what is produced by the human body/mind machine—a thing that is not pure form, cannot appear by itself, and is immediately coded.[6] As Gayle Rubin on the one hand, and Gilles Deleuze and Félix Guattari on the other have suggested, in their very different ways, this coding operation is not merely economic, it can be understood in the fields of gendering and colonialism.[7] This does not involve allegiance to the narrative of the evolution of the modes of production as the only lexicon of readability, nor the presupposition that class-analysis is the only instrument of readability. (As for the strategy for dealing with the sexism of Marxists, it seems to me not very different from that for dealing with the sexism of non- or anti-Marxists.)

Yet this counterintuitive thought of value should not make us imagine that we can ourselves escape the codes inscribing the real. We are obliged to deal in narratives of history, even believe them. In fact, it is easier to believe in Marx's historical passions than in his methodological delicacy, and many of us feel that to label one ideology and the other science is only provisionally justified in situations of political calculation. In the celebrated Postface to the second edition of *Capital I,* Marx offers us a historical narrative: he argues that Germany was unable to develop the discipline of political economy more or less because in the late eighteenth and early nineteenth centuries it had not participated in the first stages of the development of industrial capitalism. Hence Germany had no bona fide political economists, who were the ideologues of industrial capitalism. When German savants talked political economy, they produced a bizarre *Mischmasch der Kenntnisse*—a jumble of knowledges.

The peculiar historical development of German society [that the capitalist mode of production came to maturity there after its antagonistic character had already been revealed], therefore excluded any original development of "bourgeois" economics there, but did not exclude its critique. In so far as such a critique represents a class, *it can only represent* [vertreten] *the class whose historical task is the overthrow of the capitalist mode of production and the final abolition of all classes — the proletariat.*[8]

The position implicit in the work of the "Subaltern Studies" group of historians is that, since the colonies were not the theater of the development of industrial-capitalist class differentiation, if postcolonial intellectuals keep themselves strictly to the discourse of class-analysis and class-struggle, they might produce a *Mischmasch der Kenntnisse.* The peculiar historical development of colonial society, however, does not exclude the critique of class-analysis as a normative imposition of an instrument of reading. Insofar as such a critique represents a group with a name, it is the subaltern.[9]

It seems obvious to some of us that the disenfranchised *female* in decolonized space, being doubly displaced by it, is the proper carrier of a critique of pure class-analysis. Separated from the mainstream of feminism, this figure, the figure of the gendered subaltern, is singular and alone.[10] Insofar as such a figure can be represented among us, in the room where the talks published in this anthology were first given, for example, it is, first, as an object of knowledge, further, as a native-informant style subject of oral histories who is patronizingly considered incapable of strategy towards us, and finally, as imagined subject/object, in the real field of literature. There is, however, a rather insidious fourth way. It is to obliterate the differences between this figure and the indigenous elite woman abroad, and claim the subjectship of an as-yet-unreadable alternative history that is only written in the general sense I invoke above.

This fourth person is a "diasporic postcolonial." Who or what is she? (The central character of Mahasweta Devi's "The Hunt," my chief literary example of remaking history in this piece, negotiates a space that can, not only historically but philosophically, be accessible to her.)

We all know that the world was divided into three on the model of the three estates in the mid-forties when neocolonialism began.[11] We also know that, during the immediately preceding period of monopoly capitalist territorial conquest and settlement, a class of functionary-intelligentsia was often produced who acted as buffers between the foreign rulers and the ruled.[12] These are the "colonial subjects," formed with varying degrees of success, generally, though not invariably, out of the indigenous elite. At decolonization, this is the "class" (as I indicate above, class-formation in colonies is not exactly like class-formation in the metropolis) that becomes the "national bourgeoisie," with a hand in the carving out of "national identities" by methods that cannot break formally with the system of representation that offered them an episteme in the previous dispensation: a "national" buffer between the ruler and the ruled.

A good deal of this repetition of the colonial episteme in the presumed rupture of postcoloniality will come into play in Mahasweta's story. For the moment let us hold onto the fact that de-colonization does quite seriously represent a rupture for the colonized. It is counterintuitive to point at its repetitive negotiations. But it is precisely these counterintuitive imaginings that must be grasped when history is said to be remade, and a rupture is too easily declared because of the intuition of freedom that a merely political independence brings for a certain class. Such graspings will allow us to perceive that neocolonialism is a displaced repetition of many of the old lines laid down by colonialism. It will also allow us to realize that the stories (or histories) of the postcolonial world are not necessarily the same as the stories coming from "internal colonization," the way the metropolitan countries discriminate against disenfranchised groups in their midst.[13] The diasporic postcolonial can take advantage (most often unknowingly, I hasten to add) of the tendency to conflate the two in the metropolis. Thus this frequently innocent informant, identified and welcomed as the agent of an alternative history, may indeed be the site of a chiasmus, the crossing of a double contradiction: the system of production of the national bourgeoisie at home, and, abroad, the tendency to represent neocolonialism by the semiotic of "internal colonization."

Throw into this chiastic field a phenomenon I invoke often: the shift into transnationalism in the early seventies through the computerization of the big stock exchanges.[14] Of course, changes in the mode of production of value do not bring about matching changes in the constitution of the subject. But one is often surprised to notice how neatly the ruses change in that arena that engages in coding subject-production: cultural politics. And the universities, the journals, the institutes, the exhibitions, the publishers' series are rather overtly involved here. Keeping the banal predictability of the cultural apparatus in transnational society firmly in mind, it can be said that the shift into transnationalism brought a softer and more benevolent Third Worldism into the Euramerican academy. This was indeed *ricorso* from the basically conservative social scientific approach that matched the initial dismantling of the old empires. It is in this newer context that the postcolonial diasporic can have the role of an ideologue. This "person" (although we are only naming a subject-position here), belonging to a basically collaborative elite, can be uneasy for different kinds of reasons with being made the object of unquestioning benevolence as an inhabitant of the new Third World. (S)he is more at home in producing and simulating the effect of an older world constituted by the legitimizing narratives of cultural and ethnic specificity and continuity, all feeding an almost seamless national identity—a species of "retrospective hallucination."[15]

This produces a comfortable "other" for transnational postmodernity, "ground-level activity," "emergent discourses." The radical critic can turn her attention on this hyperreal Third World to find, in the name of an alternative history, an arrested space that reproaches postmodernity. In fact, most postcolonial areas have a class-specific access to the society of information-command telematics inscribed by microelectronic transnationalism. And indeed, the discourse of cultural specificity and difference, packaged for transnational consumption along the lines sketched above, is often deployed by this specific class. What is dissimulated by this broad-stroke picture is the tremendous complexity of postcolonial space, especially womanspace.[16]

As I must keep repeating, remaking history is a tall order, and we must not take collective enthusiasm or conviction as its sole guarantee. In order to emphasize this point, I will fall into the confessional mode, give you an insider's view of what it "feels like" to taste the freedom offered by political independence in its specific historical moment.

My academic generation in India, approaching fifty now, were children at the time of the Indian Independence, unlike the "midnight's children" who were born with the Independence, and served Salman Rushdie to symbolize the confusion of a new nation seeing itself only as rupture, a monstrous birth.[17] These children of the middle class have become college and university teachers, cultural workers, government servants, political activists, the women household managers with a foot in the women's movement, the professions, the arts. I know surprisingly few executives or scientists as old friends. Our childhood and adolescence were marked by a dying fall that had to be rearranged as an upbeat march. We were not old enough to analyze, indeed sometimes to know, the details of the scenario until later. Those years marked the collapse of the heritage of nineteenth-century liberalism out of which the nationalist alibi for decolonization had been painstakingly fabricated. We could not know then, although it was being bred into our bones, that the People were not behaving like a Nation, that the dubious euphoria of 1947, division and violence barely managed, was now turning into a

species of *Jawaharlalvisadayoga*—the sorrow of Jawaharlal—out of
which a chauffeur of a different kind would drive the national
automobile into a new and changed space called the Indian
Union.[18] It was beyond our grasp to *understand* that the grandeur
of an internationalist "national" commitment within a necessarily furtive left under imperialism—the undivided Communist
Party of India—was just as necessarily breaking up into a split-
level insertion into electoral politics. Yet our academic humanist
generation would bear the political melancholy of this change.
We wrote essays in our school magazines at Gandhi's murder.
Yet we had already, in the curious logic of children, settled that
the "Partition Riots" (between Hindus and Muslims at Independence), like the "Famine of '43" (artificially produced by the
British government in order to feed the military during World
War II), marked a Past that our Present had pushed firmly back.
In other words, as middle-class children and adolescents, my academic generation was thrust in the space of remaking history,
negotiating a new history. This is the subject-position of the
children of the national bourgeoisie in decolonization. The ado-
lescent imagination could be persuaded that the disturbing re-
minders of the past were no more than the ashes that the
phoenix leaves behind as she leaps into the air reborn. We were
already marked by this excusing structure (productive of unexamined allegories of nationalism) when, like everyone else, we
perceived that, in terms of religious fundamentalism as a social
formation, every declared rupture with the past is always also a
repetition.

The potential executives, scientists, and professionals from
that generation were the first big brain drain to the United
States. If, as children and adolescents, they suffered the same
contradictions that I mention above, they understood them, I
think, more in terms of broken promises.

These people, mostly men, did well in the United States.
By and large, they did not trouble themselves about the struggles

of the sixties and seventies in this country. Hard-working, ambitious, and smart, they were upwardly class mobile stuff to
begin with. They received some of the benefits of the struggles
they did not join. As the only colored community (although, like
the colonial subject of the previous dispensation, they basically
identified with the whites) in the U.S. that did not have a history
of oppression on the soil, they were often used in affirmative action employment and admission where blacks, Hispanics, and
"Asian-Americans" (meaning U.S. citizens of Chinese and Japanese extraction) were bypassed. The constitution of the Indian
community is changing rapidly, and beginning to assume some of
the more working-class and small bourgeois dimensions of the
Indian diaspora in the Afro-Caribbean and Great Britain. It can
nonetheless be said, I think, that the first generation of Indian-
Americans, just entering university, often innocently searching
for their "roots" and their "heritage" (following a route laid
down by internal colonization) are the children of the people I
have been describing. Some of these young women and men will
no doubt lend a certain confessional authenticity to Third
Worldist alternative histories in the coming years. (It might be
more interesting for them to intervene in internal colonizing *in
India,* but that suggestion is beside the point of this essay.)

The sources of the tremendous vitality of underclass *British*
subcontinental culture—rigorously to be distinguished from the
Indian academic community in Britain—are to be found in the
sort of sectarian "household" religion that has been the strength
of subaltern consciousness on the subcontinent.[19] The children
of this community (the underclass *British* subcontinentals) are
now producing the "Indy-pop" or "Panjabi New Wave" music
that can already be compared in the politics of its provenance to
jazz or soul in the U.S. These groups are now written up in
funky magazines and Sunday supplements of national dailies,
listed in *City Lights,* featured in political theater and cinema.

The Hindu majority of Indian-Americans is, in an odd sort

of way, fundamentalist. The so-called Upanishadic religion of which they promote the fundament is a version of the semitized Hinduism woven in the nineteenth century, whose most stunning achievement was its co-existence with a polytheism read as personal allegory. It is idle to deny the emancipatory energy of this innovation in its own time. In contemporary America this emancipatory force is channeled into recoding the entry into the great rational abstraction of the constitutional We the People.[20] Thus it is that the average cultured Hindu Indian-American is engaged in propagating a fantasmatic Hindu cultural heritage as the flip side of participating in the fantasy of the land of opportunity, a free society ruled by law and the Popular Mandate. The postcolonial diasporic as native informant finds a nurturing and corroborative space in this enclave in her attempts to remake history. And this group, privileged in India as the Non Resident Indian (NRI), gets investment breaks as well as invitations to opine on the Indian spiritual heritage.

This system of cultural representation and self-representation is the U.S. semiotic field of citizenship and ethnicity. The cultural fantasies of origin of the prominent "ethnic groups" in the U.S. (including the English) and their imprint on the countries of their origin are well known. (Israel, Ireland, Poland, and Cuba are four other examples.) All of these groups (excluding the English) had a history of varieties of oppression on the soil that lent an urgency to the fantasies. In the Indian case, export-import has been speeded up for reasons that I have tried to sketch.

Now, if one returns to the melancholy story of the years of Independence, whose shadow fell on my childhood, then one begins to see that cultural, communal (religious), and class heterogeneity native to the subcontinent has been asserting itself in spite of the unifying hopes on assorted sides, based on those assorted concept-metaphors: Nationalism, Secularism, Internationalism, Culturalism.

Any extended discussion of remaking history in decolonization must take into account the dangerous fragility *and* tenacity
of these concept-metaphors. Briefly, it seems possible to say that
an alternative and perhaps equally fragile mode of resistance to
them can only come through a strategic acceptance of the cen-
trifugal potential of the plurality and heterogeneity native to the
subcontinent. Yet heterogeneity is an elusive and ambivalent resource (except in metropolitan "parliamentary" or academic
space) as the recent past in India, and indeed on the globe, have
shown. Its direct manipulation for electoral or diplomatic results
constitutes devastation. (Manipulation in commercial interest can
lead to a dynamic "public culture.")

It is only in situations like this that institutionally placed
cultural workers have the obligation to speak predictively. These
scrupulous interventions are in fact our only contribution to the
project of remaking history or sustaining ever-shifting voices
with an alternative edge. In a sense our task is to make people
ready to listen, and that is not determined by argument. Indirect
and maddeningly slow, forever running the risk of demagogy and
coercion mingled with the credulous vanity and class interests of
teacher and student, it is still only institutionalized education in
the human sciences that is a long-term and collective method for
making people want to listen. As far as I can see, remaking (the
discipline of) history has its only chance on this unglamorous
and often tedious register.[21]

Therefore I propose the persistent establishment and re-
establishment, the repeated consolidating in undoing, of a strategy of education and classroom pedagogy attending to
provisional resolutions of oppositions as between secular and
nonsecular, national and subaltern, national and international,
cultural and socio/political by teasing out their complicity.[22]
Such a strategy of strategies must speak "from within" the
emancipatory master narratives even while taking a distance
from them. It must resolutely hold back from offering phan-

tasmatic hegemonic nativist counternarratives that implicitly honor the historical withholding of the "permission to narrate." The new culturalist alibi, working within a basically elitist culture industry, insisting on the continuity of a native tradition untouched by a Westernization whose failures it can help to cover, legitimizes the very thing it claims to combat.

In the longer piece of which this is a part, I go on now to deal with the emphasis on technical education in contemporary India, and suggest some alternatives. That discussion would be pertinent in comments on "remaking history" with India as its space of agency. That it is not pertinent here should remind us that our perfectly appropriate collection is still within "a parochial decanonisation debate."[23] Remaining then within the system(s) of representation negotiated by internal colonization, let me simply remark that the kind of predictive pedagogy that I engage in in the longer piece is, however hardheaded, always to come.

That peculiar space, of a future that is not a future present, can be inhabited by paralogical figures.[24] I have often attended to such paralogical figures, especially of women.[25] I have indicated in this essay why the subaltern female seems particularly meaningful within postcolonial themes. I will now look, therefore, at such a paralogical literary case, that rewrites ethnicity and reads rape appropriatively—in the strong senses of reading and writing that I brought up earlier.

I will read Mahasweta Devi's "The Hunt."[26]

In the previous pages, I have suggested that the disavowal of postcoloniality in the name of a nativist ethnicist culturalism is a species of collaboration with neocolonialism, especially in its benevolent instance. Not to be able to see error on the other side is to feed the arrogance of the benevolent neocolonialist conscience. By contrast, Mahasweta's story makes visible the suggestion that the postcolonial negotiates with the structures of violence and violation that have produced her.

History cannot be reversed or erased out of nostalgia. The remaking of history involves a negotiation with the structures that have produced the individual as agent of history. In "The Hunt," the figure for this negotiation is the rewriting of ethnicity and the reappropriation of rape. And the name of the agent of this remaking is Mary Oraon.

A word on "figure." I do not mean to read Mary as the representative of the postcolonial, or as an example of directly imitable correct practice. I am looking rather at the logic of her figuration, at the mechanics of the fabrication of the figure called Mary. I will read the fabrication of the narrative in this way as well. Our usual way of reading involves character and plot. Often we call our reading "political" if we read these two items as allegorical in the narrow sense. My reading of the figuration of Mary and her story is not unrelated to these practices, but tries to take into account that the line between aesthetics and politics is neither firm nor straight.

Mary Oraon. Oraon is the name of one of the largest of the three-hundred-odd tribes of India. In Hindi, the national language, the tribals are called *adivasi*s (original inhabitants). In English, they are referred to collectively as the "scheduled" tribes, because of the special sanctions (honored altogether in the breach) written for them in the Indian Constitution. With the "scheduled" castes, the lowest Hindu castes (the outcastes), these original inhabitants are the official subalterns of the Republic of India. In the language of the government as well as that of political activists they are the SCSTs. They are outside of the seven religions listed in the Indian national anthem: Hinduism, Buddhism, Sikhism, Jainism, Zoroastrianism, Islam, Christianity. This then is Mary, simply Oraon, simply identified with her tribe. But she was christened Mary. She is the descendant of tribals converted to Christianity by missionaries. Her father was a white planter who raped her mother before leaving India for Australia.

If we think of postcolonial, figuratively, as the living child of a rape, the making of Mary is, rather literally, its figuration. She is not a true tribal.

Mary, servant in the house of a caste Hindu, is and is not a Christian. All the appropriate categories are blurred in post-coloniality.[27] Her mother stopped being a Christian when a Hindu in independent secular rural India would not hire her for fear of caste contamination. Mary will marry a Muslim. This negotiability of "religions" is rather different from the official post-Enlightenment secularist agenda, devastated, as I have mentioned earlier, by the violent communalism on the soil.

It is not only secularism as defined through the culture of imperialism that is put into question here. The re-inscription of postcoloniality as the product of an enabling violation puts the militant "tribal" in the place of the bourgeois intellectual as its representative figuration.

Every detail in that figuration shuttles between "literal" and "metaphorical." Admiration for the courage of the white, for example, is part of the subaltern repertoire. Thus Jalim, Mary's boyfriend, comments on her insistence upon the commit-ment of marriage rather than mere cohabitation. "Yes, there is something true in Mary, the strength of Australian blood." She herself puts it with an impersonal rage against her mother that can provide a text for decoding: "When you see a white daugh-ter you kill her right away. Then there are no problems." "What about you if she'd killed," one of the tribal boys asks. "I wouldn't have been."

Describing her mindset authorially, Mahasweta writes:

She would have rebelled if they had imposed the harsh injunctions of their own society upon her. She is unhappy that they don't. In her in-most heart there is somewhere a longing to be part of the Oraons. She would have been very glad if, when she was thirteen or fourteen, some brave Oraon lad had pulled her into marriage.

Mahasweta is careful not to privilege this mindset into the self-marginalizing ethnic's project of dining out as an exile or an expression of her semi-tribal voice-consciousness. The provenance of this scenario and these sentiments is the one or two Hindi films Mary has seen. The overcoming of caste and creed barriers for the sake of love is one of the basic themes of the immensely productive Hindi film industry.[28]

The description of Mary's everyday life as a bridge between the "outside world" (represented by the obscure rural township of Tohri) and the arrested space of Kuruda (the little community on the borders of which the tribals live) is orchestrated to provide empirical sanction for Mary Oraon as the name of woman, worker, postcolonial. I will pass over that rich text and focus on the moment when, "suddenly one day, stopping the train, Collector Singh descends with Prasadji's son, and Mary's life is troubled, a storm gathers in Kuruda's quiet and impoverished existence."

The train no longer stops at Kuruda, as it did in British India, when the white planters lived there. The train is a widely current metonym for the unifying project of territorial imperialism, the "colonialism" of which Mary is the *post*colonial.[29]

"Collector"—a petty revenue collector under the British Raj—could be a proper name or a descriptive honorific. The man acts with what Lukács would have called "typicality." He violates the land by selling the Sal forests of the area, cheating the small landowners of a fair price. He violates the tribe by employing them as wage labor at a murderous rate of exploitation and entertains them with quantities of liquor and a travesty of the commodified so-called mass culture of the West. In fact, the story of the silent Sal forests is also a carefully articulated historical metonym. As follows:

The ecology of the Sal tree is thoroughly intertwined with the precapitalist communal economy and social relations of the tribes. Its transformation into colonial constant capital was per-

formed through the imposition and production of the elaborate
social relations of white planter and tribal servant. The transformation of the culture of imperialism in postcoloniality is figured
forth by the incompetent but good-natured Indians living in the
nooks and crannies of the great plantation houses. The real
legatee of the imperialist economic text, the necessary trajectory
from high bourgeois to petty bourgeois social manipulation under decolonization, is the despicable Collector Singh, who re-
mobilizes the Sal forest into constant capital and the tribals into
variable capital without inserting them into generalized commodity exchange.[30] Marx described this a hundred years ago as
"capital's mode of exploitation without its mode of production."[31] Mary Oraon, the not-quite-not-tribal, not-quite-not-
Indian, is the not-quite-not-self-conscious, not-quite-not-self-
identical agent who would defeat this continuous narrative of
exploitation.

I will not focus on this aspect of the story either. For our
present purposes, I must concentrate on Mary's appropriation of
the structure of rape as not-quite-not-man. And here, the aspect
of Collector Singh that becomes important is his attempt to vio-
late Mary sexually and his various related exchanges with Mary.
The narrative resolution of this sequence happens on the day
and night of the Spring Festival of the Oraons.

Mary, as the vigilant and alert critic of what is violating the
land and the people, rewrites the Festival, turns it from the
hunt-game to the Hunt. She brings the festival to crisis —
literalizes the metaphor — to be able to act. The "authentic" version of the tribals monumentalizes the past. There the sexual division of agency is intact. The men *know*. The women masquerade.

*They [the women] don't know why they hunt. The men know. They
have been playing the hunt for a thousand million moons on this day.
Once there were animals in the forest, life was wild, the hunt game
had meaning. Now the forest is empty, life wasted and drained, the
hunt game meaningless. Only the day's joy is real.*

If for the men the ritual of the hunt seems a functioning *meta-phor,* for the women, allowed every twelve years to perform the hunt, the ritual is staged as a *catachresis,* an analogy without an accessible historical or literal pole, in classical rhetoric a metaphor in abuse. Mary undoes this gendered opposition. She dynamically literalizes the ritual catachresis of the hunt by negotiating with the structure of rape—violation as such—and appropriates it as a weapon. For her the forest does *come* to hold an animal, and the reality of the day's joy is both "real" and "full of meaning." How does she operate this? It is the Festival that rewrites the Collector as Animal, for her, and legitimizes him as prey.

Some years ago, writing on *Jane Eyre,* I had described the scene where Jane first encounters Bertha Mason as a situation that made indeterminate the difference between human and animal so that the narrative could move Jane from the letter to the spirit of the law.[32] This is not such a making-indeterminate, but rather its opposite. Let us consider the text. Mary is returning from work, the monotone of the festival music is in the air, Collector acosts her on the lonely path.

At first Mary was scared. . . . After a good deal of struggling, Mary was able to spring out of his grasp. . . . Long sideburns, long hair, polyester trousers, pointed shoes, a dark red shirt on his back. Against the background of the Spring songs Mary thought he was an animal. A-ni-mal. The syllables beat on her mind. Suddenly Mary smiled.

Mary makes a rendezvous with him, intending to kill him. But she *cannot* kill him without help from the inscribing power or the ritual. There is, once again, a negotiation and a transformation. The tribal women at their post-hunt picnic are at that very moment getting drunk on liquor donated by Collector. For Mary he brings "imported liquor" to the tryst. This substitutes for the festival music and Mary begins to drink. "Yes the face is beginning to look like the hunted animal's." Indeed, Mary transforms

that face. She "caresses it . . . gives him love bites on the lips.
There's fire in Collector's eyes, his mouth is open, his lips wet
with spittle, his teeth glistening. Mary is watching, watching, the
face changes and changes into? Yes, becomes an animal."

One is not sure who speaks the next question: "Now take
me?" In this moment of indeterminacy, Mary appropriates rape.
She holds him, lays him down. The machete becomes the phallus
of violation. The killing of the ritual beast is also a punishment
for the violation of the people, of the land, as also a historically
displaced return for the violation of her birth: "Mary lifts the
machete, lowers it, lifts it, lowers."

Every detail seems to bristle with "meaning." Violating,
Mary feels sexually replete. This is a negotiation with the
phallus, not merely masquerading as a man. Before the kill,
dancing "she had clasped Budhni [an old tribal woman], and
said, 'I'll marry you after I play the hunt. Then I am the husband, you the wife.'" After she returns from the kill, "she
kisse[s] Budhni with her unwashed mouth."

A great deal more can be said about Mahasweta's articulation of the negotiative strategic postcolonial in the figure of the
gendered subaltern. I will do no more than comment on her use
of the word *bonno,* which I have translated as "wild" in the following passage: "A great thirst dances in her blood. Collector,
Collector, I'm almost there. Collector wants her a lot . . . With
how much violence can Collector want her? How many degrees
Fahrenheit? Is his blood as wild as Mary's? As daring?"

What blood is named "wild" here? The blood of the
forest-dwelling tribals? (The word *bonno* literally means "of the
forest.") Or the blood of the violating Australian? (In its signify-
ing scope, *bonno* also means "brute.") A group of bourgeois feminist English professors, intellectuals, and organizational activists,
strongly charged with ethnicist pride in its own place, thought
that the word could only mean Mary's return to tribal authenticity.[33] Mahasweta's peculiar burden might well be that the

wildness of the blood is both Mary and Oraon and purely
neither.

I hope it is clear by now that, in the space that I occupy in front
of you this evening, the demand that only the Indian tribal can
speak as the Indian tribal for the Indian tribal at your tribunal
tries mightily to make invisible the mechanics of production of
that space, this book. By those demands, Gayatri Spivak at-
titudinizing on the occasion of Mahasweta Devi writing about
the tribal can be at best cathartic. Attend rather to this: My contractual situation as a postcolonial is in a place where I see
claims to the subjectship of alternative histories coming, and being called for, in an often unexamined way. A literary pedagogy,
choosing texts carefully, can at least prepare another space that
makes visible the fault lines in slogans of the European
Enlightenment — nationalism, internationalism, secularism,
culturalism — the bulwark of nativism, without participating in
their destruction. This, strictly speaking, is de(con)structive pedagogy. Like all good teaching in the humanities, it is hopeful and
interminable. It presupposes and looks forward to a future ante-
rior of achieved solidarity and thus nurses "the present." In the
strictest sense, then, (para)logical: morpho-genetic (giving rise to
new ways of reading, writing, teaching *in the strongest sense*),
without terminal teleological innovation. Its "present" is a field
of value-coding, in a sense of "value" that is logically (not necessarily chronologically) prior to the economic; the political, the
economic, the affective are entangled there.

In the contractual site that holds you and me this evening,
or in this book, the remaking of history is a persistent critique,
unglamorously chipping away at the binary oppositions and continuities that emerge continuously in the supposed account of
the real. The cultural politics of repetition are in play with the
strategically necessary gesture politics of rupture attendant upon
the political independence that is the minimal requirement for

"decolonization." As it happens, generations like "my own" (I can just hear the purist murmur of "essentialism" from theoretically correct friends), straddling the transition, and groups like "my own" (again!), diasporics circulating within patterns of "internal colonization," can put one item on the agenda when they speak to a group like "yours" (again and again!), serious metropolitan radicals, when the speakers belong to the trade of cultural work: I repeat, a persistent unlearning of the privilege of the postcolonial elite in a neocolonial globe.

Notes

1. I have told the outlines of one such negotiation in "Poststructuralism, Postcoloniality, Marginality, Value," in *Literary Theory Today,* ed. Peter Collier and Helga Ryan (Cambridge: Polity, forthcoming).

2. I am drawing here upon the difficult but most perceptive passage in Gilles Deleuze and Félix Guattari, *Anti-Oedipus: Capitalism and Schizophrenia,* trans. Robert Hurley et al. (Minneapolis: University of Minnesota Press, 1983), p. 10.

3. Michel Foucault, *The History of Sexuality,* Vol. 1: *An Introduction,* trans. Robert Hurley (New York: Pantheon Books, 1978), p. 93; translation modified.

4. Karl Marx, *Capital,* trans. Ben Fowkes (New York: Vintage Books, 1977), vol. 1, p. 143.

5. I am increasingly inclined to relate the Marxian and Foucauldian enterprises in terms of a theory of value. That argument has no place here. In the spirit of the longer argument, which I hope will be soon forthcoming, let me suggest the following. Foucault's use of "utterance" *(énoncé)* in the following passage is clearly not the linguistic one. It is a "name" (not identical with what it names, thus "catachrestical" as a common noun) that is the best loan-word that can be found in the circumstances. As such, it is possible to show that it is not incoherent with Marx's analysis of capital and capitalism, although the relationship between levels and strategies are complex. Foucault's own sense of his relationship with Marx is most interesting and has to be examined according to the methods of an older intellectual history. With this in mind, let me add that I use "archives" in the sense of the following passage: "[T]he *archive* defines a particular level: that of a practice that causes a multiplicity of utterances to emerge as so many regular events . . . between tradition and oblivion, it reveals the rules of a practice that enables utterances both to survive and to undergo regular modification. It is *the general system of the formation and transformation of utter-*

ances" (Michel Foucault, *The Archaeology of Knowledge and the Discourse on Language,* trans. A. M. Sheridan Smith [New York: Harper Torchbooks, 1972], p. 130; translation modified). For another view of the relationship, see Barry Smart, *Foucault, Marxism and Critique* (London: Routledge & Kegan Paul, 1983). See Michael Ryan, "The Limits of *Capital,*" in his *Marxism and Deconstruction: A Critical Articulation* (Baltimore: Johns Hopkins University Press, 1982), pp. 82-102, for the argument that the economic and political are necessarily implicated in Marx.

6. "The value-form, whose fully developed shape is the money-form, is content-less and simple *[inhaltlos und einfach]*" (Marx, *Capital,* vol. 1, pp. 89-90). See also my "Poststructuralism, Postcoloniality, Marginality, Value."

7. Gayle Rubin, "The Traffic in Women: Notes on the 'Political Economy' of Sex," in *Toward an Anthropology of Women,* ed. Reyna R. Reiter (New York: Monthly Review Press, 1975), pp. 157-210. Deleuze and Guattari, *Anti-Oedipus.* It is curious that none of the three investigates value as such.

8. Marx, *Capital,* vol. 1, pp. 95, 98. Emphasis mine.

9. For a definition of the "subaltern," see Ranajit Guha, "On Some Aspects of the Historiography of Colonial India," and for a comment on the differential nature of Guha's definition, Gayatri Spivak, "Subaltern Studies: Deconstructing Historiography," both in *Selected Subaltern Studies,* ed. Guha and Spivak (New York: Oxford University Press, 1988), pp. 37-44, 3-32.

10. She stands unnoticed and implicit in the cracks of much carefully written documentation in the social sciences. Think, for example, of the "young wives" in Kalpana Bardhan's densely woven essay, "Women, Work, Welfare and Status: Forces of Tradition and Change in India," *South Asia Bulletin* 6 (1986): 9. Fiction can make her visible.

11. Carl E. Pletsch, "The Three Worlds, or the Division of Social Scientific Labor, circa 1950 to 1975," *Comparative Studies in Society and History* 23, no. 4 (October 1981): 565-590. For an alternative self-conception of a "third force" of nonaligned nations emerging from the Bandung Conference of 1955, see Nigel Harris, *The End of the Third World: Newly Industrializing Countries and the Decline of an Ideology* (London: I.B. Tauris, 1986).

12. For the making of this class or group in the Indian case, see Gauri Viswanathan, *The Myth of Conquest: Literary Study and British Rule in India* (New York: Columbia University Press, forthcoming).

13. Samir Amin, *Unequal Development,* trans. Brian Pearce (New York: Monthly Review Press, 1976), p. 369.

14. Most elaborately in "Scattered Speculations on the Question of Value," in *In Other Worlds: Essays in Cultural Politics,* by Gayatri Spivak (New York: Methuen, 1987), pp. 154-175. It is interesting to see that the National Governors' Report, issued in Washington on February 24, 1989, calls for more language learning and culture learning, because otherwise the U.S. will be "outcompeted."

15. Jean Baudrillard, "The Precession of Simulacra," in *Simulations,* trans. Paul Foss et al. (New York: Semiotext(e), 1983), p. 22. The following paragraph draws on Baudrillard's general argument about the divided globe.

16. It is a tribute to Hélène Cixous that her insight that "[a]s subject for history, woman always occurs simultaneously in several places" can resonate with an insight such as the following: "[d]efending women's rights 'now' (this 'now' being ANY historical moment) is always a betrayal—of the people, of the nation, of the revolution, of Islam, of national identity, of cultural roots, of the Third World . . . according to the terminologies in use *hic et nunc.*" Cixous, "The Laugh of the Medusa," in *New French Feminisms: An Anthology,* ed. Elaine Marks and Isabelle de Courtivron (Amherst: University of Massachusetts Press, 1980), p. 252. Marie-Aimé Hélie-Lucas, "Bound and Caged by the Family Code," in *Third World—Second Sex,* ed. Miranda Davies (London: Zed Press, 1987), vol. 2, p. 13. These are two of many descriptions of womanspace.

17. This section, in a slightly different form, appeared in *The Statesman* (Calcutta), August 15, 1987.

18. Literally, in Sanskrit, "The Sorrow of Jawaharlal." Jawaharlal Nehru was independent India's first prime minister. In the *Bhagavadgita,* an important sacred authoritative text of Hindu practice, "The Sorrow of Arjuna" (*Arjunavisadayoga*), opens the action. Krishna, a divine incarnation, is his charioteer and steers him onto the path of just war, a metaphor for life in the world.

19. As of this writing, the extraordinary social power of the upwardly classmobile British Muslim community displayed in the Salman Rushdie *(Satanic Verses)* case has shown that the distinction between the U.S. and British subcontinental diaspora is no longer clear-cut.

20. See Gayatri Spivak, "The Making of Americans, the Teaching of English, and the Future of Culture Studies," in *New Literary History* (forthcoming).

21. All "events"—including culture and war—remake the *material* of history. There is no such thing as remaking history as such. The discipline consolidates hegemonic remakings as history as such. The discipline of history in India— conservative in its choice of canonical method even when radical in its sentiments—resists efforts, especially from outside the discipline, to remake the disciplinary method. A random example: ". . . there is a fear that any rendering of objective history into a morphological exercise like any other art might turn an entire school of decent historians into an array of cognoscenti who are just involved with style, form and techniques of representation. Both history and art have their separate domains, one based on reality, the other fictional" (K. M. Panikkar, "History from Below," *Hindustan Times,* February 26, 1989). This is again a reminder that there are other battles to fight than just metropolitan centrism. This too is a difference between internal colonization and decolonization.

22. This awkward and heavy sentence is written for interpretive instantiation in

the classroom. By contrast, as I have argued elsewhere, clear and rousing pieces like Nancy Fraser, "Solidarity or Singularity? Richard Rorty between Romanticism and Technocracy," *Praxis International* 8, no. 3 (October 1988): 268-270, remain lists of ingredients making like recipes.

23. "Editor's Comments," *Public Culture* 1, no. 1 (Fall 1988): 3.

24. I use "paralogical" in the sense given to it by Jean-François Lyotard, *The Postmodern Condition,* trans. Geoff Bennington and Brian Massumi (Minneapolis: University of Minnesota Press, 1984), p. 61.

25. "The Rani of Sirmur," in *Europe and Its Others,* ed. Francis Barker et al. (Colchester: University of Essex Press, 1985), pp. 128-151, and "Can the Subaltern Speak?" in *Marxism and the Interpretation of Culture,* ed. Lawrence Grossberg and Cary Nelson (Urbana: University of Illinois Press, 1988), pp. 271-313.

26. Mahasweta Devi, "The Hunt," translated by Gayatri Spivak in *Imaginary Maps* (Routledge & Thema [India], forthcoming).

27. I have discussed this point at greater length in "Poststructuralism, Postcoloniality, Marginality, Value."

28. There is a description of one of these—"Bobby" by Raj Kapur—in Clark Blaise and Bharati Mukherjee, *Days and Nights in Calcutta* (Garden City, N.Y.: Doubleday, 1977), pp. 143-146.

29. For a description of this connection in Marx and Engels, see V. G. Kiernan, *Marxism and Imperialism* (Edinburgh: Edward Arnold, 1974), p. 188. Many artists, including E. M. Forster and Satyajit Ray, make this connection.

30. See Amin, *Unequal Development,* p. 380.

31. Marx, *Capital,* trans. David Fernbach (New York: Viking Books, 1981), vol. 3, p. 732. Within the narrative, Marx is describing usurer's capital.

32. "Three Women's Texts and a Critique of Imperialism," in *"Race," Writing, and Difference,* ed. Henry Louis Gates, Jr. (Chicago: University of Chicago Press, 1986), p. 266.

33. It is only if "internal colonization," and its corollary, "united ethnic voice," are the presuppositions that such a judgment can become "authoritative." Thus Ngugi wa Th'iongo: "It is important that we understand that cultural imperialism in its era of neo-colonialism is a more dangerous cancer because it takes new subtle forms and can hide even under the cloak of militant African nationalism, the cry for dead authentic cultural symbolism and other native racist self assertive banners." See "Literature and Society," in his *Writers in Politics* (London: Heinemann, 1981), p. 25.

Janet Abu-Lughod is an urbanist and historian, and a professor of sociology at the New School for Social Research, New York. She is the author of *Rabat: Urban Apartheid in Morocco* (1980) and *Before Europe's Hegemony* (1989).

Homi K. Bhabha teaches English literature and literary theory at Sussex University. He is the editor of *Nation and Narration* (1989) and writes frequently on postcolonial discourse.

Victoria de Grazia is a historian of twentieth-century Europe. She is the author of *The Culture of Consent: The Organization of Leisure in Fascist Italy* (1981) and an editor of *Radical History Review*.

J. Hoberman is a staff writer for the *Village Voice,* writes a column for *Artforum,* and is a co-author of *Midnight Movies* (1983).

Alice Yaeger Kaplan is the author of *Reproductions of Banality* (1986) and, most recently, "Paul de Man, *Le Soir,* and the Francophone Collaboration (1940-1942)," in *Responses: On Paul de Man's Wartime Journalism* (1989). She teaches French literature at Duke University.

Edward W. Said is Parr Professor of English and Comparative Literature, Columbia University, and the author of *Orientalism* (1978), *The Question of Palestine* (1979), *The World, the Text, and the Critic* (1983), and co-editor of *Blaming the Victims* (1987).

Gayatri Chakravorty Spivak, author of *In Other Worlds: Essays in Cultural Politics* (1987), is Andrew W. Mellon Professor, Department of English, University of Pittsburgh.

Carol Squiers is a writer and curator and has written about photographic representation in publications such as *Manhattan, Inc., The Village Voice, Vogue,* and *Artforum.* She is an associate editor at *American Photographer* and editor of *The Critical Image: Essays in Contemporary Photography* (forthcoming).

Paula A. Treichler teaches at the University of Illinois at Urbana-Champaign in the College of Medicine, Institute of Communications Research and Women's Studies. She is co-author of *A Feminist Dictionary* (1985) and *Language, Gender, and Professional Writing* (1989).

Bernard Tschumi, architectural theorist and chief architect of Parc de la Villette, Paris, is the dean of the School of Architecture, Columbia University.

Michele Wallace is a writer and cultural critic. She is the author of *Black Macho: The Myth of the Superwoman* (1979) and writes frequently on black politics and culture.

Cornel West is professor of religion and director of the Afro-American Studies Program, Princeton University. He is on the editorial board of *Social Text* and is co-editor of *Out There* (forthcoming).